The Presidential Contest

The Presidential Contest
With a Guide to the
1992 Presidential Race

Fourth Edition

Joseph A. Pika
University of Delaware

Zelma Mosley
University of Delaware

Richard A. Watson
Emeritus, University of Missouri—Columbia

A Division of Congressional Quarterly Inc.
Washington, D.C.

Cover design: Paula Anderson

Library of Congress Cataloging-in-Publication Data

Pika, Joseph August, 1947-
    The presidential contest : with a guide to the 1992 presidential
race. -- 4th ed. / Joseph A. Pika, Zelma Mosley, Richard A. Watson.
        p.   cm.
    Rev. ed. of: The presidential contest / Richard A. Watson. 3rd ed.
c1988.
    Includes bibliographical references and index.
    ISBN 0-87187-623-X : $14.95
    1. Presidents--United States--Election.   I. Mosley, Zelma.
II. Watson, Richard Abernathy, 1923- . III. Watson, Richard
Abernathy, 1923- Presidential contest. IV. Title.
JK524.W38 1992
324.973'092--dc20   91-35612
                                                            CIP

To our parents:
Rosa L. Mosley
David L. Mosley
Joseph A. Pika, Jr.

Contents

Contents

Tables and Figures ════════════════

Tables

Figures

Preface

Presidential elections are multifaceted events—part spectacle, part governance, part fun, and part tedium. Particularly since 1968, there has been an explosion of detail that one might cover in a book like this, but we have chosen to remain true to the approach followed in three previous editions of this work by adhering to a concise, coherent framework for organizing the major features of the presidential selection process. This approach provides instructors with ample opportunity to expand and elaborate on those features of the process they find most intriguing.

The book really contains two frameworks. New to the fourth edition is an explicit chronological framework that centers on stages in a typical presidential election cycle. This four-part time line is briefly set forth in the introduction and followed throughout. Readers should find it a useful device in orienting discussions of previous contests and of contemporary developments in the election cycle. We have also retained the parallel, analytic framework so successfully employed in previous editions. Thus, common topics (such as campaign finance) can be compared and contrasted for the nomination and general election phases of the contest.

The Presidential Contest is designed to be a supplementary text in regular college courses—particularly those focusing on American government, political parties, and the American presidency—as well as in special election-year courses dealing with the president's selection. It should also prove helpful to journalists, politicians, and citizens in this country and abroad seeking a concise treatment of this elaborate process.

All topics in this revision of the book have been thoroughly updated through the 1988 election with an eye to the upcoming 1992 contest. In addition, there are expanded discussions of selected aspects of group voting behavior (specifically, developments associated with race and sex); new reflections on the question of realignment; and a largely new concluding chapter that examines dissatisfaction with both the nomination and election stages of the presidential contest and proposals to reform them.

We wish to thank a number of persons whose assistance has been important for this edition. Richard Watson, sole author of the previous editions of this work, was not involved in preparing the fourth edition, but readers of the earlier editions will note that his basic approach and treatment remain central throughout. We also thank Brenda Carter, Dave Tarr, and their coworkers at Congressional Quarterly for having been particularly helpful. We benefited from the reviews of John Kilkelly and a second reviewer who preferred to remain anonymous.

Introduction

In a democratic society, elections are the principal means by which those "outside" the government can judge the performance of those "inside" the government and redirect the efforts of government officials. Major officeholders must periodically come before the populace to renew their right to exercise political power. Voters may also select an alternative group of leaders if they are dissatisfied with the performance of those currently in office. As Joseph Schumpeter observed, in a democracy individuals acquire the right to make political decisions by means of a "competitive struggle for the people's vote." [1]

This "competitive struggle" is a continuous process in which leaders in and out of power attempt to convince the voters that they will fare better under their particular administration. The major effort to win over the electorate, however, is concentrated in the period immediately before the election. During this time, candidates mount campaigns using a variety of political appeals designed to motivate the general public to take the time and effort to vote, and to vote for them.

According to democratic theory, political campaigns and elections perform several important functions in society. As Stephen Hess points out, they are primarily a process of "personnel selection," with the electorate operating as a "gigantic search committee" for the nation's political leaders. [2] However, campaigns and elections also serve other purposes. They offer a "corrective" for past electoral mistakes—the chance to "throw the rascals out" and give a new team the opportunity to govern the nation. Campaigns also provide a means to identify the principal problems in a society and to consider policies and programs for dealing with such problems; viewed in this way, campaigns are "educational," a civics lesson for the electorate. The electoral process can also be a catharsis, enabling societal conflicts to be made public and thereby faced squarely. Such a process may lead to another function of demo-

1

cratic elections: the development of attitudes of political compromise and the promotion of social consensus.[3]

Although elections of major public officials are important in any democratic society, they are doubly so in the United States because of its presidential form of government. Under the parliamentary system used in most other democracies in the world, the voters do not directly choose the nation's executive officials. Instead they choose the members of the legislative body, who bargain with one another over the composition of the cabinet, including its leader, who is usually called the prime minister. But in the United States, the presidential election is separate from legislative contests and voters are able to pass judgment on the candidates for the nation's highest office (although their influence on the selection remains indirect, mediated through the electoral college).[4] Because the United States has a two-party instead of a multiparty system, most votes go to the two major candidates, with the winner generally receiving a majority of the total popular vote.

Another distinguishing feature of U.S. presidential contests is the significant role the voters play in *nominating* candidates for the nation's highest office. In most other democratic societies, political party leaders, acting through committees or conferences, choose persons to represent them in the general election. This was also the case throughout most of U.S. history as delegates from the states gathered at the national conventions of the two principal parties to select their candidates. However, the choice of delegates in recent years has been vested more and more in rank-and-file voters instead of traditional party activists. As a result, the nomination as well as the election of the president has become a contest in which candidates must establish their popularity with voters.

The presidential selection process is also a unifying ritual, an opportunity for citizens from across the nation to engage in a common civic experience. Although their perspectives on candidates and problems may be shaped by very different concerns, there is a shared opportunity to help shape the nation's future.

This book is organized around four stages in the presidential selection process: 1) defining the pool of candidates; 2) securing the nomination of one of the major political parties—a stage in which citizens and party professionals select delegates to the national party conventions, after which those delegates select a nominee; 3) waging the general election campaign; and 4) validating election results in the electoral college.

No two presidential election cycles are identical, but the time line is relatively predictable. Potential candidates maneuver for position during the one or two years preceding the election year. Selection of convention delegates begins in January or February of the election year, with conventions typically scheduled in mid-July for the out-party and mid-August for the party that controls the presidency. For 1992 the Democrats chose New York City and the Republicans chose Houston as convention sites. Traditionally the general election campaign begins on Labor Day and runs to the first Tuesday following the second Monday of November, but recent campaigns have begun as soon as the identity of major party nominees has become clear, sometimes before the conventions have been held. Finally, electors cast ballots in their state capitals in mid-December; those ballots are officially tabulated in the first week of January during a joint session of the U.S. Congress over which preside the incumbent vice president and Speaker of the House of Representatives. The time line for a typical presidential election cycle is presented in Figure I-1. The following chapters follow this time line, although some features will be considered out of sequence, for example, the electoral college.

Chapter 1 provides background information on the rules of the nomination process, the ways they have evolved over the years, and their current nature and impact. It also discusses the pool of candidates from which the voters draw their presidential aspirants. Chapter 2 analyzes the nomination campaign itself: the early maneuvering for position, the targeting of the primary and caucus-convention states, the manipulation of political appeals, the communication of those appeals through the media and campaign workers, the handling of campaign finances, and the ultimate decision—the selection of the presidential and vice-presidential candidates at the parties' national conventions.

Chapter 3 shifts to the general election, analyzing it in the same framework that was used for the nomination process. This enables the reader to see similarities and differences in the two phases of the presidential contest. Chapter 4, which deals with voting in presidential elections, first traces the progressive extension of the franchise to more and more Americans and then analyzes the extent to which persons have actually exercised their right to vote in recent elections. The chapter then examines the effect of political party affiliation, social group and class identification, candidate appeal, issues, events, and presidential performance on the voting decisions of the American people. The concluding section of the chapter analyzes the consequences of presidential elections for the political party system and for policy making in the United States.

These four chapters thus chronicle the entire presidential contest, reporting and integrating a wide variety of studies of the subject. By contrast, Chapter 5 takes the form of an extended essay or editorial; it presents our assessment of what is right and wrong about the way the nation's highest political official is chosen and of what can be done to

Figure I-1 The Presidential Contest Time Line

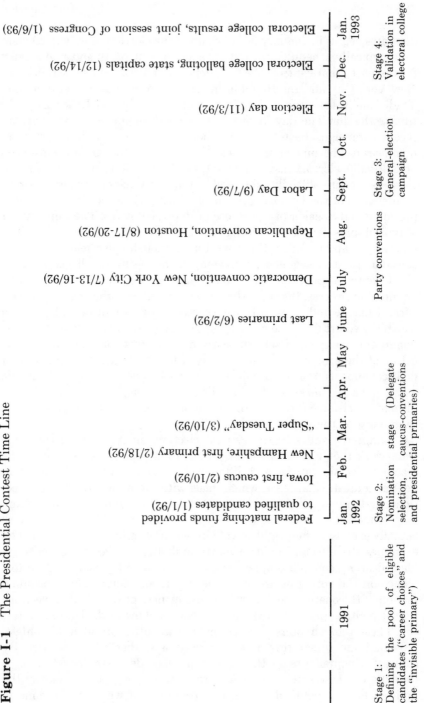

1991	Jan. 1992	Feb.	Mar.	Apr. May June	July	Aug.	Sept.	Oct.	Nov.	Dec.	Jan. 1993

Federal matching funds provided to qualified candidates (1/1/92)

Iowa, first caucus (2/10/92)

New Hampshire, first primary (2/18/92)

"Super Tuesday" (3/10/92)

Last primaries (6/2/92)

Democratic convention, New York City (7/13-16/92)

Republican convention, Houston (8/17-20/92)

Labor Day (9/7/92)

Election day (11/3/92)

Electoral college balloting, state capitals (12/14/92)

Electoral college results, joint session of Congress (1/6/93)

Stage 1:
Defining the pool of eligible candidates ("career choices" and the "invisible primary")

Stage 2:
Nomination stage   (Delegate selection,   caucus-conventions and presidential primaries)

Party conventions

Stage 3:
General-election campaign

Stage 4:
Validation in electoral college

improve the process.

The appendixes contain supplemental information on the presidential contest. Appendix A is a schedule of the 1992 primaries and caucuses; Appendix B contains profiles of major candidates likely to contest the 1992 election; Appendix C presents the results of the 1988 presidential primaries; and Appendix D tabulates the results of presidential contests from 1932 through 1988.

Notes

1. Joseph Schumpeter, *Capitalism, Socialism, and Democracy,* 3d ed. (New York: Harper and Row, 1950), 269. As discussed in Chapter 4, the concept of the "people's vote" has changed over the years in the United States as the franchise has been extended to more and more groups; this trend toward broader public participation is also a feature of democratic elections.
2. Stephen Hess, *The Presidential Campaign* (Washington, D.C.: Brookings, 1974), chap. 4.
3. Morris Janowitz and Dwaine Marvick, *Competitive Pressure and Democratic Consent* (Ann Arbor, Mich.: Bureau of Government, Institute of Public Administration, 1956), 2.
4. The winning presidential candidate must receive a majority of the votes in the electoral college. (See Chapter 3.) Since the Civil War, the winner in the electoral college has always received at least 40 percent and usually more than 50 percent of the popular vote.

Nomination Rules and Candidates 1

It operated so simply in 1789 and 1792. In both instances, George Washington was selected president by unanimous votes in the electoral college.[1] John Adams, the second-place finisher both times, became vice president. In 1789, electors were chosen on the first Wednesday of January and met in their respective states to vote on the first Wednesday in February. The votes were counted on April 6, a month later than intended because of delays in convening Congress. The election calendar for 1792 was made more flexible by allowing electors to be chosen within thirty-four days of the first Wednesday in December, when ballots would be cast.[2]

Today's presidential aspirants and their supporters confront a far more complicated task. They must first win their party's nomination in a contest that may test their endurance as much as their ability. Then they must mount a nationwide campaign to gain victory over the opposing candidates in the general election. It is now customary for candidates to begin their nomination campaigns two years or more before the decisive moment and to spend millions of dollars in the effort. As the contrast with Washington's selection illustrates, the process has evolved substantially over time. Dividing the presidential contest into two phases lengthens the electoral process and requires candidates to wage two separate campaigns under quite different sets of rules. Moreover, campaign strategies and techniques must be tailored for the two distinct stages of the presidential battle. Not even the participants in the two contests are the same: Hugh Heclo has labeled the much smaller group of persons who help choose presidential nominees the "selectorate," in contrast to the "electorate," who vote in the general election.[3]

The Founders never contemplated this separation in the procedure they devised for choosing the chief executive. Major developments in the young nation, however, soon divided the selection process into two parts,

7

and after the process was divided, changes continued to occur in both nomination and election procedures. This chapter first describes the development of the nomination process, from the establishment of the congressional caucus in 1796 until the national convention system was instituted in the 1830s and expanded in the 1840s. It then explains the nature and impact of current nomination rules. The final section analyzes the backgrounds of presidential candidates, "the pool of eligibles."

Evolution of the Nomination Process

As noted above, the presidential elections of 1789 and 1792 were conducted without a separate nominating procedure. The system operated as the Founders intended: members of the political elite from the various states, acting through the mechanism of the electoral college, chose George Washington to lead the country. Persons of diverse political views agreed that the nation's wartime hero was a "patriot king" who would rule in the interest of all the people.

In Congress, however, no such political consensus prevailed. In 1790 Alexander Hamilton, the first secretary of the treasury in the Washington administration, presented an economic program that would establish a national bank and a tariff to protect U.S. manufacturers and merchants from foreign competition. Thomas Jefferson, then secretary of state, and James Madison, a member of Congress, opposed the program on the grounds that it benefited only mercantile interests and not the nation's farmers, for whom they had great admiration. Subsequently, Jefferson and Madison also differed with Hamilton over the Jay Treaty. Negotiated with England in 1794, the treaty obliged the British to withdraw their troops from forts in the Northwest. However, it failed to satisfy two grievances of Jefferson and Madison: the lack of compensation for slaves carried away by British soldiers during the Revolution and the impressment into the British Navy of sailors from U.S. ships seized by Britain for trading with the French (then at war with Britain).

Out of these controversies over domestic and foreign policy emerged an important institution not provided for by the U.S. Constitution— political parties. The Federalist party had formed by the early 1790s, with Hamilton acting as the principal initiator of policies in Congress and Washington as the popular leader who could rally support for such policies. Federalists soon were running for Congress and, once in office, voting for Hamilton's programs.[4] Jefferson's resignation from the Washington administration in 1793 and Madison's congressional disputes with Hamilton paved the way for a rival political party, the Republicans.[5] By the mid-1790s cohesive pro- and antiadministration blocs were voting against each other in Congress, and congressional candidates were being identified as Republicans as well as Federalists.[6] George Washington's retirement at the end of his second term in 1797 enabled party politics to spread from Congress to the presidency.

The creation of political parties in the United States thus ended the brief period in which the political elite of the day selected the president. From then on, party politics would determine the nation's chief executive, a development that required the parties to devise a means of choosing, or nominating, candidates to run under the party name. Over time, influence over presidential nominations has shifted and broadened within the parties, moving first from members of Congress to local party leaders, and later to a broad base of party activists and supporters of the candidates.

Congressional Caucuses

In 1796 the Federalists chose their candidate, John Adams, through consultation among their prominent leaders. The Republicans turned to their party members in Congress, who nominated Thomas Jefferson as their standard-bearer. Four years later the Federalists followed suit, and the congressional caucus became the nominating mechanism for both parties.

The congressional caucus offered several practical advantages in this early stage of party development. Members of Congress, already assembled in the nation's capital, faced minimal transportation problems in meeting to select a nominee. With so few members participating, the nominating task was kept manageable. Legislators were familiar with potential presidential candidates from all parts of the new country, making them logical agents for choosing candidates for an office with a nationwide constituency, and the caucus provided an organizational base for launching coordinated campaigns. Finally, caucuses provided a means to exercise peer review of candidates' credentials as one group of politicians assessed another's skills and abilities.

But the congressional caucus had serious flaws that eventually proved fatal. First, it violated the separation-of-powers principle of the Constitution in giving members of the legislative body a routine role in choosing the president, a role much wider than the narrow one provided in the Constitution in the event of an electoral college deadlock. Second, the caucus could not represent areas in which the party had lost the previous congressional election. Third, interested and informed citizens who participated in grass-roots party activities (especially campaigns) had no means to participate in congressional caucus deliberations.

The Federalists were the first to be affected by the system's limitations. With the decline of their political fortunes, the size of the party's congressional delegation shrank so much that it ceased to provide geographic representation. The party turned to alternative nominating devices, employing what one political scientist calls "primitive national conventions" in 1808 and 1812 and holding no organized caucus or convention in 1816, the last presidential contest the Federalists contested.[7] The Republicans used the congressional caucus effectively, though not without criticism, between 1800 and 1820 to nominate three Virginians who had previously served as secretary of state: Thomas Jefferson in 1800 and 1804, James Madison in 1808 and 1812, and James Monroe in 1816 and 1820. In 1824, however, three-fourths of the Republican members of Congress boycotted the caucus to protest an attempt to nominate Secretary of the Treasury William Crawford, who was seriously ill.

The 1824 election brought an end to the congressional caucus nomination system. That year, five presidential candidates were nominated, principally by state legislatures. One candidate was Andrew Jackson, who was proposed by the Tennessee legislature. Jackson won more popular votes and more electoral votes than any other candidate, but failed to achieve a majority of the electoral votes; as a result, the election was thrown into the House of Representatives where former secretary of state John Quincy Adams achieved victory through a political deal with House Speaker Henry Clay, another of the candidates. Clay threw his considerable House support to Adams in return for being named secretary of state. "King Caucus," as it had come to be called by critics, was permanently discredited by these shenanigans.

In 1828 responsibility for presidential nominations was vested entirely in the states; legislatures and conventions chose "favorite sons" such as Jackson and Adams as candidates. Although the congressional caucus had been too centralized to represent the state and local party units, the new system proved too decentralized to select national candidates. Some device was needed that would represent party elements throughout the country and at the same time facilitate the nomination of a common candidate.

National Party Conventions

The nomination method that emerged to satisfy these needs was the party convention, a truly national meeting that included delegates from all the states. Rail transportation made such assemblies feasible; expanding citizen participation in presidential elections made them necessary. With the advent of the convention, influence over selection of the party nominee shifted to state and local party leaders, particularly those able to commit large blocs of delegate support to a given candidate.

Two minor parties with no appreciable representation in Congress paved the way. The Anti-Masons and National Republicans convened national assemblies in 1831.[8] The Democratic-Republicans, as Jefferson's Republicans had come to be known, held a national convention in 1832 under President Andrew Jackson. Jackson, first elected in 1828, viewed the convention as an ideal way of rallying support and securing the vice-presidential nomination for his handpicked candidate, Martin Van Buren.

Since the early 1830s, major political parties have nominated their presidential and vice-presidential candidates by holding national conventions. National committees have called the presidential nominating conventions into session and conventions have adopted a platform of common policy positions since the 1850s.[9] Two basic features of the early conventions have persisted to the present day, though in modified form: delegates are still selected by states and allocated primarily on the basis of each state's representation in Congress (senators plus House members). In other respects, however, conventions have undergone substantial change. Until early in the twentieth century, national conventions were periods of intense bargaining among local party leaders from throughout the nation who were willing to trade the voting support of their state delegations in exchange for jobs and other benefits controlled by the federal government. In the era of "brokered conventions" nominees were chosen through negotiations among a relatively small number of party chiefs. Early in the century, with the emergence and spread of presidential primaries as a means to select convention delegates, convention procedures became more open and deliberations less susceptible to tight control by party leaders. Nonetheless, party leaders continued to dominate convention business—including the presidential nomination— through 1968.

Although today's nominating conventions resemble those that developed more than 150 years ago, the entire nomination process has undergone drastic change since 1968. Influence over the nomination decision has effectively shifted from party leaders to those who participate in presidential primaries or presidential caucuses. (Although convention delegates chosen through these methods do not formally select the nominee until the party convention, for all intents and purposes the decision has been made before the convention begins.) Because the presidential nomination process is so fluid and complex, party leaders, especially

11

among the Democrats, have been tempted to engage in "institutional tinkering" by changing the rules. But as observers have noted, the same complexity and fluidity produce "great latitude for unintended consequences." [10] The next section of this chapter focuses on the current rules governing the nomination of candidates and recent changes in those rules.

Current Nomination Rules

The rules that govern any political contest are important. Rules both prescribe behavior in political contests and influence election outcomes. By determining the strategies and tactics that participants adopt to improve their chances of winning, rules shape the nominating process. Yet they are shaped by the process as well. As people seek advantage for their particular interests, rules become the focus of struggles for change. The prevailing rules are seldom neutral: inevitably they favor some individuals and interests over others—sometimes by design, sometimes not.

Since the late 1960s the rules of the presidential nomination contest have become especially important. They are highly complicated because they come from a variety of sources—one-hundred state political parties and fifty legislatures, the national political parties, and the Congress. (Sometimes individuals also turn to the courts to interpret provisions of these regulations and to reconcile conflicts among them.) In addition, the rules have been changed so drastically and so often, particularly in the Democratic party, that it is difficult for candidates and their supporters to keep up with the changes. These changes have created confusion and uncertainty for many participants and have favored those who somehow manage to puzzle their way through the welter of rules. Indeed, some contend that Sen. George McGovern won the 1972 Democratic nomination partly because of his close association with the changes made in the nomination rules of that year. (As discussed later in this chapter, McGovern chaired the commission that helped bring about changes in the 1972 nomination contest.)

The following three sections examine the rules for apportioning convention delegates among the states, selecting delegates within the states, and financing nomination campaigns.

Allocating National Convention Delegates

A presidential candidate starts out with a well-defined goal: to win a majority of the votes at the party's national convention and so be nominated for the presidency. To win the nomination at the 1988 conventions the Republican nominee needed 1,139 votes out of 2,277 and the Democratic nominee required 2,082 out of 4,162.

Although the numbers of convention votes differ, the parties use similar formulas to decide how many votes each state is entitled to cast at the convention. The parties take into account the size of a state's congressional delegation or its population in determining its basic vote allocation, and its record in supporting the party's candidates in recent years in allocating extra, or "bonus," votes to each state. The methods that parties use to determine these bonus votes benefit some states at the expense of others.

The Republican party is interested in a state's recent record in voting not only for the presidential nominee but also for governors, senators, and representatives; however, the party does not take into account the *size* of the popular vote for these officials, but simply whether or not they win. The smaller states, especially those in which the Republican party dominates the nonpresidential elections, therefore wield disproportionate influence at the GOP convention. For example, Utah, a state with a small population that has elected a large number of Republican officials, is benefited, even though its small size means that it can cast relatively few popular votes for Republican candidates for president. A large two-party state such as New York, however, is at a disadvantage. Democratic candidates may win elections for governor, U.S. senator, or U.S. representative, costing the state Republican party bonus votes at the convention. The large number of popular votes the state has cast over the years for Republican presidential candidates is not taken into account, only whether the Republican candidate carried the state.

In contrast, the Democratic party focuses on a state's voting record in recent presidential elections to the exclusion of gubernatorial and congressional contests; moreover, the party is concerned with the total number of popular votes cast for its presidential candidates. A populous two-party state such as New York is favored by the system. Its size means that it will cast a large number of popular votes for the Democratic presidential candidate (whether the candidate carries the state or not); the fact that Democratic candidates lose nonpresidential elections will not work to the state's disadvantage at the convention. However, a small state in which the Democrats are dominant, such as Rhode Island, is disadvantaged. Democratic presidential candidates, while carrying the state, do not win a large number of popular votes, and Democratic victories in nonpresidential elections earn the state no bonus votes.

Selecting Delegates

State delegates to the national conventions of both parties are chosen by one of three methods. In some states *party leaders* such as members of the state central committee, the party chairperson, or the governor (if the party controls that office) select the delegates. In others, a *state convention* composed of persons themselves elected at caucuses and conventions held in smaller geographical areas, such as precincts, wards, counties, and congressional districts makes the selection. Finally, in many states the voters select delegates directly in *presidential primaries*. States sometimes combine methods, using a primary to elect district delegates but allowing their state committees or state conventions to choose "at-large" delegates representing the whole state.

Traditionally, persons active in party affairs—public and party officials referred to as "professionals"—dominated the selection of delegates. This was only natural under the first method, in which party officials formally appoint the delegates. Professionals also dominated under the second system because they manipulated the caucuses and conventions into choosing themselves and their loyal supporters as delegates. Moreover, professionals remained influential even after the introduction of presidential primaries by running for delegate positions. Because many states did not require delegates to vote for the candidate favored by rank-and-file voters in the primary, delegates were free to vote their own presidential preferences instead of the public's.

Between 1968 and 1980, however, there was a definite trend away from control by party professionals and toward increased participation by rank-and-file voters. In 1968 only seventeen states chose delegates by a presidential primary; in 1980, thirty-one did so. Meanwhile, the proportion of total national convention delegates chosen by both parties in primaries climbed from 38 percent to 72 percent. In the process, the primary replaced the state convention system as the dominant method for choosing delegates to the national convention. During the 1988 nomination campaign, 76.9 percent of the Republican convention delegates were selected in thirty-five Republican primaries. Thirty-four Democratic primaries chose 66.6 percent of the Democratic delegates.[11] Clearly, today's candidates for the presidential nomination of either party must court the support of voters more than that of party chieftains.

Many of the new primary laws passed between 1968 and 1980 increased the influence of rank-and-file voters over their party's ultimate choice for president. States encouraged delegates chosen in primaries to indicate which candidate they supported for president so that voters could predict how their delegates would vote at the national convention.

Some states also permitted voters to indicate their personal preference for president and legally bound the delegates to support the preferred candidates for one or more ballots at the convention. Moreover, under many of the new state laws, a presidential candidate's name was placed on the ballot if his or her candidacy was recognized by the national news media. A candidate who wanted to be removed from the race in such states had to file an affidavit swearing that he or she was not a candidate in any state. This system prevented candidates from choosing the state primaries they would enter, thus allowing voters to pass judgment on a broader range of potential nominees than would otherwise have been available to them.

The trend toward greater influence for rank-and-file voters retreated briefly between 1980 and 1984 as six jurisdictions abandoned the primary in favor of the caucus-convention for selecting delegates to the national convention. As a result, the proportion of delegates for the two major parties' conventions chosen by state presidential primaries declined from 72 percent to 54 percent. But these changes proved short-lived; the 1988 election saw a return to the primary method.

During the twenty-year period 1968-1988 the system of choosing delegates to the national convention underwent massive change. (See Figure 1-1.) The use of primaries spread, and many were scheduled earlier in the year. Still, the system was a "mixed" one, with thirty-five states and the District of Columbia using primaries and twenty states using caucus-conventions. These totals exceed fifty because in five states (Idaho, North Dakota, South Carolina, Texas, and Virginia) Republicans and Democrats used different methods to select delegates. (Vermont held a nonbinding primary to gauge voter preferences but not to select delegates.) As one can see in Figure 1-1, there were some regional variations in the use of the two methods: the West remained the only region to rely more heavily on caucus-conventions, whereas primaries outnumbered caucus-conventions in both midwestern and northeastern states. Primaries were used to select convention delegates from every state in the southern region except for Democrats in Delaware and South Carolina and Republicans in Virginia who continued to use the convention-caucus method.

In addition to the passage of laws by state legislatures, the national political parties have taken action to reform the process for selecting delegates to the national conventions.

Democrats. The vast changes in the Democratic party's procedures after 1968 can be traced to that year's convention in Chicago. It was an assembly marked by acrimonious debates over the Vietnam War

Figure 1-1   Presidential Primaries: More and Earlier

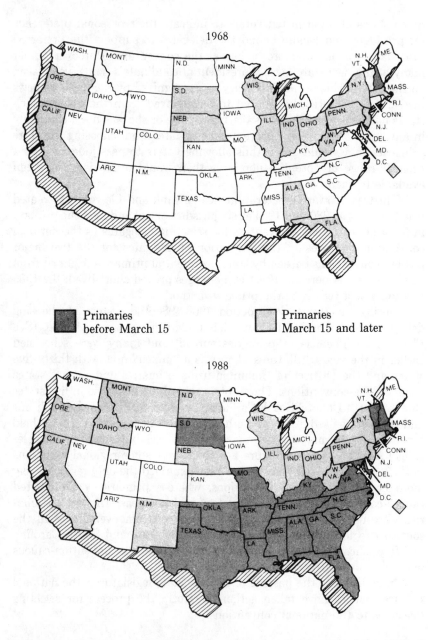

1968

Primaries
before March 15

Primaries
March 15 and later

1988

Note: Both maps include "binding" primaries that selected delegates and "nonbinding" primaries that were beauty contests only. Neither Alaska nor Hawaii holds presidential primaries. South Carolina held a primary for Republicans only.

Source: The Elections of 1988, ed. Michael Nelson (Washington, D.C.: CQ Press, 1989), figure 2-1, 30.

within the convention hall and by bloody battles outside the convention arena between war protesters and the police. Sen. Hubert Humphrey won the nomination without entering a single statewide presidential primary, because party leaders favoring him dominated the delegations of the caucus-convention states. The 1968 delegates were concerned that much of the chaos of that convention occurred because the regular party organization was impervious to the will of rank-and-file Democrats. The delegates consequently adopted a resolution requiring state parties to give "all Democrats a full, meaningful, and timely opportunity to partici-pate" in the selection of delegates. Not long after, the Democratic Na-tional Committee (DNC) established a commission chaired by Senator McGovern of South Dakota to assist state parties in meeting that re-quirement. This action established a pattern: following the 1972 conven-tion a new commission, this time under the leadership of Baltimore councilwoman Barbara Mikulski, continued the effort to change the delegate selection process. After the 1976 national convention, the party organized still a third commission, chaired by Morley Winograd (state chairperson of the Michigan Democratic party). In each case the commis-sion recommended changes in rules affecting the selection of convention delegates for the next convention; most of these were adopted by the DNC and ultimately by the Democratic national convention.

For the most part, the battle lines in this series of rules changes were drawn between party professionals and political "amateurs," persons not traditionally active in party affairs but who became involved because of an interest in a particular candidate or issue. The amateurs won the struggle to open up the selection process when the McGovern Commis-sion recommended that states remove restrictive voter registration laws so that non-Democrats and unaffiliated voters could become party mem-bers. At the same time, the control of traditional party leaders over caucuses and conventions was reduced by regulations that forbade them to serve automatically as ex officio delegates and by requirements for written party rules, adequate public notice of meetings, and the elimina-tion of proxy voting.

A second issue that plagued all three party commissions was the representation of particular groups within state delegations to the na-tional convention. The amateurs scored an initial victory when the Mc-Govern Commission recommended that minority groups, women, and young people (those age eighteen to thirty) be represented in state delegations "in reasonable relationship to the groups' presence in the state." This recommendation led many states to adopt a quota system when they chose their delegates to the 1972 convention. Other minority groups, however, such as those of Italian and Polish descent, who had traditionally supported the party, questioned why they had not been included in the quotas. Other Democrats opposed the idea of quotas altogether because the quotas determined the results of the political process rather than merely the opportunity to participate in it—the traditional American concept of political equality. The Mikulski Commission adopted the latter concept by eliminating the quotas in favor of more inclusive "affirmative action plans," whereby each state party undertook to encourage "minorities, Native Americans, women, and other traditionally underrepresented groups to participate and to be represented in the delegate selection process and all party affairs." The idea of quotas resurfaced as professionals and amateurs battled over representation at the 1980 convention. This time each achieved a victory: the professionals won an increase in the size of state delegations by 10 percent to permit selection of state party and elected officials; the amateurs won the adoption of a rule requiring that state delegations comprise equal numbers of men and women.

A third major problem for all three party commissions was the division of state delegation votes among the various contending candidates. The McGovern Commission recommended that states abolish the "winner-take-all" primaries—whereby the candidate who received a plurality of the popular vote was awarded all the delegates—in favor of a provision for the "fair representation of minority views on presidential candidates." California refused to follow this recommendation (the commission only "urged" rather than "required" the action). At the 1972 convention, McGovern received all 271 votes of the California delegates, although he had beaten Humphrey in the primary by only 45 to 39 percent of the popular vote. The irony of that development led the Democrats to abolish statewide winner-take-all contests in 1976, so that candidates winning at least 15 percent of the votes in presidential primaries and caucus-convention meetings would receive their proportional share of a state's delegate votes. For the 1980 nomination, Democrats extended the proportional representation principle to district contests. The minimum cutoff figure for candidates entitled to delegate votes was determined by dividing the number of district delegates by one hundred. (In a district with five delegates, for example, the cutoff would be 20 percent.) In no case, however, was the cutoff figure to be higher than 25 percent, regardless of the number of delegates elected in a district.

The battle over rules for the selection of delegates to Democratic national conventions continued in the 1980s. The DNC again appointed a commission—this one chaired by Gov. James B. Hunt, Jr., of North Carolina—to develop rules for the 1984 nomination contest. This time party professionals were determined to establish rules that would give them a greater role in the nomination process and also facilitate the selection of "their" kind of candidate rather than an "outsider" like McGovern or Jimmy Carter. They clearly prevailed over the political amateurs in the changes proposed by the Hunt Commission and later adopted by the national committee and the 1984 convention. A bloc of "superdelegates" composed of party and elected officials (constituting some 14 percent of the convention votes in 1984 and 16 percent in 1988) was created; state officials and Democratic members of the House and Senate were responsible for choosing these superdelegates (typically themselves), who were to go to the 1984 convention uncommitted. Another change also favored the states, particularly populous ones, by allowing them to use once again the winner-take-all principle in district contests and thereby reward a front-runner with a large bloc of delegate votes.[12] Finally, the new rules abolished a provision that bound all delegates to the 1980 national convention to vote on the first ballot for the candidate to whom they were linked in the state's delegate selection process. (The vital part this provision played in the 1980 convention will be discussed in Chapter 2.) The 1984 delegates were therefore legally free to vote as they desired at that year's convention.

Because unsuccessful Democratic candidates Gary Hart and Jesse Jackson were dissatisfied with the 1984 rules (which, they said, favored Walter Mondale), the national convention created the Fairness Commission to study their complaints. The commission, chaired by Donald L. Fowler of South Carolina, sought primarily to develop rules that would enable the party to build consensus behind a candidate in 1988.

In the end, only minor changes were made in the 1984 rules. The commission actually increased the number of superdelegates from about 550 to some 650, which meant that all the Democratic governors, all the members of the DNC, and 80 percent of the Democratic members of Congress occupied delegate seats at the 1988 convention. The Fairness Commission also relaxed the 1984 rule that restricted participation in the nomination process to Democrats, so that a number of states such as Wisconsin and Montana were able to conduct "open" primaries in 1988 with the approval of the national party. In 1988, ten states employed open primaries that allowed voters to participate in either the Democratic or Republican party's primary election and another eight states allowed independents to participate in the primaries but prohibited registered members of the other party from "crossing over."

As a concession to the major critics of the 1984 rules—principally backers of Jesse Jackson—the proportion of votes a candidate had to receive in a primary or caucus to qualify for delegates was lowered from 20 to 15 percent. To advance party unity, rules changes for 1992 were considered even before the 1988 convention began. Jackson supporters won two changes they hoped would benefit their candidate: primary winners would no longer be awarded bonus delegates (something that had been done in eight states, including Florida, New York, and Ohio) and the number of superdelegates would be reduced substantially, perhaps to as few as four hundred, by withdrawing seats previously reserved for members of the DNC. In subsequent planning for 1992, however, Democrats later reconsidered these agreements; the prohibition on bonus delegates was retained but DNC members were once again made automatic uncommitted delegates for the next convention.

Compared to previous rules changes, those for 1992 are relatively minor. In 1984 and 1988, the Democrats, for the first time in a generation, operated under essentially the same rules in back-to-back contests; the string will be extended to three consecutive contests in 1992. In 1988, for the first time since 1968, a postelection commission was not empaneled to review the rules of the nomination struggle.

Republicans. The Republican party also has made changes in its delegate selection process even though its leaders have not faced the pressures for reform that confronted Democratic leaders. A committee chaired by Rosemary Ginn, a Missouri member of the Republican National Committee (RNC), recommended proposals that were implemented in the choosing of delegates to the 1976 convention. Included were provisions, similar to those of the McGovern Commission, that reduced the influence of traditional party leaders by eliminating them as ex officio delegates, that regularized the nomination process by informing citizens how to participate in it, and that increased participation by opening the primaries and the state conventions to all qualified citizens.

At the same time, the Republican party has not attempted to regulate selection of national convention delegates nearly as extensively as has the Democratic party. The 1972 Republican national convention turned down recommendations of the Ginn Committee to include in future conventions persons under twenty-five years of age in "numerical equity to their voting strength in a state" and to have one man, one woman, one person under twenty-five, and one member of a minority group on each of the convention's principal committees. In 1975 the RNC refused to adopt the recommendation of a new committee chaired by Rep. William Steiger of Wisconsin that all states be required to have their affirmative action plans approved by the national committee. Nor have the Republicans moved to abolish winner-take-all primaries, like the one in California. The winner-take-all principle proved especially important to the 1988 campaign of George Bush, who finished first in each of the sixteen Republican primaries conducted on March 8, the day known as Super Tuesday. Thus the national Republican party has been much less willing than its Democratic counterpart to intervene in state decisions on the selection of delegates to the national convention.

Effect of Changes in Delegate Selection Rules

The rules changes made from 1968 to 1980 had a profound effect on the choosing of presidential nominees, particularly for the Democratic party. The proliferation of primaries and the deliberate lessening of the influence of party leaders in caucus-convention states made these leaders far less influential in the nomination process. Such professionals, who traditionally used their skills to select persons considered electable and loyal to the party (such as Humphrey), were largely replaced by political amateurs who supported "issue-oriented" and "antiestablishment" candidates for the presidency (such as McGovern and Carter). Despite these changes, the backgrounds of the new breed of candidates were consistent with those of earlier presidents.

Democratic rules designed to increase the representation of traditionally disadvantaged groups in the nomination process also brought the intended results. Women in particular benefited. In 1968, before the Democratic reforms, women constituted only 13 percent of the delegates at the Democratic convention. In 1972 that figure nearly tripled to 38 percent and, after a slight decline to 33 percent in 1976, rose to almost 50 percent in 1980. It remained at that level in 1984 and 1988 as a consequence of the party's decision to require that both sexes be equally represented at the Democratic national convention. More women delegates have also attended the Republican convention, but the increase has not been as startling. Women made up 33 percent of delegates at the 1988 Republican convention. The number of African-American delegates has risen dramatically at Democratic conventions (from 5 percent of delegates in 1968 to 23 percent in 1988, while the Republican percentage rose from 2 to 4 percent over the same period). In early 1989, the Democrats chose Ronald H. Brown as the new DNC Chairman. Brown is the first black to hold the post in either party.

Finally, Democratic rules changes ending the winner-take-all primary in favor of a proportional division of states' convention votes made victories in states such as California less important than they used to be. Although George McGovern owed his convention victory in 1972 to the 271 votes he won from that state, Jimmy Carter won his party's nomination in 1976 and in 1980 without winning California. (Gov. Jerry

21

Brown carried the state in 1976; Kennedy carried it in 1980.) The proportional rule also encouraged candidates to participate in state primaries they did not expect to win, because they had a chance to receive some convention votes rather than being shut out completely, as had occurred in winner-take-all contests.

The rules favored by the party professionals in 1984 also brought about the desired effects. Walter Mondale—the candidate they preferred—benefited by the new rules. He received an overwhelming share of the votes at the national convention from the superdelegates and did very well in states that used the winner-take-all principle to allocate delegates in district contests. In states that used caucuses to select their delegates he won a greater number of votes than did Gary Hart or Jesse Jackson (recall that more states adopted this method in 1984). As a result, Mondale prevailed at the convention, even though his two rivals received a combined share of 55 percent of the votes cast in the primaries. Prior to 1988 Hart and Jackson supporters successfully pushed for rules changes they hoped would help their candidates, but Gary Hart withdrew from the race in early 1987 and Dukakis went on to best Jesse Jackson. During the 1988 contest, Dukakis won 42 percent of all votes cast in Democratic primaries and carried 271 of the 445 districts in which votes were cast.[13] Jesse Jackson's convention support was greater among delegates selected through caucuses (36 percent) than among delegates chosen through primaries (28 percent), but Dukakis had substantial margins in both categories.[14]

Financing Presidential Nomination Campaigns

Historically, restrictions on contributions to presidential campaigns have not worked. The federal government passed legislation in 1907 forbidding corporations to contribute money to presidential candidates, but corporations easily circumvented the law by paying executives extra compensation, which they and their families subsequently contributed in their own name. The 1947 Taft-Hartley Act prohibited contributions by labor unions, but unions, too, evaded the restrictions by forming political action committees (PACs) to solicit voluntary donations from members and to spend the funds in the committee's name. Finally, the Hatch Act of 1940 (which limited individual contributions to a candidate for federal office to $5,000) and a federal tax law that imposed progressive tax rates on contributions of more than $3,000 to a single committee both proved ineffective because numerous committees were formed for a single candidate, and each committee was entitled to accept a $5,000 contribution.

The move for campaign reform began with President John F. Kennedy, who knew the advantages wealth gave a candidate.[15] He appointed the Commission on Campaign Costs, which in 1962 issued a report proposing public reporting of campaign expenditures, tax incentives for contributors, and matching funds for presidential candidates. Nothing came of the proposals during the 1960s, but they laid the groundwork for the wave of reform that swept the country in the 1970s. In 1971 and again in 1974 Congress passed legislation affecting campaign financing. In January 1976, however, in *Buckley v. Valeo,* the Supreme Court ruled certain provisions of the legislation unconstitutional;[16] later that year Congress responded by enacting still further regulations governing the use of money in federal elections. Finally, in 1979 Congress added more amendments to the campaign finance legislation.

A variety of financial regulations therefore govern the conduct of presidential campaigns. The following sections discuss the major ones affecting the nomination process. (Some of the provisions also apply to the general election campaign, which is treated in Chapter 3.)

Disclosure of Information. Presidential candidates and committees are required to provide full information on the financing of their campaigns. They must report the names of all contributors who give at least $200 and must itemize expenses of $200 or more. This information is filed with the Federal Election Commission (FEC), the agency responsible for administering the campaign legislation. The FEC is a bipartisan body of six members nominated by the president and confirmed by the Senate.

Limits on Contributions. Individuals may contribute no more than $1,000 to a presidential candidate for each election (the nomination and general election are considered separate contests), $5,000 to a political action committee (one that contributes to more than one candidate), and $20,000 to the national committee of a political party. The total contribution may not exceed $25,000 a year. Presidential candidates are free to spend an unlimited amount of their own money and their immediate family's money on their campaigns, but if they accept public financing, their contributions to their own campaign are limited to $50,000 per election.

Limits on Spending. Candidates may spend as much as they wish on presidential campaigns unless they accept public financing, in which case limitations apply. For the 1988 presidential campaign, limits for the nomination process included a national ceiling of $23.05 million plus $4.6 million for fund-raising costs—a total of $27.65 million. In addition, state spending limitations based on population applied. In 1988, California had the highest spending limit ($7.1 million); the lowest figure, which applied to a number of small states, was $444,600. These figures will be adjusted in 1992 to reflect population and inflation data.

Independent Campaign Expenditures. There is no limitation on independent campaign expenditures, that is, those made by individuals or political committees advocating the defeat or election of a candidate but not made in conjunction with the candidate's campaign. However, individuals or committees making such expenditures in amounts of more than $250 must file a report with the FEC and must state, under penalty of perjury, that the expenditure was not made in collusion with the candidate. Such expenditures have been more significant during the general election than during the nomination process.

Public Financing. Candidates for the presidential nomination who are able to raise $100,000 in individual contributions, with at least $5,000 collected in twenty different states, receive federal matching funds equal to the total amount of contributions of $250 or less. By checking a box on their federal income tax forms, taxpayers authorize the federal government to set aside one dollar of their tax payments for public financing of campaigns, but that voluntary financing arrangement may be in danger of insolvency. (See Chapter 5.) In 1988, candidates could qualify for a maximum of just over $11.5 million in federal matching funds (50 percent of the base cap) for the nomination process. Sixteen candidates qualified for a total of $67.5 million in matching funds. The federal government also provided $9.2 million to the Democratic and Republican parties to finance their nominating conventions.

Like delegate selection rules, campaign finance laws have had a significant effect on presidential nominations. The sources and techniques for raising funds have changed radically. Rather than depending upon a few "fat cats" to finance their campaigns (in 1968 insurance executive W. Clement Stone gave $2.8 million to Richard Nixon's campaign), candidates now raise funds from a large number of small individual contributors, primarily through direct mail solicitation.[17] Public funds also make it possible for persons who formerly could not afford to mount a nomination campaign to do so. Sen. Fred Harris had to abandon a presidential bid in 1972 because he could not raise money from large contributors; but with federal matching funds available, he was able to run in 1976. Moreover, even Right to Life candidate Ellen McCormack was able to qualify for federal funds that year, as was Leonora Fulani of the New Alliance Party in 1988. At the same time, the new method of raising money from a large number of individuals and thereby qualifying for federal matching funds means that candidates tend to start their campaigns earlier than they formerly did. Finally, as election specialist Herbert Alexander suggests, public funding also helps "free each candidate's personal organization from the party hierarchy." [18]

Thus a variety of rules help shape the nomination contest. The remainder of the chapter focuses on the people directly affected by such rules—the presidential candidates themselves.

Defining the Pool of Candidates

Unlike the rules governing the nomination process, those relating to the qualifications of presidential candidates are minimal. To be eligible for the presidency, individuals need to meet only three requirements, set forth in Article II, Section 1, of the Constitution. One must be a "natural born" citizen,[19] at least thirty-five years of age, and a resident of the United States for fourteen years or longer. In 1987, Michael Nelson estimated that some 87 million Americans met these constitutional requirements, a figure that will be even higher under the 1990 census results. But the pool of "plausible" candidates is far smaller than that of "possible" candidates.[20]

Although there are few *formal* requirements for the presidency, there are major *informal* ones. Persons who entertain presidential ambitions (the bug is considered to be virtually incurable once it strikes) must possess what is generally called "political availability"; that is, they must have the political experiences and personal characteristics that presumably make them attractive to political activists and to the general voting public. Although there is no simple checklist of job qualifications for the presidency, one can gain an understanding of the political experiences and personal characteristics that put an individual in line for a presidential nomination by looking at past candidates. Even this approach poses some difficulties, since the attitudes of political leaders and the American public change over time. The following discussion, which focuses on the period since the election of Franklin D. Roosevelt in 1932, analyzes the informal standards of presidential "availability" that operated during that era, including how some of those standards have changed in the past half-century.

Political Experience of Presidential Candidates

In terms of the electoral timeline, we can think of candidates' strategic career decisions as occurring over an extended period long before the election year begins. Like their predecessors, most nominees and other major presidential candidates since 1932 (see Appendix C for a list of the 1992 Democratic aspirants) had previous service in a civilian, elective, political office. The two exceptions among nominees were Wendell Willkie, who was president of a public utility company when he was nominated by the Republicans in 1940, and Dwight D. Eisenhower, a career military man and World War II hero who became the successful GOP candidate in 1952. The campaign in 1988 included an unusually large number of aspirants who lacked experience in elected office. Campaigns were mounted by Jesse Jackson, a civil rights organizer; Marion G. (Pat) Robertson, a television evangelist and businessman; and Alexander Haig, a retired military officer. Lee Iacocca, chairman of the Chrysler Corporation, was often mentioned as a candidate early in the campaign.

Ordinarily, nominees and most major candidates can claim to have occupied a variety of political posts during the course of their political careers, but the particular offices they held immediately before becoming presidential candidates are relatively limited. As the following discussion indicates, candidates of the party out of power follow paths somewhat different from those of the party holding the presidency, but when one looks back to the last half of the nineteenth century, it is striking how little the background characteristics of nominees has changed.[21]

Since 1932 a principal recruiting ground for the party out of power—one long popular in U.S. politics—has been a *state governorship*. Throughout this era, both major parties have looked to governors as promising candidates. From 1932 through 1956 governors tended to become the nominees: Democrat Franklin Roosevelt of New York in 1932 and Republicans Alfred Landon of Kansas in 1936 and Thomas Dewey of New York in 1944. After a hiatus from 1960 through 1972, the state governorship once again emerged as the dominant background for successful presidential nominees of the party out of power: former Georgia governor Jimmy Carter won the Democratic presidential nomination in 1976; former California governor Ronald Reagan became the Republican standard-bearer in 1980; and the sitting governor of Massachusetts, Michael Dukakis, was the Democratic nominee in 1988. Only in 1984, when Democrats nominated former Vice President Walter Mondale, did the party out of power not turn to a governor during this period, although Mondale shared a significant common characteristic with Carter and Reagan—none of the three held an elected office at the time he sought the nomination; thus each had the freedom to run a full-time campaign.

The other major source of presidential candidates for the party out of power since 1932 is the *U.S. Senate*. Many senators have been presidential candidates throughout the period, particularly between 1960 and 1972. During these years, the Democrats nominated senators John Kennedy of Massachusetts in 1960 and George McGovern of South Dakota in 1972, and the Republicans chose Barry Goldwater of Arizona in 1964.[22] Lyndon Johnson and Richard Nixon, respectively the Democratic and Republican nominees in 1964 and 1968, had served in the Senate before moving on to the vice presidency.

Several factors have increased the importance of the Senate as a recruiting ground for presidents. As Nelson Polsby points out, the nationalization of American politics has tended to shift political attention away from the state capitals to Washington, D.C., and senators have taken advantage of the opportunity to project themselves over the national news media concentrated there.[23] Senators increasingly have associated themselves with major public policies, a development that provides them great political visibility. In particular, the nation's increasing involvement in foreign affairs since World War II has placed the Senate in the public eye because of its influential role in the conduct of relations with other countries. Moreover, the six-year term of senators enables them to try for the presidency without giving up their legislative seat: of the senators who have run for the presidency since 1922, only Barry Goldwater lost his place in the upper chamber as a result of his candidacy.[24] Despite these factors, only twice have senators been elected directly to the White House (Harding in 1920 and Kennedy in 1960).[25]

Although prominent since 1972, the position of governors seeking the presidency may be weaker today than it was in the past. State chief executives no longer hold as crucial a position in the presidential selection process as they did when, as heads of state delegations, they negotiated with their peers at the national convention to choose the party's nominee, who frequently turned out to be a governor. Another handicap of recent governors who aspire to the presidency is that only those from states with large cities serving as communications centers for the nation, such as New York, Los Angeles, and Chicago, receive as much publicity as national officials in Washington, D.C. In addition, governors have no significant responsibilities in foreign affairs and frequently do not appear well-versed in such matters. They also are more tied to their home states (particularly when the state legislature is in session) than are senators, who are expected to move freely about the country. Finally, many governors serve short stints in office—in some cases because of legal limitations on their tenure, in others because they fail to meet public expectations that they will solve major domestic problems without increasing taxes. They therefore find it difficult to become sufficiently well known to be viable presidential candidates.

Carter's election in 1976 and Reagan's bid for the nomination that year and election in 1980 indicate that governors possess some advantages as candidates, particularly if they are *not* occupying the governor's mansion at the time they seek the presidency (a point driven home by Dukakis's defeat). Unlike Dukakis, Carter and Reagan were free to devote full time to the demanding task of winning the nomination, an opportunity not available to senators with heavy legislative duties who sought the presidency in both of those years (for example, Democrats Frank Church and Henry Jackson in 1976, Republicans Howard Baker and Robert Dole in 1980, and Dole again in 1988). Both Carter and Reagan also benefited from the anti-Washington mood of the voters, which made voters receptive to candidates who had not served in a national office. Citizen concern with the burgeoning costs of government and the problems of controlling the federal bureaucracy could continue to make governors attractive presidential candidates: governors can claim valuable executive experience in managing large-scale public enterprises and thousands of state government employees, in contrast to a senator's legislative duties and small personal staff. Finally, the decline in the public's concern over foreign affairs compared with the domestic economy during the 1976-1988 period may counteract the advantages senators held over governors as presidential candidates before the end of the Vietnam War. The defeat of Michael Dukakis in 1988 does not necessarily signal the end of this era, as his loss could be attributed to a faulty campaign, division within the Democratic party following the heated primary contest, and voter satisfaction with the Republican record.

It is probable that the offices of both U.S. senator and state governor will continue to be major recruitment grounds for presidential candidates of the party out of power. At this writing (April 1991), prominently mentioned Democratic hopefuls include three sitting governors (Bill Clinton of Arkansas, Mario Cuomo of New York, and L. Douglas Wilder of Virginia) as well as six senators (Lloyd Bentsen of Texas, Bill Bradley of New Jersey, Al Gore of Tennessee, Tom Harkin of Iowa, Robert Kerrey of Nebraska, and Sam Nunn of Georgia). A seventh interested senator, John D. (Jay) Rockefeller of West Virginia, formerly served two terms as governor of that state. Also known to be interested are Rep. Richard A. Gephardt of Missouri and civil rights activist Jesse Jackson, not to mention several other candidates from the senate and governor's mansion who were unable to win the nomination in 1988. Former senator Paul Tsongas of Massachusetts was the first to announce his candidacy in 1991. (See Appendix B for the backgrounds of major candidates in the Democratic party.)

For the party that occupies the presidency, *that office itself* is the major source of candidates. In only four instances since 1932 has the incumbent chief executive not been his party's subsequent nominee. In 1960 and 1988 Republican incumbents Dwight Eisenhower and Ronald Reagan were precluded from running again by the Twenty-second Amendment, and in 1952 and 1968 Democratic presidents Harry S. Truman and Lyndon B. Johnson chose not to seek another term. The exact reasons for Truman's and Johnson's decisions are unknown, but both held office at the time of highly unpopular wars in Korea and in Vietnam. In addition, both had been challenged and embarrassed politically in the New Hampshire primary, Truman by Sen. Estes Kefauver of Tennessee and Johnson by Sen. Eugene McCarthy of Minnesota.

When the incumbent president decides not to run or is constitutionally barred from doing so, recent experiences indicate that the office of *vice president* becomes the major source of presidential candidates for the party in power. In 1960 the Republicans chose Richard Nixon, who won the nomination virtually without opposition. (Governor Nelson Rockefeller of New York had considered making a bid that year but decided not to run when he determined early on that the vice president had the nomination locked up.) In 1968, the Democrats chose Vice President Hubert Humphrey as their nominee, but only after he had overcome the challenge of Senator McCarthy and after the assassination of Sen. Robert Kennedy of New York in early June had ended Kennedy's candidacy. George Bush overcame five major challengers from a variety of political backgrounds—Kansas senator Robert Dole, former Delaware governor Pierre (Pete) du Pont, New York representative Jack Kemp, former secretary of state Alexander Haig, and evangelist/businessman Marion G. (Pat) Robertson—to win the nomination in 1988 and the opportunity to succeed Ronald Reagan. Only in 1952 was the incumbent vice president, Alben Barkley, denied the presidential nomination. At the time he was seventy-five years old and not considered to be a major figure in the party.[26] In that instance, the principal candidates came from the traditional training grounds already discussed: the party's nominee, Adlai Stevenson, was the governor of Illinois; contenders Estes Kefauver of Tennessee and Richard Russell of Georgia represented their states in the U.S. Senate.

Incumbent presidents have natural advantages when it comes to winning their party's nomination. It is difficult for a party to admit to the voters that it made a mistake four years before when it nominated the candidate who won the presidency. As discussed in the next chapter, incumbents also have several political weapons they can use against candidates who seek to deny them their party's nomination. As a result, even unpopular presidents tend to be renominated. The Republicans chose Herbert Hoover again in 1932 in the midst of the Great Depression; and the Democrats renominated Jimmy Carter in 1980 when both inflation and unemployment were high, Americans were being held hostage in Iran, and Soviet troops occupied Afghanistan. Since 1932, three vice presidents who succeeded to the presidency on the death or resignation of their predecessors were subsequently nominated by their party—Democrats Harry Truman and Lyndon Johnson and Republican Gerald R. Ford. This record suggests that George Bush should expect smooth sailing to the 1992 Republican nomination, but the experiences of Truman and Johnson, who confronted intraparty opposition during an unpopular war, must have given Bush's political strategists a reason to pause after the initiation of hostilities with Iraq in January 1991. The widespread popularity of that conflict and its stunning military success suggest that Bush is likely to avoid a similar fate.

Recent developments also help explain why incumbent vice presidents are now more likely to win their party's nomination in their own right than they were in the past.[27] Presidential candidates of late tend to choose more capable running mates, individuals who are viable prospects for the presidency itself. In addition, recent presidents are assigning their vice presidents more meaningful responsibilities than did their predecessors. These duties include participating in political party activities (especially campaigning in off-year elections), which helps them forge ties with party chieftains; serving as liaisons with social groups, which draws vice presidents to the attention of group leaders; and acting as emissaries to foreign countries, which makes them visible to the general public. In the postwar era, however, vice presidents seemed to be winning nominations but losing the general election. Nixon and Humphrey lost in 1960 and 1968, as did Walter Mondale in 1984. In 1988 George Bush broke a long string of failed campaign efforts when he became the first incumbent vice president to win the presidency since Martin Van Buren in 1836.

Personal Characteristics of Presidential Candidates

Although nearly 90 million people meet the formal requirements for president, far fewer meet the informal criteria that have been commonly employed. Most constraining have been the limitations of gender and race. No woman and no African-American has ever been nominated for president by a national convention, although in the past twenty years several have waged national campaigns. Geraldine Ferraro was part of the Democrats' national ticket in 1984 as a vice-presidential nominee. Other "tests" based on personal characteristics have also been applied to presidential aspirants. Journalist Sidney Hyman listed several of these informal qualifications in 1959.[28] It is instructive to consider this list to appreciate how much has changed in the eight presidential contests that have occurred since that time. Hyman drew the following conclusions:

- Preferred candidates come from states that have a large electoral vote and a two-party voting record.
- Candidates from big northern states are favored over those from southern states.
- Conventions nominate only persons who are, or who can be made to appear, hospitable to the many economic interests in the nation.
- Presidential candidates, like the English Crown, are expected to represent an idealized version of home and family life.
- Although the majority of Americans live in large urban centers, preferred candidates come from small towns.
- Preferred candidates come from English ethnic stock.
- Nominating conventions have created an extraconstitutional religious test by their decisive preference for Protestant hopefuls.

Although many of the candidates in presidential contests since 1960 satisfied the above tests, some clearly did not. Past geographical preferences for nominees from northern, two-party states with a large electoral vote failed to prevent the nomination of Barry Goldwater, from Arizona; Johnson and Bush, from Texas; Humphrey and Mondale, from Minnesota; McGovern, from South Dakota; Carter, from Georgia; or Dukakis, from Massachusetts, a Democratic bastion. Nor were all the candidates from small towns. Nixon grew up on the outskirts of Los Angeles; John and Robert Kennedy, as well as Dukakis, were raised in the Boston area. Goldwater spent his young adult years in Phoenix, Humphrey in Minneapolis, and Edmund (Jerry) Brown in Sacramento. Reagan was raised in the small town of Dixon, Illinois, but his political career had its roots in the Los Angeles area.

Other of Hyman's tests pertaining to the social backgrounds of candidates also fail to apply to several candidates since 1960. John Kennedy's candidacy in 1960 violated the traditional preference for Protestants. Once he won, little was made of the fact that his brothers Robert and Edward were also Roman Catholic, as were other Democratic hopefuls—Eugene McCarthy and Edmund Brown (who even received training as a Jesuit priest). Nor did Republicans seem concerned that Senator Goldwater, though an Episcopalian, had a Jewish background on one side of his family. The related, traditional preference for English stock did little to deter the candidacies of the Kennedys, McCarthy, and Reagan of Irish background, Goldwater of Russian background, Mondale of Norwegian background, or Dukakis of Greek heritage.

In addition, several presidential candidates since 1960 could not be said to represent an idealized version of home and family life. In 1963 Nelson Rockefeller divorced his wife of over thirty years and remarried a much younger woman, a divorcée whose previous husband won custody of the children of that marriage. In 1976 Democratic candidate Morris Udall was divorced, and in 1980 it was widely known that Edward Kennedy's marriage was in serious trouble (he and his wife subsequently separated). Edmund Brown was unmarried and at one time was reputed to be having an affair with rock singer Linda Ronstadt. Although none of these candidates won their party's nomination, Reagan, also divorced, was both nominated and elected in the 1980 contest and thereby became the country's first president to have divorced and remarried. However, Gary Hart's widely reported relationship with Donna Rice, a younger woman, ended his 1988 presidential hopes even though he had entered the campaign as the front-runner.

Finally, several recent presidential candidates failed to meet Hyman's 1959 test of being or appearing to be hospitable to the many economic interests in the nation. Goldwater had private business interests (his family owned a department store), and Nixon had close political ties to conservative California businessmen, as did Reagan, who, like Goldwater, also clearly embraced the tenets of private enterprise. Bush made a fortune as an oil drilling contractor in Texas before turning to politics.

Humphrey, Edward Kennedy, and Mondale were allied closely with organized labor; McGovern was identified with economic underdogs, as indicated in the 1972 campaign by his espousal of a $1,000 grant for all Americans.

Thus, none of Hyman's informal qualifications have stood the test of time. Changes in the nomination process itself as well as broader currents in U.S. society have altered many of the major considerations underlying the choice of presidential candidates. Divorce is far more prevalent and acceptable today than in the past. The proliferation of presidential primaries "provides a forum in which prejudices can be addressed openly," [29] and the vice presidential nomination offers a way to address such social views indirectly, as was the case with Geraldine Ferraro's nomination in 1984. The development of a more common culture and the nationalization of American life in general, brought about by improved means of communication and transportation, have reduced the importance of parochial concerns—the religious, ethnic, or geographical background of a candidate—and increased the emphasis on the experience presidential candidates have had in the national political arena and their association with national issues. Moreover, as other groups that are still socially or politically disadvantaged—blacks, women, immigrants from Mexico, eastern and southern Europe, and the Far East—begin to occupy governorships and seats in the U.S. Senate, from which U.S. chief executives traditionally have been recruited, they will increase their chances of becoming serious candidates for the presidency.[30]

Notes

1. James Monroe is the only other candidate to have approached this distinction. He won all but one electoral vote in 1820.
2. Michael Nelson, *Guide to the American Presidency* (Washington, D.C.: CQ Press, 1990), 266-267, 1403.
3. Hugh Heclo, "Presidential and Prime Ministerial Selection," in *Perspectives on Presidential Selection,* ed. Donald R. Matthews (Washington, D.C.: Brookings, 1973), 25.
4. William Chambers, *Political Parties in a New Nation: The American Experience, 1776-1809* (New York: Oxford University Press, 1963), chap. 2.
5. In the early 1820s the Republican party became known as the Democratic-Republicans and in 1840 was officially designated as the Democratic party. Paul David, Ralph Goldman, and Richard Bain, *The Politics of National Party Conventions* (New York: Vintage, 1964), chap. 3.
6. Joseph Charles, *The Origins of the American Party System* (New York: Harper Torch, 1956), 83-94.
7. Gerald Pomper, *Nominating the President: The Politics of Convention Choice* (New York: Norton, 1966), 17.
8. David, Goldman, and Bain, *Politics of National Party Conventions,* 50. The National Republican party was soon to give way to the Whigs, with many Whig supporters joining the modern Republican party when it was formed in the 1850s.
9. Ibid., 61.
10. Alexander Heard and Michael Nelson, "Change and Stability in Choosing Presidents," in *Presidential Selection,* ed. Heard and Nelson (Durham, N.C.: Duke University Press, 1987), 5.
11. Rhodes Cook, "The Nominating Process," in *The Elections of 1988,* ed. Michael Nelson (Washington, D.C.: CQ Press, 1989) 28.
12. Some states used another variant in 1984 and 1988, the "winner-take-more" principle, whereby the leading candidate in a district received a "bonus" delegate, and the remainder of the delegates were divided among the candidates in proportion to the votes they received.
13. Cook, "The Nominating Process," 53.

14. Harold G. Stanley and Richard G. Niemi, *Vital Statistics on American Politics*, 2d ed. (Washington, D.C.: CQ Press, 1990), 98.
15. Herbert E. Alexander, *Financing Politics: Money, Elections and Political Reform*, 2d ed. (Washington, D.C.: CQ Press, 1980), 27.
16. 424 U.S. 1 (1976).
17. Although political action committees can help finance nomination campaigns, their contributions, unlike those of individuals, are not matched by federal funds.
18. Alexander, *Financing Politics*, 98.
19. Naturalized citizens (such as former secretary of state Henry Kissinger, who was born in Germany) do not meet this requirement. There is some question whether persons born abroad of American citizens (such as George Romney, former governor of Michigan and 1968 presidential aspirant, who was born of American parents in France) are also legally barred from the presidency by this stipulation.
20. Michael Nelson, "Who Vies for President?," in *Presidential Selection*, ed. Heard and Nelson, 129.
21. John Aldrich, "Methods and Actors: The Relationship of Processes to Candidates," in *Presidential Selection*, ed. Heard and Nelson.
22. It should be noted that on occasion the party out of power draws on a third source for candidates—*defeated presidential candidates*. Since 1932, the Republicans have chosen Thomas Dewey and Richard Nixon, and the Democrats, Adlai Stevenson, to run for the presidency a second time. Only Nixon was successful.
23. Nelson Polsby, *Congress and the Presidency*, 3d ed. (Englewood Cliffs, N.J.: Prentice-Hall, 1976), 99-102.
24. William Keech and Donald Matthews, *The Party's Choice* (Washington, D.C.: Brookings, 1976), 23. During the early 1980s, aspiring nominees believed that unemployment was an advantage to seeking the nomination, causing several potential candidates to avoid seeking election or reelection to the senate. This was true for Senators Howard Baker and Gary Hart who declined to seek reelection in 1984 and 1986, as well as for former senator and vice president Walter Mondale who declined to pursue a vacant Senate seat from Minnesota in 1982.
25. Roland Elving, "The Senators' Lane to the Presidency," *Congressional Quarterly Weekly Report*, May 20, 1989, 1218.
26. It should also be noted that a former vice president may ultimately become a presidential candidate: Richard Nixon ran successfully in 1968 after losing in 1960, and Walter Mondale served in that office from 1977 to 1981 and became the Democratic presidential candidate in 1984.
27. Before Richard Nixon's selection in 1960, the last incumbent vice president to be nominated was Martin Van Buren in 1836.
28. Sidney Hyman, "Nine Tests for the Presidential Hopeful," *New York Times*, January 4, 1959, sec. 5, 1-11.
29. Michael Nelson, "Who Vies for President?," in *Presidential Selection*, 144.
30. Jesse Jackson finished third behind Walter Mondale and Gary Hart for the 1984 Democratic nomination and second for the 1988 nomination. In the 1988 contest Rep. Patricia Schroeder of Colorado was widely mentioned as a possible Democratic candidate.

Selected Readings

Alexander, Herbert E. *Financing Politics: Money, Elections, and Political Reform.* 3d ed. Washington, D.C.: CQ Press, 1984.

Crotty, William, and John S. Jackson III. *Presidential Primaries and Nominations.* Washington, D.C.: CQ Press, 1985.

Grassmuck, George, ed. *Before Nomination: Our Primary Problems.* Washington, D.C.: American Enterprise Institute, 1985.

Heard, Alexander and Michael Nelson, eds., *Presidential Selection.* Durham, N.C.: Duke University Press, 1987.

Shafer, Byron E. *Quiet Revolution: The Struggle for the Democratic Party and the Shaping of Post-Reform Politics.* New York: Russell Sage Foundation, 1983.

The Nomination Campaign 2

Potentially damaging issues faced the Republicans as the 1988 campaign approached. After eight years of Republican control of the White House, the federal deficit had doubled. The stock market crash on October 19, 1987, had signaled bad economic times. The Senate had rejected two Reagan nominations to the Supreme Court (Robert Bork and Douglas Ginsburg) and the administration had become embroiled in a secret and illegal arms-for-hostages deal with Iran. Although the president had enjoyed unprecedented popularity throughout his two terms, his approval rating was down slightly as the 1988 nomination campaign approached. Nevertheless, the deficit had not resulted in high inflation and unemployment was low. On the whole, the American people felt the economy was going well. Overall, the Republican party was in a favorable position going into the 1988 nomination campaign, whereas the Democrats were in disarray.

The nomination campaign is a long, winnowing process in which each of the two major parties chooses from a large pool of potential candidates the one person who will represent it in the general election. As political scientist Austin Ranney points out, the nomination phase is more important than the election stage of the campaign, because "the parties' nominating processes eliminate far more presidential possibilities than do the voters' electing processes." [1]

There are several important differences between the campaign for the nomination and the campaign preceding the general election. A nomination campaign is much less structured than a general election campaign. Rather than contending with one known opponent representing the other major political party, aspirants for their party's nomination typically do not know how many opponents they will face or who they will be. In contrast to the general election's relatively short campaign period (extending roughly from Labor Day in early September to election day in early November), the nomination campaign is long and indefinite. Candidates start their quest for the presidency up to two years before election year. Unlike the general election campaign, which occurs in all fifty states simultaneously, the nomination campaign takes place in stages, and candidates must hopscotch the nation in pursuit of votes. Finally, presidential nominees can use their party label to attract votes and can count on party leaders to work in their campaign, but candidates for the party's nomination must develop other types of political appeals to attract the support of the "selectorate" and a personal organization to work on their behalf.

The highly unstructured nature of the presidential nominating process causes great uncertainties for candidates in planning and conducting the campaign. A further complication is that most first-time candidates must organize a nationwide political campaign, a task that, by comparison, dwarfs the effort of winning a Senate seat or governorship in even the largest states. As the following discussion indicates, important decisions have to be made all along the road to the party's nomination.

Early Maneuvering

Although the formal nomination process does not start until the beginning of the election year (the Iowa caucuses in February have been the kickoff event since 1976), political maneuvering takes place long before that time. A few days after the 1972 presidential election, for example, Jimmy Carter's staff laid out a plan for winning the 1976 Democratic nomination. Shortly after vice-presidential candidate Walter Mondale lost the 1980 election, he began his quest for the 1984 Democratic presidential nomination.

Journalist Arthur Hadley calls this political interval between the election of one president and the first primary before the next presidential election "the invisible primary." [2] By this he means that a political contest occurs during this time that has many of the characteristics of the actual state primaries. The major difference between the two types of primary is that the invisible one takes place behind the scenes as far as the general public is concerned, whereas American voters are very conscious of the regular primaries.

The invisible primary is a testing ground for the would-be president to determine whether his candidacy is viable. One factor that Hadley emphasizes is a psychological one: is the candidate willing to undergo the grueling process needed to win, a process characterized by extended absences from home, long hours on the campaign trail, and short, sometimes sleepless nights? Vice President Walter Mondale, an early casualty of the period preceding the 1976 election, withdrew from the race in November 1974 with the following statement: "I found I did not have the overwhelming desire to be President which is essential for the kind of campaign that is required. I don't think anyone should be President who is not willing to go through fire." [3]

An important task for the presidential candidate at this stage is assembling a staff to plan the campaign strategy and a group that Hadley calls a "constituency," a larger group of workers who are willing to do the advance work necessary to organize states for the upcoming primary and caucus-convention contests. Recent Democratic party nominees benefited from having dedicated supporters who began their organizational activities very early. A full one and one-half years before the Wisconsin primary in April 1972, a young member of George McGovern's staff, Eugene Pokorny, began to build a base of operation there;[4] in early 1975 a Carter staffer, Tim Kraft, began putting together a Carter organization for the Iowa precinct caucuses to be held in January 1976;[5] and in 1979 Terry Turner was made director of Carter's field operations in Iowa for the 1980 election.

Perhaps the most important factor in this early phase is how would-be candidates fare with the media. As columnist Russell Baker notes, the members of the media are the "great mentioner," the source of name recognition and favorable publicity. Candidates who are ignored because reporters and commentators do not regard them as serious contenders find it almost impossible to emerge as viable presidential possibilities. Adverse comments can also seriously damage a candidacy: in his quest for the 1980 Democratic nomination, Edmund (Jerry) Brown was portrayed by the media as a "spacey," "far-out" politician whose ideas, rhetoric, and life-style disqualified him for the presidency. In that same contest, Edward Kennedy's 1979 interview with CBS commentator Roger Mudd turned into a disaster as the senator seemed unable to give an adequate explanation of his actions in the drowning of Mary Jo Kopechne in 1969; of his strained relationship with his wife, Joan, and his alleged affairs with other women; and of why he wanted to be president and how his policies and political views differed from those of President Carter. Many observers concluded that the Massachusetts senator never recovered from that interview, which occurred before his official presidential campaign even began.

Personal character became a key factor in evaluating presidential candidates when two candidates withdrew from the race in 1987. Gary Hart, the early Democratic front-runner, was unable to defuse womanizing charges stemming from a story that appeared in the *Miami Herald.*

The paper reported that he had hosted Donna Rice, an attractive model and actress, in his Washington town house while his wife was in Colorado. To make matters worse, it was reported that Rice had accompanied Hart on an overnight boat trip to Bimini. Hart was forced to withdraw in May of 1987 when it was revealed that the *Washington Post* was developing a story about a relationship with yet another woman. He reentered the race at the end of the year in time to file for the New Hampshire primary but later withdrew. The campaign of Senator Joseph Biden, Jr., was similarly plagued by a negative media image and questions of personal character. Biden admitted plagiarizing a law review article while attending the Syracuse Law School in 1965. He also admitted quoting Robert F. Kennedy, Hubert H. Humphrey, and British Labour party leader Neil Kinnock without attribution. Although the latter practice is not unusual among politicians, media attention to his misstatements overshadowed his candidacy. Biden, too, withdrew from the 1988 race even before it really began.

In contrast, candidates who tend to do well in the invisible primary exploit the advantages provided by the media. Early in his 1976 campaign Carter's staff recommended that he cultivate important political columnists and editors—such as *New York Times* columnist Tom Wicker and *Washington Post* chairman Katharine Graham—by making favorable comments on their articles and columns and, if possible, by scheduling visits with them. Some candidates enhance their presence in the print media through magazine articles or books published either earlier in their careers or during the nomination campaign itself; examples include John F. Kennedy's *Profiles in Courage,* Richard Nixon's *Six Crises,* and Jimmy Carter's *Why Not The Best?* They also use television and radio, appearing regularly on shows such as "Meet the Press." They may even use a syndicated radio program or news column of their own, as Ronald Reagan did to advance his political views and, indirectly, his candidacy.

People with presidential ambitions typically take additional steps to enhance their prospects with leaders of their party as well as with the public. In anticipation of the 1972 election, Edmund Muskie, Hubert Humphrey's running mate in 1968, began accepting speaking engagements outside his home state of Maine soon after he and Humphrey were defeated. Looking toward the 1976 election, Jimmy Carter assumed the position of coordinator of the 1974 Democratic congressional campaign, a job that took him to thirty states, where he had the opportunity to get acquainted with Democratic leaders. A trip abroad may also keep candidates in the news and, if they have not had much experience in foreign affairs, help to counteract the charge that they are not knowledgeable in this vital area that consumes so much of the U.S. president's time.

Another key aspect of the invisible primary is the raising of funds necessary for the nomination campaign. As previously explained, the new finance legislation, which favors raising money in small amounts from many individuals, requires candidates to get an early start in soliciting funds. In fact, financial maneuvering may precede the candidate's own personal campaign. In January 1977, with $1 million left over from his 1976 campaign, Ronald Reagan established a political action committee (PAC) called Citizens for the Republic. In 1978 the organization contributed more than $600,000 to four hundred Republican candidates in federal, state, and local elections, but the remainder of its total expenditure of $4.5 million went to pay operating expenses and traveling costs for Reagan, who served as the principal speaker at political gatherings for the GOP candidates. Thus Reagan himself was the major beneficiary of Citizens for the Republic: he ingratiated himself with the Republican candidates who received contributions from the organization while gaining valuable contacts with Republican party supporters and the contributors to Citizens for the Republic, natural targets for his own fund raising for the 1980 presidential campaign. Walter Mondale established a PAC, Committee for the Future of America, that raised $24 million and contributed to more than two hundred House, Senate, and gubernatorial candidates in 1982.

As the presidential election year approaches, campaign fund raising moves into high gear. During the last three months of 1979, seven candidates each raised more than $1 million: Republicans Connally, Reagan, Bush, and Dole and Democrats Kennedy, Carter, and Brown. Ultimately, six of the seven received federal matching funds (Connally is the only major candidate since 1976 to finance his campaign from private sources alone), as did Republican candidates John Anderson, Howard Baker, and Philip Crane, and Democratic long shot Lyndon LaRouche. Financing for the 1984 contest got off to an even earlier start: during the first three months of 1983, Mondale raised more than $2 million; Reubin Askew, $800,000; Gary Hart, $465,000; Alan Cranston, $440,000; and Ernest Hollings, almost $250,000. At the end of 1987 Bush (with $18.1 million), Robertson ($14.2 million), and Dukakis ($10.2 million) led the field in collecting individual campaign contributions, thus freeing them to compete in more of the early nomination contests.

In recent years presidential candidates have also found it wise to enter prenomination "popularity" contests held in some states, even though such contests have no legal effect on the composition of the state delegation to the national convention. The Carter forces packed a Jefferson-Jackson Day fund-raising dinner held in Iowa in October 1975 and, consequently, won the straw poll taken there. Four years later members of Carter's staff worked hard to get his supporters elected as delegates to the Florida Democratic state convention held in November 1979; as a result, he soundly defeated Senator Kennedy in a straw vote taken at the convention. At the same time, Ronald Reagan was scoring a triumph over his Republican opponents in a comparable poll taken at the Republican state convention in Florida. Such popularity contests started early in the 1984 race: in January 1983, native son Alan Cranston won a preferential poll at a Democratic party state convention in California; in April of that year, Mondale came out first in a similar poll conducted at a party convention in Kennedy's home state of Massachusetts. The following June, Cranston also scored victories in straw polls in Wisconsin and Alabama, and in October Mondale won in Maine. Pat Robertson scored a surprise victory in the Iowa straw poll sponsored by the state GOP in September 1987. He formally entered the race the following month.

The early phase of the 1984 contest took on a new dimension when both the AFL-CIO, with its 14 million members and 98 affiliated unions, and the National Education Association (NEA), the nation's largest individual labor union with 1.7 million members, endorsed Mondale as the Democratic candidate before the official state contests. Shortly thereafter, the National Organization of Women endorsed Mondale as well. These early endorsements later became a target of Republican criticism, and the Democratic national chairman asked organized interests to refrain during the 1988 contest from endorsing any candidate prior to the state contests.

Although it appeared in mid-1987 that straw polls and interest group endorsements would be less prevalent in the 1988 nomination contest, particularly for Democrats, other developments emerged early in that race. Besides the difficulties of Hart and Biden, long shot Bruce Babbitt, the former Arizona governor, began television advertising in Iowa far earlier than usual, hoping to create curiosity about his candidacy among party activists who would dominate the precinct caucuses there. He also engaged in an interparty debate with Republican candidate Pierre (Pete) du Pont, who, like Babbitt, was given little chance of winning his party's nomination. Two more prominent candidates, Richard A. Gephardt (D-Mo.) and Jack F. Kemp (R-N.Y.), also participated in an interparty debate. All seven Democratic candidates appeared in a televised debate on William F. Buckley's program, "Firing Line."

The early phase of the nomination campaign, which political scientist Donald Matthews refers to as "the emergence of presidential possibilities," serves as a testing period for would-be candidates, especially those in the party out of office.[6] An eligible incumbent president is typically the front-running candidate for the nomination of the party in power. Some

Table 2-1 Leading Presidential Candidates and Nominees, 1936-1988

	Party in power			Party out of power		
Year	Party	Leading candidate at beginning of election year[a]	Nominee	Party	Leading candidate at beginning of election year[a]	Nominee
1936	D	Roosevelt	Roosevelt	R	Landon	Landon
1940	D	Roosevelt	Roosevelt	R	—	Willkie
1944	D	Roosevelt	Roosevelt	R	Dewey	Dewey
1948	D	Truman	Truman	R	Dewey-Taft	Dewey
1952	D	Truman	Stevenson	R	Eisenhower-Taft	Eisenhower
1956	R	Eisenhower	Eisenhower	D	Stevenson	Stevenson
1960	R	Nixon	Nixon	D	Kennedy	Kennedy
1964	D	Johnson	Johnson	R	—	Goldwater
1968	D	Johnson	Humphrey	R	Nixon	Nixon
1972	R	Nixon	Nixon	D	Muskie	McGovern
1976	R	Ford[b]	Ford	D	Humphrey[b]	Carter
1980	D	Carter[c]	Carter	R	—[c]	Reagan
1984	R	Reagan[d]	Reagan	D	Mondale[d]	Mondale
1988	R	Bush	Bush	D	—[e]	Dukakis

Source: Donald Matthews, "Presidential Nominations: Process and Outcomes," in *Choosing the President*, ed. James David Barber (Englewood Cliffs, N.J.: Prentice-Hall, 1974), 54.

[a] Dash (—) indicates that no single candidate led in the polls.

[b] The 1976 information was taken from the January Gallup poll.

[c] Carter led Kennedy in all Gallup polls conducted after the seizure of the hostages by Iran in November 1979. In a February 1980 Gallup poll listing eight candidates, 34 percent of Republican voters named Reagan as their first choice and 32 percent chose Ford; however, when the choice was narrowed to those two candidates, 56 percent preferred Ford and 40 percent, Reagan.

[d] Since President Reagan was unopposed for the Republican nomination, no preference poll was taken. A Gallup poll in mid-February 1984 showed, however, that 86 percent of Republicans approved the president's performance in office. The Gallup poll indicating Mondale to be the leading candidate among Democrats was taken in mid-November 1983.

[e] In an October 1987 Gallup poll, Jackson led Dukakis 22-14 percent but after Hart reentered the contest, he vaulted to the lead in a January 1988 poll with 23 percent to 16 for Dukakis and 15 for Jackson. By mid-March, after Hart's second withdrawal, Dukakis moved into a 32-23 percent lead over Jackson.

drop out before the official campaign begins, as did Democratic senator Walter Mondale in 1975, Republican senator Lowell Weicker in 1979, and Democrats Hart and Biden in 1987. Others establish themselves as leaders in the public opinion polls taken at the beginning of the year and go on to win their party's nomination. As Table 2-1 shows, this was the prevailing pattern from 1936 through 1968. In three recent instances, however, the front-runner was ultimately replaced by a dark horse— McGovern, who was preferred by only 3 percent of the Democrats in January 1972, and Carter, the choice of only 4 percent in January 1976. Michael Dukakis was preferred by only 3 percent of Democrats in a January 1987 Gallup poll that showed Hart to be the choice of a full 53 percent. By January 1988, Hart led by a narrow margin of 23 percent to 16 percent. Dukakis increased his support to 32 percent when Hart dropped out of the race for the second time. Leaders in the polls therefore cannot afford to relax after achieving early popularity: the final choice of the nominee depends on presidential primaries as well as on caucus-convention contests.

Targeting the Nomination Campaign

Developments since 1968 have increased the number of state contests in which candidates participate. Primary laws in some states automatically place nationally recognized candidates on the ballot, thus forcing them to participate in contests they may prefer to bypass. The proportional representation feature of the national Democratic party rules and similar provisions in some Republican state contests encourage candidates to enter races they do not expect to win, because they receive some delegate votes even when they lose. Moreover, the selectorate expects candidates to show that they have political support in all parts of the country. As a result, in 1980 both Jimmy Carter and Edward Kennedy were on the ballot in thirty-four of the thirty-five Democratic preference primaries (ignoring only Michigan, where the primary results were not binding and delegates were chosen in separate caucuses). Republican George Bush entered all thirty-four of the GOP preference primaries, and Ronald Reagan entered thirty-two (he was not on the ballot in Puerto Rico or the District of Columbia). In 1984, Mondale and Hart entered all twenty-five primaries, and Jesse Jackson, twenty-four (he was not on the ballot in Puerto Rico). In 1988, Dukakis and Jackson were on the ballot in thirty-eight primaries. George Bush entered all thirty-seven GOP primaries, and Robert Dole entered thirty-three (he was not on the ballot in West Virginia, Idaho, New Jersey, or North Dakota).

A candidate's name may appear on a state ballot, but that does not mean he or she will wage an all-out campaign in that state. Limitations of time and energy prevent active campaigning in every state. The allocation of money also becomes a major problem. Not only is there an overall restriction on spending ($27.65 million was the limit for those accepting public financing in 1988), but spending limits also apply in each state.

Such considerations require presidential candidates to establish priorities among the large number of primaries and caucus-convention contests. The primaries, in particular, are important, because they determine more than half of the delegates to the national conventions. Moreover, candidates are much more likely to campaign personally and spend more money in states that hold primaries than in those that have caucus-conventions.[7]

Candidates take several factors into account when deciding which primaries they should emphasize in their nomination campaigns. One is the date of the primary. The earliest contest, traditionally New Hampshire, usually attracts most of the major contenders because it is the first popular test of voter sentiment. Although the number of New Hampshire delegates is small (in 1988, only 18 of 4,162 Democratic delegates and 27 of 2,277 Republicans), it focuses immediate attention on the winner, as it did on John Kennedy in 1960 and Carter in 1976. Even if a candidate loses in New Hampshire but draws a greater percentage of the vote than expected the media may interpret the results as a "moral" victory, a judgment that benefited Eugene McCarthy in 1968 and George McGovern in 1972.

New Hampshire appeals to presidential candidates for another reason: its small area and population make campaigning there manageable. Slightly more than 120,000 Democrats were registered in 1976, and the Carter organization stated that it contacted about 95 percent of them.[8] The state was therefore ideal for the former governor in the early stages of the nomination contest: he had not yet acquired substantial financial resources for media expenditures and his contingent of Georgia volunteers could conduct an effective door-to-door campaign.

In the 1988 campaign, the primaries held on Tuesday, March 8, presented a formidable strategic hurdle for the candidates. On Super Tuesday delegates were selected from twenty states, most of them in the South. Southern politicos hoped that Super Tuesday would provide momentum early in the nomination process for a candidate to the liking of southern voters. Al Gore (D-Tenn.), the only southerner in the race, mounted minimal efforts in the New Hampshire and Iowa events and focused on Super Tuesday. But he won only five states (the same success enjoyed by Jesse Jackson) and suspended his campaign six weeks later.

All of the candidates concentrated on remaining viable until the Super Tuesday contest and after; however, no Democratic candidate came out a clear regionwide winner.[9] For the Republican Party, Super Tuesday became a crucial contest between Bush and Dole. Bush had suffered a major defeat when Dole won in Iowa, but the vice president later swamped Dole in the New Hampshire contest. Bush needed a Super Tuesday victory to take advantage of the momentum gained in New Hampshire. Bush assured himself the Republican nomination by winning each of the sixteen Republican primaries.

Other primaries provide a late indication of voter preference. The California primary, for example, has traditionally occurred near the end of the primary season, although there have been extensive discussions about changing the date in 1992. If the earlier primaries have not produced a clear favorite, Golden State voters are often in a position to determine who the party's nominee will be. Both Goldwater in 1964 and McGovern in 1972 owed their selection to their primary victories in California, which showed them as "winners" shortly before delegates throughout the country went to the national convention. In recent years the California primary has been less important in determining the nominee. Dukakis in 1988 became the first front-running Democrat since 1964 to win the California primary and subsequently get the party's nomination.[10] The rules of the nomination contest nevertheless make California an attractive target for presidential candidates. It has the largest number of state delegates at both of the party conventions and, for Republicans, a winner-take-all provision that delivers those delegates in a solid bloc to the winner of the primary.

Other considerations besides timing and delegate strength affect candidates' decisions about where to concentrate campaign efforts. Naturally, candidates try to choose states, beyond Iowa and New Hampshire, where they think they have the best chance of winning. In 1976 and again in 1980 the Carter forces concentrated major efforts in their candidate's native South. In 1976 Henry Jackson chose Massachusetts and New York as special targets because both states contained many Catholics, Jews, and labor union members with whom the Washington senator had close political ties. In 1984 Walter Mondale selected Pennsylvania and Illinois for the same reasons. Morris Udall in 1976, John Anderson in 1980, and Gary Hart in 1984 focused on Massachusetts and Wisconsin because they expected to do well in the liberal academic communities concentrated in those states. The two Republican contenders in 1976, Gerald R. Ford and Ronald Reagan, worked hard in their home states of Michigan and California to advance their candidacies, as did 1980 Democratic candidates Jimmy Carter in Georgia and Edward Kennedy in Massachusetts.

Both Albert Gore and Jesse Jackson targeted southern states in the 1988 Super Tuesday contests. Gore hoped to transform favorite son status into nationwide support, and Jackson to mobilize his black support throughout the region.

At times, however, candidates may deliberately choose to contest primaries that are not considered advantageous to them to demonstrate that they have a broader appeal than is generally recognized. John Kennedy went into the West Virginia primary in 1960 to prove that a Catholic could win in a state in which the population was 95 percent Protestant. In 1976 Jimmy Carter chose the Pennsylvania primary to show that a southern Baptist could do well in a northern industrial state with a large Catholic population. Both risks proved to be good ones that greatly advanced the Kennedy and Carter candidacies.

A major problem for candidates is properly managing a primary they clearly expect to lose. Many contenders have found that the most successful approach is to convince the public and particularly the media that they are not contesting the primary, so that a loss is not considered a genuine defeat. George McGovern successfully pursued that ploy in the Florida primary in 1972, as did Ronald Reagan in Wisconsin in 1976. This strategy also enables candidates to save their resources for more promising primaries.

Most important, candidates must avoid raising false expectations during the nomination campaign. In 1976, shortly before the New Hampshire primary, the Reagan staff released the results of a public opinion poll showing him to be ahead of Ford. When the California governor lost that primary by a single percentage point, the media interpreted the results as a serious defeat for him and a major victory for Ford. In 1980 John Connally decided to focus on the South Carolina primary as the one that would establish his candidacy; when he lost to Reagan there, the Texas governor felt obliged to withdraw from the race altogether.

Even though since 1972 primaries usually have been more consequential than caucus-convention contests in nomination campaigns, in some instances caucus-conventions become crucial. Since 1976 the Iowa caucuses have taken on major importance because they are the first test of the candidates' political strength, and the media therefore attach great significance to an Iowa victory.[11] In 1976 Jimmy Carter's successful campaign in Iowa established him as the Democratic pack leader; in 1980 his victory over Senator Kennedy in that state gave him a psychological edge in the New Hampshire primary a month later. The importance of the Iowa caucuses as a launching pad for presidential contenders diminished in 1988. The winners, Gephardt for the Democrats and Dole for the Republicans, dropped out of the nomination contest by the end of March.

Republican Pat Robertson, who finished second with 25 percent of the vote, received a great deal of favorable media coverage because he had not been expected to do that well, but he failed to transform the coverage he earned by "exceeding expectations" into later success.

Caucus-convention states also become important if no clear victor emerges in the presidential primaries. In 1976 both Gerald Ford and Ronald Reagan diligently pursued delegates chosen in Republican party caucuses and conventions, especially in the period immediately preceding the Republican convention. In the end, Ford owed his nomination to previously uncommitted delegations, such as that of Mississippi, that cast their ballots for him at the national convention.

Manipulating Political Appeals

No candidate in the nomination campaign has the option of using the party label against opponents in the same way he or she can in the general election. However, a president seeking renomination and facing possible challenges can emphasize that he is currently the representative of his party. He can suggest that persons who challenge him for the nomination are casting doubts on the good judgment of the party, which nominated him four years previously, and that a challenge would divide the party in the upcoming general election. The president can even imply that attacks on him constitute attacks on the country. President Carter and his spokespersons employed all these tactics in his 1980 contest with his major opponent, Senator Kennedy.

In contrast, the challenger of an incumbent president must make the challenge appear legitimate. Several ways are possible. One is to suggest that the incumbent president is not providing the leadership the nation requires. Another is to intimate that the president is such a weak candidate that he will take the party and its congressional, state, and local candidates down to defeat in November. A third is to avow that the president has not kept the promises he made in his previous campaign and that he has strayed from the traditional policies of the party. Senator Kennedy used all these appeals in his unsuccessful attempt to wrest the 1980 Democratic nomination from President Carter.

In a nomination campaign, the incumbent president also can use the powers of his office to great advantage. In a speech early in the 1980 campaign Senator Kennedy charged that the Carter administration's offer of $7 million to relieve starvation in Cambodia was woefully inadequate; two hours later the president called in television camera crews to announce that $69 million would be given to combat famine and to resettle Cambodian refugees in Thailand. Throughout the campaign, the president invited Democratic leaders to the White House, and their acceptance was considered an endorsement of Carter's renomination. Aware of Carter's power to approve or disapprove federal grants to states and cities, almost five hundred mayors, governors, and members of Congress attended these meetings to demonstrate their support for his candidacy. As the campaign progressed, the president continued to use the prerogatives of his office. The Sunday before the Iowa caucuses, he appeared on "Meet the Press" and announced that he would insist that U.S. athletes boycott the summer Olympics unless the Soviet Union withdrew its troops from Afghanistan. On the eve of the New Hampshire primary the president invited the U.S. Olympic hockey team to the White House for a televised congratulatory ceremony for its victory over the Soviet team. On the morning of the Wisconsin and Kansas primaries, Carter made a public announcement of a "positive step" toward the release of the hostages in Iran.

The incumbent president therefore has a clear advantage in a nomination campaign. Not only can he invoke the symbol of party unity; he can also manipulate events to benefit his candidacy. Incumbency is particularly advantageous if foreign crises occur during the campaign period, for Americans tend to "rally 'round the flag," and hence their president, as they initially did in 1980 for Carter when Americans were taken hostage in Iran. A review of U.S. history clearly shows the superior campaign position of the incumbent: Franklin Pierce was the last president who actively sought his party's renomination and failed to obtain it: James Buchanan won the Democratic nomination from him in 1856. President Chester Arthur lost the GOP nomination in 1884 but there is some question about how actively he sought the nomination.

Presidential candidates in the party out of power face an entirely different campaign situation. Although they do not have the problem of how legitimately to challenge an incumbent president, they do experience other difficulties. Typically, many candidates vie for their party's nomination, and each aspirant must find a way to distinguish himself from his opponents. Tables 2-2 and 2-3 present information on the range of persons who sought the 1988 Democratic and Republican nominations. A further complication is that the range of political views of the selectorate in the nomination campaign is narrower than that of the electorate in the general election: most Republicans participating in the nomination process are more conservative than the average Republican voter; most Democratic participants are more liberal than the average Democratic voter.

The limited range of the selectorate's views creates problems and

Table 2-2 Major Candidates for 1988 Democratic Nomination

Candidate	Background	Political Views	Assets	Liabilities
Bruce Babbitt	Lawyer, former governor of Arizona, born June 27, 1938	Offered nonmainstream ideas, such as means testing for federal benefit programs and a national consumption tax; pushed opponents on how to balance the budget.	Not burdened by orthodox positions; fresh and candid style; two terms as a governor; no experience in Washington.	Finished last in fund raising; lacked a clear constituency within the party, particularly among activists; poor television appearance.
Michael Dukakis	Lawyer, governor of Massachusetts, born Nov. 3, 1933	Generally liberal stands on civil liberties but new approach to job creation through public-private partnerships and job training; increase tax revenues through enforcement; claimed personal "competence."	Home state was thriving economically; led field in fund raising with appeal to both Greek and Jewish communities; expected to win in neighboring New Hampshire; strong in Northeast, generally.	Three terms as governor provided ample ammunition for criticism; problems in setting campaign strategy especially after early campaign conflict with Biden camp damaged reputation.
Richard Gephardt	Lawyer, U.S. representative from Missouri, born Jan. 31, 1941	Outspoken proponent of legislation to protect American jobs from unfair foreign competition; softened his personal anti-abortion stand.	Bright, with outstanding record of leadership in Congress on issues such as tax reform; youthful appearance; enormous time and effort spent in Iowa, a neighboring state (visited all 99 counties).	First Democrat to enter race; had difficulty raising funds and sustaining momentum from Iowa victory (finished second in New Hampshire, poor showing on Super Tuesday); was the candidate of Washington "insiders."

Candidate	Background	Positions/Themes	Strategy	Assessment
Albert Gore, Jr.	Journalist, home builder, U.S. senator from Tennessee, born Mar. 31, 1948	Relatively hawkish on defense and foreign policy but liberal on economic and social issues; proposed new nuclear deterrent based on mobile missiles; developed themes of economic populism late in campaign.	One of only two candidates from the South and more moderate than Jackson; hoped to benefit from Super Tuesday.	Decision to bypass New Hampshire and Iowa probably a mistake; youngest candidate (39); initially stiff in television appearances; success on Super Tuesday overshadowed by Bush's victories.
Gary Hart	Lawyer, former senator from Colorado, born Nov. 28, 1936	Hoped to continue appeal based on "new ideas," on defense, nuclear arms control, revitalizing industry, and competing with Japan.	Led all candidates in Jan. 1987 polls, reflecting 1984 success; retired from Senate in 1986 to pursue presidency full time.	Doubts about character from 1984 were renewed in furor over marital problems and extramarital affairs; left race in May 1987 but returned in December; campaign debts carried over from 1984.
Jesse Jackson	Minister, civil rights activist, born Oct. 8, 1941	Most liberal candidate; appealed to coalition of minorities and poor.	Previous experience in presidential campaign; enthusiastic supporters; appealed to party activists; supported by black voters, especially in South and urban areas; personal roots in South and in Chicago.	Had never held elective public office; some resentment among party officials over 1984 wrangling; question of electability—whether nation was ready to elect a black to the presidency.
Paul Simon	Journalist, U.S. senator from Illinois, born Nov. 29, 1928	Traditional liberal appeals on jobs, health care, and education.	From major industrial state critical in presidential elections.	Oldest candidate; low name recognition; somewhat dated image (bow ties); competed for votes at crowded end of the political spectrum without distinctive message.

Table 2-3 Major Candidates for 1988 Republican Nomination

Candidate	Background	Political Views	Assets	Liabilities
George Bush	Businessman, vice president of the United States, born June 12, 1924	A convert to the Reagan agenda, Bush moved toward a stronger anti-abortion stand and supported tax and spending cuts although he had a "moderate" image; promised to focus on education.	Association with Reagan's record and popularity; best financed, best organized; experience in government.	Nagging questions about role as vice president and character ("wimp" label); conservatives distrustful of positions; aristocratic background; consummate Washington insider during period when outsiders had become winners.
Robert Dole	Lawyer, U.S. senator from Kansas, born July 22, 1923	Had difficulty projecting a clear programmatic vision; tended to focus on questions regarding Bush's conduct in office and issues surrounding Iran-contra incident.	Image of strength, record of accomplishment in Congress (28 years); support in Iowa.	Hatchet-man image from 1976 campaign; continuing responsibilities as Senate minority leader; pragmatic style that inhibited articulating a program; overmanaged his own campaign.
Pierre (Pete) du Pont	Lawyer, businessman, former governor of Delaware, born Jan. 22, 1935	Sought attention by endorsing controversial positions to make social security optional, test for drugs, discontinue farm price supports, abolish Aid to Families with Dependent Children; reduce the role of government.	Eight years of executive experience; out of office; first candidate to declare.	Experience limited to small state; name, where recognized, associated with privileged wealth.

Name	Background	Positions	Strengths	Weaknesses
Alexander Haig	Career military officer, businessman, born Dec. 2, 1924	Assertive defense policy, caution in dealing with the Soviet Union.	Military experience.	No base of party support; service in Nixon's White House during Watergate defense period; stormy departure from Reagan cabinet.
Jack Kemp	Pro football player, U.S. representative from New York, born July 13, 1935	Avid supporter of supply-side economic policy; pushed for innovative programs to help "empower" minorities with urban enterprise zones; fervent anti-abortion position; strong support for Strategic Defense Initiative and free trade.	Appeal to blue collar and minorities unique in party; name recognition.	Strong competition for conservative support; difficulty projecting a clear, focused image with "windy" speeches; House background lacked stature of competitors' backgrounds.
Marion (Pat) Robertson	Minister, businessman, born Mar. 22, 1930	"Restore American greatness through moral strength."	Enthusiastic support of fundamentalist Christians; second to Bush in fund raising.	Able to compete better in caucuses than primaries; questions raised about service in military coincided with teleministry scandals; lacked experience in elective political office.

opportunities for those who try to advance their candidacy by taking stands on the issues. A candidate who departs from the standard positions runs the risk of alienating a large number of party members; yet one who does not do so remains indistinguishable from the other candidates. Thus it was difficult for Democratic voters in 1984 to differentiate among the policy positions of liberal candidates Mondale, Cranston, and McGovern. The same was true in 1980 for Republicans attempting to distinguish among the political views of conservative candidates Reagan, Crane, Dole, and Connally. In contrast, Republican representative John Anderson in 1980 took policy positions very different from those of conservative Republicans. (He favored, for example, gun control, the Equal Rights Amendment, the imposition of an import fee on gasoline to discourage consumption, and the public funding of abortions.) As a result, he alienated many Republican voters and had to drop out of the Republican race and run as an independent candidate.

The dynamics of the relationship between the parties can affect political dialogue in the nominating campaign. A diminished Democratic advantage in voter loyalty and Republican victories in the off-year elections of 1986, coupled with massive budget deficits and the Reagan legacy of reduced federal involvement in domestic activities, set the stage for programmatic appeals in the 1988 nomination campaign. The final contest between Dukakis, Gore, and Jackson represented an atypical choice for Democratic voters. No expensive new programs were advanced by the candidates. Gore sought to distinguish himself from rival Democrats with "tough" defense and foreign policy stands. Dukakis, the more moderate of the leading contenders, sought to reassure more liberal Democratic voters by noting his membership in the American Civil Liberties Union and his longstanding opposition to U.S. military interventions. Jackson espoused the views of the more progressive wing of the party.[12]

On the Republican side, eight years of party control of the White House had diminished ideological divisions within the party. Each of the candidates embraced elements of the Reagan legacy. Though Bush had attacked Reagan's proposals in 1980 as "voodoo economics," in 1988 he emphasized his commitment to all of Reagan's programs. Both Vice President Bush and Senator Dole sought to associate themselves with the administration record. Reverend Robertson focused on the administration's support of traditionalist values and life-styles.

Facing the problems associated with taking stands on issues, candidates develop other types of political appeals in nomination campaigns. Most important is the projection of a personal image that reflects their most attractive attributes. In 1980 Senator Kennedy, for example, pictured himself as a strong leader who could handle the nation's mounting economic and foreign policy problems. Four years earlier Jimmy Carter had sought to take advantage of the nation's distrust of public officials after the Vietnam War and Watergate by creating the image of an honest person and promising to make the government as "truthful, capable, and filled with love as the American people." In 1988 Dukakis sought to take advantage of his experience as governor of Massachusetts as a way to demonstrate competence in handling difficult economic matters. Thus candidates seek to link their personal characteristics with the perceived needs of the times.

Another important technique used in nomination campaigns is to project oneself as a "winner." This appeal usually is adopted by candidates who do well in the early nomination contests. Confident after his victory over Reagan in the 1980 Iowa caucuses, Bush suddenly announced that his campaign had momentum, or what he referred to as "Big Mo." Unfortunately for Bush, Big Mo lasted only until the New Hampshire primary, which Reagan clearly won. Similarly, in the 1984 Democratic contest Walter Mondale asserted his invincibility after his decisive victory in Iowa; one week later, however, he was upset by Gary Hart in New Hampshire. Momentum developed by Dole and Gephardt in the early contests in 1988 could not be sustained. Robert Dole won the Republican caucuses in Iowa, but his campaign faltered the following week in New Hampshire. Gephardt similarly fell by the wayside.

Presidential nomination campaigns, therefore, are characterized more by the manipulation of personal images and claims of winner status than by a discussion of the issues. Contributing greatly to this situation is the influence of the media in the nomination process.

Communicating Political Appeals

In 1988, more than 23 million voters participated in the Democratic primaries. To communicate with this vast number of people, candidates must turn to the mass media and novel ways of commanding public attention. Candidates in the 1988 campaign prepared videotapes for distribution at gatherings they were unable to attend. Televised call-in shows beamed up to a satellite allowed candidates to link up with voters and reporters around the country.[13] These innovations complemented the usual techniques of modern campaigning.

Major candidates depend heavily on short television commercials to carry their messages. In 1980, Jimmy Carter's advertisements stressed his character: one showed the president with his family and concluded with the statement, "Husband, Father, President. He's done these three jobs with distinction." Edward Kennedy's commercials carried a leadership theme: they focused on the senator looking forceful in Senate hearings and walking through enthusiastic crowds. In 1984, advertisements took a more negative tone: one for Mondale showed a blinking red telephone on the president's desk, raising the fear that Hart could not be entrusted with the "most awesome, powerful responsibility in the world." Hart countered with a political commercial that showed a burning fuse, as a voice suggested that Mondale would risk another Vietnam in Central America by leaving U.S. troops there and by "using our sons as bargaining chips." After suffering a 37 to 19 percent defeat to Robert Dole in the Iowa caucuses in 1988, Bush began a hard-hitting advertising campaign against Dole in the New Hampshire contest.

Candidate debates became important in the 1980 GOP nomination contest. Reagan refused to participate in the initial nationally televised debate held in Iowa on the grounds that such verbal encounters would destroy party unity; George Bush did well in the debate (paraphrasing Yogi Berra in asserting that Carter had made the "wrong mistake" by imposing an embargo on grain shipments to the Soviet Union) and went on to win the caucuses there. Reagan then switched tactics and engaged in two debates in New Hampshire. In the second one, originally scheduled to include only Reagan and Bush, the California governor outmaneuvered his opponent by suggesting that the debate be opened to other candidates; when Bush insisted on sticking to the terms of the original two-person encounter, he came across as selfish to the other Republican contenders and to many voters as well. Reagan won the New Hampshire primary and also prevailed in Illinois, where he did well in a multicandidate debate that included John Anderson of Illinois.

The Democratic candidates held about a dozen debates in 1984, but none proved as crucial as the Reagan-Bush New Hampshire debate of 1980. One problem, particularly early in the nomination campaign, was the large number of candidates. With eight in the debate that preceded the Iowa caucus it was difficult for viewers to keep straight which candidate said what. Nonetheless, these verbal encounters, called "media events" [14] by one scholar, did enable the candidates to confront one another with interesting questions. In Iowa, Hart asked Mondale to indicate a single, major domestic issue on which he disagreed with the AFL-CIO; in Atlanta, Mondale challenged Hart to spell out the substance of his "new ideas," making his point by using the famous line from the Wendy's commercial, "Where's the beef?" During the 1988 nominating season, approximately one-hundred candidate debates were held; toward the end of the campaign, several weary candidates began declining invitations to participate.

More important than candidate commercials or debates in campaign communications is the coverage of the nomination process by the news media. Particularly influential are nationally syndicated newspaper columnists, such as David Broder, Jack Germond, and Jules Witcover; many people, including writers for local newspapers, take their cues about the candidates and the nomination contest itself from these media "heavies." (One observer refers to this tendency as "pack journalism." [15]) Principal network newscasters, such as Dan Rather, Peter Jennings, and Tom Brokaw, also have played an important role in recent nomination campaigns, as television evening news is the main source of political information for most voters. Early in 1988 George Bush and Dan Rather confronted one another in a live interview on "The CBS Evening News." Rather persistently pressed Bush on his role in the Iran-contra scandal, particularly his knowledge about the details of the arms-for-hostages trade. Bush refused to answer directly and seized the opportunity to dispel his image as a "wimp." Alluding to one evening when Rather had walked away from his desk to protest a late beginning to the newscast, Bush said that people should be judged by their entire records, not by a single event in their careers. Rather had seemed intent on using the interview to embarass Bush, but the vice president successfully managed to turn the tables and use the encounter to his political advantage.

Such dramatic encounters are rare. As political scientist Thomas Patterson maintains, the mass media focus primarily on the presidential "game"—who is winning and losing, campaign strategy and logistics, and appearances and "hoopla." [16] Thus the chances of the contestants are calculated and their candidacies assessed by the extent to which they surpass or fall short of the media's predictions. The media also attempt to analyze the strategies of the candidates and how successful they are likely to be. Television in particular concentrates its attention on candidate appearances and crowd reactions to such appearances, as it tries to convey the visually exciting aspects of the campaign.[17] Patterson contends that the media devote far less coverage to what he calls the "substance" of the campaign—discussion of issues and policies, the traits and records of the candidates, and endorsements by political leaders.

The media downplay political issues and policies in nomination campaigns for several reasons. As previously discussed, it is difficult to focus effectively on issues when a number of candidates in a nomination contest hold very similar views. Moreover, today's nomination campaigns are so long that candidates' speeches become, from the media's point of view, "unnewsworthy," as the contenders repeat their stands on the issues again and again. Finally, many media representatives assume that most voters are not interested in the issues; in any event, it is difficult to present issues in depth—especially on television, where the average evening news story lasts only a little longer than one minute.

Patterson points out that the media are, however, interested in two kinds of issues.[18] One is the "clear-cut" issue, in which candidates take diametrically opposed stands on a matter of public policy. This opposition creates controversy, on which the media thrive. The other is the "campaign" issue, one involving an error of judgment by a candidate, such as Jimmy Carter's remark in 1976 about the desirability of preserving the "ethnic purity" of city neighborhoods. A graphic illustration of the media's preoccupation with campaign issues rather than policy issues is Roger Mudd's previously mentioned interview with Edward Kennedy: it concentrated primarily on Mary Jo Kopechne's death at Chappaquiddick and barely touched on Kennedy's voting record in his seventeen years in the Senate.

According to C. Anthony Broh, "the roles in which television presents candidates affect the expectations of the members of the public who watch the programs."[19] Thus, the media can shape public perceptions about a candidate's viability. Jesse Jackson's candidacy in 1984 and 1988 presented a special challenge for reporters. Broh's analysis of television's treatment of Jackson in 1984 found that reporters gave Jackson less presidential "game" coverage than the other candidates in the Democratic field. Stories focused on his personality and on his role as an outsider with little chance for the nomination. Though the media presented Jackson as a legitimate candidate, they also implied that he was different from the other candidates in the race, reinforcing the idea that he had little chance of nomination.

The media also devote little attention to how candidates have done in prior public offices. Before the state caucuses and primaries begin, commentators give some coverage to the candidates' records, but that interest declines when the presidential "game" begins. Only when a hiatus occurs in the primary campaign do the media generally return to an examination of the record. In April 1980, for example, during the three weeks between the Wisconsin and Pennsylvania primaries, the media suddenly began producing detailed comparisons of Reagan's campaign statements and his actual performance as the governor of California.

Thus the media shape the nature of the nomination campaign. They tend to focus attention on the game aspects of the early contests, particularly those in Iowa and New Hampshire. According to Patterson, they typically employ a winner-take-all principle that gives virtually all the publicity, regardless of how narrow the victory or the number of popular votes involved, to the victorious candidate in a state contest. In the 1976 Iowa caucuses Carter's capture of about 14,000 voters (just 28 percent of the 50,000 cast) was interpreted by Roger Mudd as making the Georgia governor a "clear winner" and as opening the "ground between himself and the rest of the so-called pack." [20] At times, however, the media may provide greater coverage to the runner-up: after winning a mere 16 percent of the votes in the Iowa caucuses in 1984, Hart received as much publicity as Mondale, who captured three times as many votes.[21]

Campaign Organization and Workers

Although the mass media play a major role in communicating political appeals to the selectorate, interpersonal contacts remain an important element in nomination campaigns. This is particularly true in states that use caucus-conventions to choose their delegates to the national convention. In those states voters do not simply cast their ballots; rather, they often participate in lengthy meetings and sometimes in confrontations with supporters of other candidates. A series of meetings usually takes place throughout the state political system until a state convention chooses the national convention delegates. Most people are unwilling to commit that much time and effort to the nomination process unless campaign workers contact them personally.

As the campaign progresses, a candidate must expand the previously mentioned "constituency" that developed in the early, prenomination stage of the process. In the past, candidates often turned to political professionals to sponsor and organize their campaign, as Hubert Humphrey did in 1968. The endorsement of party professionals, however, does not always ensure the nomination. In 1972, for example, the early endorsement of Sen. Edmund Muskie by a number of Democratic party and public officials did not prevent the party from choosing George McGovern, a candidate with whom many professionals were uncomfortable. In 1976, an "outsider," Jimmy Carter, won the Democratic nomination, even though he had virtually no initial support from his fellow governors or other members of the Democratic political establishment. Among Republicans, Sen. Barry Goldwater won the 1964 nomination despite the opposition of many party leaders and public officials.

Probably the only candidate today who is in a position to line up the support of party professionals is an incumbent president, for he can use his influence over the dispensation of federal grants as political leverage against his opponents. Even this weapon is not always successful, however. Mayor Jane Byrne of Chicago (successor to the most powerful political boss of recent times, Richard Daley) endorsed Senator Kennedy, not President Carter, in the 1980 Democratic contest. Moreover, even when an incumbent president does receive the political blessing of a key political figure, it may not be decisive: Carter lost the 1980 New York primary to Kennedy even though the president had been endorsed by Mayor Edward Koch of New York City.

Today's candidates generally build their personal organization with political amateurs who offer support because they agree with a candidate's stands on the issues or are attracted to his or her personality or political style. Amateurs constituted the base for the Goldwater movement in 1964, for Eugene McCarthy's "Children's Crusade" in 1968, for McGovern's "guerrilla army" in 1972, and for Reagan's conservative constituency in 1976 and again in 1980. Political scientist Jeane Kirkpatrick refers to such activists as a "new presidential elite." [22] Usually members of the upper middle class, such people have neither experience in nor loyalty to traditional party organizations. As Kirkpatrick contends, they typically take a keen interest in the intellectual and moral aspects of politics and use their verbal skills to great advantage in nomination politics.

At times, members of interest groups also endorse presidential candidates and furnish campaign workers for them. Some major labor unions participated actively in the 1980 Democratic contest. Edward Kennedy drew support from the International Association of Machinists and Aerospace Workers, and the National Education Association worked hard on President Carter's behalf. Both the AFL-CIO and the NEA endorsed Walter Mondale before the formal 1984 nomination process began and then played an important part in helping him secure the Democratic nomination. Mondale was subsequently labeled the "candidate of the special interests" because of his interest group endorsements.

Campaign Finance

Presidential candidates since the 1970s have begun to raise funds for their campaigns before the state contests begin. The solicitation of funds continues during the official campaign period. Candidates who do not do well in the first few primaries, however, tend to drop out of the race early on. One reason is that, under the campaign finance law, federal matching funds must be cut off within thirty days if a candidate obtains less than 10 percent of the votes in two consecutive primaries. Even candidates who do not depend on matching funds may decide that a contest is hopeless; John Connally withdrew from the Republican race in early March 1980 after losing the South Carolina Republican primary to Reagan. (By that time the former Texas governor had spent $11 million of privately raised money and had won only one convention delegate.) Even candidates who score some successes in primaries may nonetheless develop financial problems if their opponents are doing even better. In 1980 Senator Kennedy found that President Carter was outspending him in virtually every state, including his home state of Massachusetts (New Hampshire was one exception). That same year, Bush was forced to take out a bank loan of $2.8 million after losing to Reagan in several primaries.

Candidates must decide not only how to raise funds but also how to spend them. The overall spending limits for the entire campaign ($17.6 million in 1980, $24.4 million in 1984, and $27.7 million in 1988), as well as expenditure limits in each state, require that money be carefully allocated. Because they want to win in initial primaries and caucuses, candidates are inclined to spend heavily in the very early stages of the campaign. By February 26, 1980, the date of the New Hampshire primary, Reagan had spent two-thirds of his allowable limit for a campaign consisting of thirty-four primaries.[23]

Summary of Developments in Recent Nomination Campaigns

As suggested in the preceding sections, presidential nomination campaigns are highly complex operations that call for a variety of specialists. Pollsters help candidates assess their nomination prospects and provide vital feedback on the reactions of voters to the candidates and their campaigns, on the issues that people are thinking about, and on the attitudes of social and economic groups about such issues. Media consultants help candidates develop a favorable image, write their speeches, and plan their television appearances. Direct-mail specialists help raise money and get out the vote. Since the 1952 presidential election, candidates have turned more and more to political consultants to organize these diverse operations, to develop strategy, and to manage the overall campaign.

Since the late 1960s control over the fate of presidential candidates has passed from a relatively few party professionals to rank-and-file voters. The attitudes of these voters evolve during the course of the nomination contest, in large part under the influence of the media. In the early stages of the contest the media help determine who the viable candidates are; then, once the state primaries and caucuses begin, they label the "winners" and "losers," often influencing the results of future state contests, for voters gravitate toward the winners and desert the losers. Periodic public opinion polls reflect the presidential preferences of U.S. voters, as do the results of state primaries and caucuses.

Moreover, the attitudes of voters, the media, the polls, and the state contest results influence one another. Candidates who receive favorable treatment from the media tend to do well in the primaries, and their showing there, in turn, raises their standings in the polls. Favorable polls impress representatives of the media as well as political activists and many rank-and-file voters, leading to more victories for the poll leaders in both nonprimary and primary contests. Usually, the result of this reinforcement process is that one candidate has emerged by the time the delegates gather for their party's national convention. This candidate has received the most extensive and the most favorable media coverage, has led in the polls, and has won more primary and caucus-convention contests than any other candidate.[24] However, one more hurdle remains for the front-runner to cross—the party's national convention.

The National Convention

The national convention is important to presidential candidates for two reasons. First, whatever may have happened before, the actual nomination occurs at the convention. Second, the convention provides opportunities for candidates to strengthen their chances to win the general election the following November.

Rules and Politics of the Proceedings

Several decisions that precede the balloting for the nomination can affect significantly both the choice of nominee and the outcome of the general election. Sometimes the location of the convention is important. (The party's national committee officially makes this decision: for the party out of power, the national committee chairperson has the greatest say in the matter; for the party in power, the U.S. president does.) The welcoming speech of Illinois governor Adlai Stevenson to the Democratic delegates assembled in Chicago in 1952 is credited with influencing their decision to nominate him that year. In 1968 the confrontation in Chicago between protestors and Mayor Daley's police contributed to Hubert Humphrey's defeat in the general election.

Also important are the struggles between rival slates of delegates from states where the process of selecting delegates was disputed. At the 1952 Republican convention, the party's credentials committee awarded Robert Taft a majority of the delegates in several southern states, but this decision was overturned on the floor of the convention in favor of the ultimate nominee, Dwight Eisenhower. At the 1972 Democratic convention, there were eighty-two separate challenges involving thirty states and more than 40 percent of the delegates; most of the disputes stemmed from alleged violations of the McGovern Commission guidelines. Eventually, all but two were settled by the credentials committee; these went to the convention floor and were resolved in Senator McGovern's favor. He was awarded all of California's delegate votes even though, as previously noted, he won only 45 percent of that state's primary vote. Another dispute led to a convention decision to seat the delegation favoring the senator, and not the regular Illinois delegation linked with Mayor Daley of Chicago, on the grounds that the latter did not contain an adequate representation of youth, women, and minorities and was chosen through improper processes.

Fights over rules of convention proceedings sometimes take on great significance. One such battle occurred at the 1976 Republican convention when the Reagan forces moved to amend the rules so as to require candidates to name their vice-presidential choice before the balloting on presidential candidates; they hoped thereby to force Ford to name a running mate and thus risk the loss of supporters who would be disappointed with his decision. (Before the convention Reagan had chosen liberal-to-moderate Pennsylvania senator Richard Schweiker as his vice president, a move calculated to bring him needed support from uncommitted delegates in large eastern states such as New York and Pennsylvania.) The defeat of that amendment helped pave the way for President Ford's victory on the first ballot that year. In 1980 Edward Kennedy's forces attempted to persuade the Democratic convention delegates to vote down a rule, first proposed by the Winograd Commission and later adopted by the Democratic National Committee, that required delegates to vote on the first ballot for a presidential candidate to whom they were pledged in their home state's primary or caucus-convention. When the convention upheld the rule, the Massachusetts senator knew he had no chance of winning the Democratic nomination, for a majority of the delegates were pledged to Carter. Kennedy immediately withdrew his candidacy. The 1988 Democratic convention witnessed a reversal in the effect of rules changes on the convention. Jesse Jackson realized he had lost the nomination that year but sought to win concessions on the rules governing the 1992 contest. Rather than risk a publicly embarrassing and potentially unity-shattering battle over the rules, the Dukakis forces gave Jackson what he wanted. Delegate selection was tied more closely to the share of the vote earned in the primary and caucus contests, and the number of superdelegates was reduced.

Writing and adopting the party platform entails other important convention decisions. Although critics have ridiculed the platforms for containing promises the party does not intend to keep, presidents of both parties have used their influence to enact the promises into law.[25] Moreover, many delegates and party leaders take them seriously.[26] In 1948 some of the delegates to the Democratic convention felt that the platform was too liberal on civil rights; twenty years later the Democrats bitterly debated the Vietnam plank in the platform. Republicans also have experienced major conflicts over their party platform: in 1964 the conservative Goldwater forces, who controlled that convention, refused to make any concessions to party moderates, such as governors Nelson Rockefeller of New York and George Romney of Michigan, on civil rights and political extremism.

One of the problems of platform fights is that the intraparty conflict may influence the general election campaign. In 1948 a group of southerners headed by South Carolina governor J. Strom Thurmond formed the States' Rights party, which actually carried four southern states— Alabama, Louisiana, Mississippi, and South Carolina. Republican governors Nelson Rockefeller and George Romney did little to help Goldwater in 1964, and many Democrats opposed to the proadministration Vietnam plank in the party's 1968 platform did not rouse themselves in the general election campaign that year.

Because of the possibility of splitting the party in the fall campaign, presidential candidates and their supporters sometimes decide not to fight their major rivals over the platform. After defeating Ronald Reagan for the 1976 Republican nomination, President Ford allowed the views of the California governor to prevail in several major provisions of the platform, including advocating a "moral" foreign policy in contrast to the Ford administration's policy of détente with the Soviet Union. In 1980 President Carter followed a similar procedure in permitting the Kennedy forces to add to the Democratic platform a provision for a $12-billion, antirecession job program. In 1984 Mondale allowed Hart to add a plank spelling out the conditions under which a Democratic president would use U.S. forces abroad and permitted Jackson to add a provision for "affirmative action goals and timetables and other verifiable measurements." In 1988 three of Jackson's proposed platform amendments were not included, but the Dukakis forces accepted modified versions of nine other Jackson planks in exchange for Jackson's acceptance of a short platform.

Credentials contests, the adoption of rules of procedure, and the writing of the party platform are tests of strength for the candidates and often determine who will prevail in the most important decision of the convention—the balloting for president, which typically takes place on the third day of the proceedings. In the interim, preparations are made for the roll-call vote. Presidential hopefuls frequently call caucuses of state delegations and sometimes contact individual delegates for their support. Polls are taken of delegates so that candidates know how many votes they can count on and from whom they may pick up additional support. In 1960 Edward Kennedy retained contacts with the Wyoming delegates he had worked with the previous spring and was in their midst when that delegation cast its decisive vote for his brother on the first ballot.[27] Also in 1960, Richard Nixon arranged to have his picture taken with each delegate at the Republican convention.[28]

The strategy a candidate employs in the balloting depends on the amount of delegate support he has. If he is the front-runner, as President Ford asserted he was in 1976, he concentrates on holding the votes he has been promised and on picking up any additional votes needed to win a majority on the initial ballot. The candidate and his workers use the bandwagon technique to achieve this goal—that is, they argue that because he will win the nomination anyway, smart delegation chairpersons or individual members should come out early for his candidacy rather than wait until the matter has already been settled. The candidate, the workers imply, will remember early support in the future when he is in a position to do political favors. Franklin Roosevelt did so quite specifically after he was elected in 1932, determining whether a person seeking a political position had backed him "before Chicago" (where the convention had been held).

Candidates with less delegate support attempt to counter the bandwagon technique with their own strategies. They try to create the impression that the nomination is still uncertain, as the Reagan forces did at the 1976 Republican convention. At times, they may encourage delegates who do not support them to cast their ballots for favorite sons or other minor candidates; their objective is to hold down the vote for the front-runner on the first roll call. Candidates also attempt to forge alliances to stop the leader. They may agree, for example, that at some time during the balloting, those who fall behind in the voting will throw their support to others. The difficulty with making such an arrangement is that minor candidates frequently have greater differences among themselves than they have with the leader. The only alliance that conceivably might have stopped Richard Nixon at the 1968 Republican convention would have been one between Nelson Rockefeller and Ronald Reagan. However, given their divergent views on vital issues of the day, and Rockefeller's failure to support Goldwater in 1964 (in contrast to Reagan's famous convention speech on Goldwater's behalf), the two governors were hardly a compatible political combination.

The leader, along with other candidates, offers various enticements in bargaining with possible political supporters. Some delegates may be interested in persuading the party to take a particular stand on the platform. Others may have more tangible concerns: senators or governors may seek the candidate's support in their own campaigns; other political leaders may be looking toward a cabinet post. Although a presidential candidate himself may refuse to make such commitments so that he can go before his party and the electorate as a "free" man beholden to none, his supporters do not hesitate to make promises. One delegate to the 1960 convention claimed to be the nineteenth person to whom the Kennedy forces had offered the vice presidency.[29]

A definite trend in recent conventions is early victory for the candidate who arrives at the convention with the greatest number of pledged delegates. In the twenty-two conventions the two major parties have held since World War II, only two nominees—Thomas Dewey in 1948 and Adlai Stevenson in 1952—failed to win a majority of the convention votes on the first ballot. Thus, the convention has become a body that typically legitimizes a decision made some time before the delegates gather to confer the nomination upon their candidate.

The selection of the vice-presidential nominee is the final decision of the convention. Although in theory the delegates make the choice, it has been political custom since 1940 to allow presidential nominees to pick their own running mates. On rare occasions nominees may decide not to express their preference and to permit the convention to make an open choice, as Adlai Stevenson did in 1956. The typical presidential nominee, however, confers with leaders whose judgment he trusts, and, when he makes the decision, the word is passed on to the delegates. Even though some delegates may resist a particular vice-presidential candidate, nominees generally get their way. In 1940 Franklin Roosevelt threatened to refuse the presidential nomination unless Henry Wallace were chosen as his vice president. In 1960 John Kennedy insisted on Lyndon Johnson as his running mate over the objections of some liberal members of the party, including his brother Robert. In effect, the vice president is the first political appointment of the winning presidential nominee.

Various considerations underlie the choice of a vice-presidential candidate. Parties traditionally attempt to balance the ticket—that is, to select a person who differs in certain ways from the presidential nominee. For example, the two candidates may come from separate parts of the country. Over the years, the Democratic party often has chosen southerners to run with presidential nominees who were typically from other, two-party regions; the Kennedy-Johnson ticket in 1960 and the Dukakis-Bentsen ticket in 1988 were two such combinations. In 1976, when a southerner, Jimmy Carter, won the Democratic presidential contest for the first time since before the Civil War, the process worked in reverse; he chose as his running mate Walter Mondale from the northern state of Minnesota. In 1972 George McGovern originally chose Sen. Thomas Eagleton as his running mate, because the Missourian possessed certain characteristics the South Dakotan lacked: affiliation with the Roman Catholic church, ties to organized labor, and previous residence in a large city (St. Louis). In 1980 Ronald Reagan chose George Bush (whom he reportedly did not much admire) in order to win the support of moderates in the Republican party. In 1984 Mondale selected as his running mate Rep. Geraldine Ferraro of New York, who not only complemented the ticket geographically but also was the first woman and first Italian-American to serve as a major party candidate in a presidential contest. The ticket is balanced in these ways to broaden its appeal and thereby strengthen the party's chances in the general election.

At least some presidential nominees consider how the vice-presidential candidate will perform in office. The trend toward assigning important responsibilities to the second in command has led some candidates to choose running mates with whom they feel they can work effectively. This was the main reason Carter chose Walter Mondale over other northern liberal senators he had interviewed for the position, including Edmund Muskie of Maine, Frank Church of Idaho, John Glenn of Ohio, and Adlai Stevenson III of Illinois. The possibility of succession also has led presidents to choose the running mate who seems most able to assume the duties of the nation's highest office. John Kennedy reportedly chose Lyndon Johnson not only because he balanced the Democratic ticket in 1960 but also because Kennedy considered the Texan to be the most capable leader among his rivals for the presidential nomination.

Whatever the considerations that prompt the choice of a running mate, there is no doubt that presidential nominees often make the decision too quickly, and frequently without complete knowledge of the candidate's background. A notable example is McGovern's choice of Eagleton in 1972. McGovern and his staff met the morning after his nomination (many of them having had only two or three hours of sleep), and by five o'clock that afternoon they settled on Eagleton. The Missourian accepted the nomination after several other persons had either turned it down, could not be contacted, or were vetoed by key McGovern supporters. During that time no one on the candidate's staff discovered Eagleton's history of mental illness, which ultimately led McGovern to force him off the ticket after a storm of public controversy. Media reaction to the choice made by a presidential nominee can become a complication for the ticket. In 1988 the reaction to Bush's selection of Dan Quayle nearly overshadowed the Republican convention. Questions were raised about Quayle's ability to perform as president should the need arise, his service in the National Guard during the Vietnam War, and the circumstances of his admission to law school. Following the controversy, Quayle may have temporarily benefited from a sympathetic backlash to the media's "feeding frenzy," but his problems at the outset of the campaign probably explain why he virtually disappeared during the general election.

The Democrats' choice also produced problems in 1988, though of a different sort. Dukakis and Bentsen had substantial policy differences that attracted immediate Republican comment. More significantly, however, Jesse Jackson was rebuffed in his pointed pursuit of the vice-presidential nomination, a position to which he felt entitled given his second-place finish in the competition for the presidential nomination. Dukakis not only denied Jackson this chance but managed to alienate Jackson and many of his supporters in the process. Jackson had expected Dukakis to give him the courtesy of a telephone call before announcing his choice, but the decision was announced publicly before Jackson could be reached. The bad feelings carried over into the fall campaign.

After the vice-presidential candidate is chosen, the final night of the convention proceedings is given over to acceptance speeches. On this occasion the presidential nominee tries to reunite the candidates and various party elements that have confronted one another during the long preconvention campaign and the hectic days of the convention. Major party figures usually come to the convention stage and pledge their support for the winner in the upcoming campaign. At times, however, personal feelings run too high and wounds fail to heal sufficiently for a show of party unity. In 1964, for example, important members of the liberal wing of the Republican party did not support the GOP standard-bearer, Barry Goldwater. In 1968 many McCarthyites (including McCarthy himself) refused, at least immediately, to endorse the Democrats' nominee, Hubert Humphrey. In 1972 prominent Democratic leaders, including George Meany of the AFL-CIO, did not support McGovern. Senator Kennedy and many of his followers did not enthusiastically endorse President Carter on the final night of the 1980 Democratic convention. Thus, the convention does not always achieve one of its main objectives: to rally the party faithful for the general election.

Recent Changes in Conventions

As noted in Chapter 1, the principal activities of today's national conventions are the same as those developed one hundred and fifty years ago: devising the rules of procedure, adopting platforms, and, most important, nominating presidential and vice-presidential candidates. Recent developments, however, particularly since the mid-1960s, have radically changed the character of party conventions.

The most basic change is the way political power is organized and exercised at the convention. In the past, to win their party's nomination, presidential candidates were forced to negotiate with party leaders, particularly with those who chaired state delegations (often governors). Today, however, candidates' personal organizations dominate the convention proceedings and contact individual delegates directly rather than working through the leaders who chair state delegations. Thus the growth in importance of candidate (rather than party) organizations, which has occurred in presidential nomination campaigns, has carried over into the national convention itself.

The character of convention delegates also changed in the late 1960s and 1970s. Students of those conventions have identified a basic split in both parties between amateur and professional delegates, the former motivated primarily by candidates' stands on the issues and the latter by their ability to unite the party and win in November.[30] In the 1980s, however, the distinction between the two types of delegates has blurred as former amateurs share power with professionals and take on many of the latter's characteristics. Two political scientists call these people the "new professionals." [31]

Also becoming more prominent are delegate caucuses that transcend state boundaries, such as those organized by women, blacks, and Chicanos. In some instances these groups take the leadership in platform fights, as women did at the 1976 Republican convention over the ratification of the Equal Rights Amendment (ERA) and at the 1980 Democratic convention over the use of Medicaid funds for abortions and the denial of financial and technical campaign support to candidates not supporting ERA. Also surfacing as power blocs are those organized by interest groups: the AFL-CIO had 405 delegates and the National Education Association 302 delegates at the 1980 Democratic convention.[32]

Finally, technological developments have affected recent nominating conventions. Sophisticated electronic equipment enables centralized candidate organizations to communicate directly with their organizers and with individual delegates on the crowded convention floor. Even more important is the mass media's thorough and immediate coverage of convention proceedings. Such coverage has forced the parties to stage proceedings in a way that appeals to a nationwide audience; visually important events must be scheduled to take advantage of prime-time viewing. The media's close attention also has made it difficult for the parties to carry on delicate negotiations. As columnist David Broder has pointed out, not since 1952 (when, he suggests, television "took over" the convention hall) has either major party used more than one ballot to nominate its presidential candidate. He attributes this consequence to the party members' inability "to take the time for the slow and sometimes secretive bargaining that in the past allowed their national conventions to function successfully as coalition-building institutions." [33] Some observers of the 1980 Republican convention believe that the reason the GOP failed to consummate the "dream ticket" of Reagan and Ford was the media's relentless pressure to cover and thereby to shape the delicate negotiations surrounding that important decision.

Notes

1. Austin Ranney, "Changing the Rules of the Nominating Game," in *Choosing the President,* ed. James David Barber (Englewood Cliffs, N.J.: Prentice-Hall, 1974), 71.
2. Arthur Hadley, *The Invisible Primary* (Englewood Cliffs, N.J.: Prentice-Hall, 1976).
3. Jules Witcover, "Sen. Mondale Won't Seek Presidential Nomination," *Washington Post,* November 22, 1974, A1.
4. Theodore H. White, *The Making of the President, 1972* (New York: Bantam, 1973), 127.
5. Martin Schram, *Running for President 1976: The Carter Campaign* (New York: Stein and Day, 1977), 8.
6. Donald Matthews, "Presidential Nominations: Process and Outcomes," in *Race for the Presidency: The Media and the Nominating Process,* ed. James David Barber (Englewood Cliffs, N.J.: Prentice-Hall, 1978), 39.
7. John Aldrich, *Before the Convention: A Theory of Presidential Nomination Campaigns* (Chicago: University of Chicago Press, 1980), 70.
8. Schram, *Running for President,* 20.
9. Thomas B. Edsall and Richard Marin, "Super Tuesday's Showing," *Washington Post National Weekly Edition,* March 14-20, 1988, 37.
10. Gerald Pomper, "The Presidential Nominations," in *The Election of 1988,* ed. Gerald Pomper (Chatham, N.J.: Chatham House, 1989), 47.
11. Former Tennessee senator Howard Baker noted that this development has made the Iowa caucuses the "functional equivalent of a primary." Lou Cannon and William Peterson, "GOP," in *The Pursuit of the Presidency,* ed. Richard Harwood (New York: Berkeley, 1980), 129.
12. Walter Dean Burnham, "The Reagan Heritage," 34-35; Gerald M. Pomper, "The Presidential Nominations," in *The Election of 1988,* 56-57.
13. Pat Dunham, *Electoral Behavior in the United States* (Englewood Cliffs, N.J.: Prentice-Hall, 1991), 163. "Beaming at the Voters," *Time,* February 15, 1988, 78-79.
14. Michael W. Traugott, "The Media and the Nominating Process," in *Before Nomination: Our Primary Problems,* ed. George Grassmuck (Washington,

D.C.: American Enterprise Institute, 1985), 111-112.

15. Timothy Crouse, *The Boys on the Bus* (New York: Ballantine Books, 1972).

16. Thomas Patterson, *The Mass Media Election: How Americans Choose Their President* (New York: Praeger, 1980), chap. 3.

17. Television reporters refer to coverage of candidates arriving at and departing from airports as "here he comes, there he goes" stories.

18. Patterson, *Mass Media Election,* chap. 4.

19. C. Anthony Broh, *A Horse of a Different Color: Television's Treatment of Jesse Jackson's 1984 Presidential Campaign* (Washington, D.C.: Joint Center for Political Studies, 1987), 4.

20. Ibid., 44.

21. William C. Adams, "Media Coverage of Campaign '84: A Preliminary Report," *Public Opinion,* April-May 1984, 10-11, cited in Gary R. Orren, "The Nomination Process: Vicissitudes of Candidate Selection," in *The Elections of 1984,* ed. Michael Nelson (Washington, D.C.: CQ Press, 1985), 53.

22. Jeane Kirkpatrick, *The New Presidential Elite: Men and Women in National Politics* (New York: Russell Sage Foundation and the Twentieth Century Fund, 1976).

23. Cannon and Peterson, "GOP," 128.

24. Recent exceptions to that trend, when two candidates ended the preconvention period fairly even in all respects, are Ford and Reagan in 1976, McGovern and Humphrey in 1972, and Mondale and Hart in 1984.

25. Gerald Pomper and Susan Lederman, *Elections in America: Control and Influence in Democratic Politics,* 2d ed. (New York: Longman, 1980), chap. 8.

26. Judith Parris, *The Convention Problem: Issues in Reform of Presidential Nominating Procedures* (Washington, D.C.: Brookings, 1972), 110.

27. Theodore H. White, *The Making of the President, 1960* (New York: Pocket Books, 1961), 203.

28. Nelson Polsby and Aaron Wildavsky, *Presidential Elections: Strategies of American Electoral Politics* (New York: Scribners, 1964), 82.

29. Ibid., 4th ed. (1976), 144.

30. Robert Robach, "Amateurs and Professionals: Delegates to the 1972 Republican National Convention," *Journal of Politics* 37 (May 1975): 436-469; John Soule and Wilma McGrath, "A Comparative Study of Presidential Nominations: The Democrats, 1968 and 1972," *American Journal of Political Science* 19 (August 1975): 501-517; Robert Nakamura, "Beyond Purism and Professionalism: Styles of Convention Delegate Followership," *American Journal of Political Science* 24 (May 1980): 207-232.

31. William Crotty and John S. Jackson III, *Presidential Primaries and Nominations,* Washington, D.C.: CQ Press, 1985), 122.

32. Michael Malbin, "The Conventions, Platforms, and Issue Activists," in *The American Elections of 1980,* ed. Austin Ranney (Washington, D.C.: American Enterprise Institute, 1981), 128.

33. David Broder, "Political Reporters in Presidential Politics," in *Inside the System,* 2d ed., ed. Charles Peters and John Rothchild (New York: Praeger, 1973), 7.

Selected Readings

Bartels, Larry M. *Presidential Primaries and the Dynamics of Public Choice.* Princeton, N.J.: Princeton University Press, 1988.

Geer, John G. *Nominating Presidents: An Evaluation of Voters and Primaries.* New York: Greenwood Press, 1989.

Kessel, John. *Presidential Campaign Politics.* Homewood, Ill.: Dorsey, 1988.

Nelson, Michael, ed. *The Elections of 1988.* Washington, D.C.: CQ Press, 1989.

Pomper, Gerald, ed. *The Election of 1988.* Chatham, N.J.: Chatham House, 1989.

Wayne, Stephen J. *The Road to the White House: The Politics of Presidential Elections.* 3d ed. New York: St. Martin's, 1988.

Election Rules and the Election Campaign 3

George Herbert Walker Bush was officially declared the nation's forty-first president on January 4, 1989, when ballots from members of the electoral college were opened and recorded during a joint session of Congress. Electors had met in their respective state capitals on December 19, 1988, to cast presidential and vice-presidential ballots. Bush was inaugurated on January 20, 1989, in accordance with the timetable set forth in the Twentieth Amendment to the Constitution, ratified in 1933. These events validated the popular vote outcome reported by the media on election night and brought to a conclusion the election phase of the selection process, a phase in which candidates face very different problems from those confronted in winning the nomination.

New political appeals must be developed for this new stage of the campaign, which is essentially a one-on-one contest pitting the nominees of the two major parties against each other, although, on occasion, a strong third party candidate may run. The audience of the campaign increases greatly—more than twice as many people vote in the general election as participate in the nomination process.[1] Candidates and staff members therefore must decide how they can win the support of these new voters as well as those who backed losing candidates in the nomination process. A further complication is the length of the campaign: this new, expanded phase of the presidential contest is compressed into the ten weeks extending from Labor Day to election day.

The first section of this chapter traces the evolution of the electoral college system and explains how it and recent campaign finance laws affect the general election campaign. The second section analyzes the campaign in the same framework as was used in Chapter 1 for the nomination contest: its early stages and targeting efforts, the kinds of political appeals directed toward the electorate, the communication of these appeals through the media and campaign workers, and the sources and types of expenditures.

Rules of the Election Contest

Rules covering the general election phase differ in two central respects from those governing the nomination phase: the constitutional requirement that the electoral college choose the president and the distinctive provisions of the campaign finance laws. The constitutional requirements have been remarkably stable over time, particularly when compared to the extensive changes found in the nomination process, but campaign finance laws have undergone significant change over the past twenty-five years.

The Electoral College

The method of selecting the president was among the most difficult problems the delegates to the Constitutional Convention faced.[2] A variety of plans were proposed, the two most important being selection by the Congress and direct election by the people. The first, derived from the practice in most states of the legislature's choosing the governor, had the backing of a number of delegates, including Roger Sherman of Connecticut. It was eventually discarded because of fear of legislative supremacy and also because the delegates could not choose between "state-unit voting," which favored the small states, and joint action of the two chambers, which benefited the large states with their greater voting power in the House of Representatives. Three of the most influential members of the convention—James Madison of Virginia and James Wilson and Gouverneur Morris of Pennsylvania—supported direct popular election, but most delegates considered that method too democratic. As George Mason of Virginia said, "It would be as unnatural to refer the choice of a proper magistrate to the people as it would to refer a trial of colors to a blind man."

Having decided against both popular election and selection by legislative bodies, the delegates proceeded to adopt an entirely new plan put forth by one of their own committees. The proposal, which some historians believe was based on a method used in Maryland to elect state senators, specified that each state legislature could choose electors, by whatever means it desired, equal to its total number of senators and representatives in Congress, but that none of the electors could be members of Congress or hold other national office.[3] The individual electors would assemble at a fixed time in their respective state capitals and cast two votes each for president. These votes were then to be transmitted to Washington, D.C., where they would be opened and counted during a joint session of Congress. Whoever received the largest number of electoral votes would be declared president, provided an absolute majority (one more than half) had been obtained; if no candidate received a majority, the House of Representatives, voting by states (with each state delegation having one vote), would choose the president from among the five candidates receiving the highest number of electoral votes. After the president was chosen, the person with the next highest number of electoral votes would be declared vice president. If two or more contenders received an equal number of electoral votes, the Senate would choose the vice president from among them.

This complicated procedure reflected values and assumptions about human nature enunciated in *The Federalist Papers,* Number 68. Number 68 is attributed to Alexander Hamilton, whose views were somewhat more elitist than those of the majority of the delegates to the Constitutional Convention. Nevertheless, most of the Founders believed that the average person did not have the ability to make sound judgments about the qualifications of the presidential candidates and that the decision therefore should be left to a small group of electors—a political elite who would have both the information and the wisdom necessary to choose the best persons for the nation's two highest offices. Because the electors could not be national officeholders with connections to the president, they could approach their task without bias; because they assembled separately in their respective state capitals rather than as a single body, there would be less chance of their being corrupted or exposed to popular unrest. Moreover, because they were convened for a single purpose and would be dissolved when their task was completed, the possibility of tampering with them in advance or rewarding them with future favors was eliminated.

Philosophy shaped the presidential selection process adopted by the delegates, but so did a recognition of political factors. One student of the subject suggests that some of the delegates did not expect the electors to be entirely insulated from popular preferences.[4] They anticipated that each state's electors would cast one vote for a "native son," a locally popular political figure, and the other for a "continental character," an individual with a national reputation known to members of the political elite if not to the average citizen. (Evidence for this assumption is provided by Article II, Section 1, of the Constitution, which states that at least one of the two persons for whom an elector votes must not be an inhabitant of the elector's state.)

The Founders also expected that after George Washington's presidency, the electoral votes would be so widely distributed that few candidates would receive a majority, and, therefore, most elections (Mason estimated nineteen out of twenty) would ultimately be decided by the

House of Representatives. The electors would thus serve to "screen" (or, in today's terms, "nominate") the candidates, and the House would choose (elect) the president from among them. The conflict between large and small states, which was settled by the Connecticut Compromise on the composition of the Senate and House, also arose in the plan the delegates worked out for the selection of the chief executive. In the initial vote by the electors, the large states had the advantage, because the number of each state's votes reflected the size of its House delegation. If no candidate received a majority, the small states were favored in the second selection, because the contingent vote was by states, not by the number of representatives.

As was true of so many issues decided by the Founders, the method of selecting the president was a compromise. In addition to resolving the large-state/small-state conflict, the electoral college device took into account the attitudes of the advocates of states' rights by allowing the state legislatures to decide how the electors should be chosen. It also held open, for those who favored letting the people choose the president, the possibility of the electors' actually reflecting the popular vote for the president in their state. As political scientist John Roche has pointed out, the intermediate elector scheme gave "everybody a piece of the cake"; he also notes, however, that "the future was left to cope with the problem of what to do with this Rube Goldberg mechanism." [5]

Events soon nullified both the philosophical and political assumptions underlying the Founders' vision of the electoral college and forced them to cope with the "Rube Goldberg mechanism." The formation and organization of political parties in the 1790s proceeded so quickly that by the election of 1800, the electors no longer served as independent persons exercising their own judgments on candidates' capabilities; instead, they acted as agents of political parties and the general public. In 1800, the Republican party was so disciplined that all Republican electors cast their two votes for Thomas Jefferson and Aaron Burr. Although it was generally understood that Jefferson was the Republican candidate for president and Burr the candidate for vice president, the Constitution provided no means for the electors to make that distinction on their ballots. The result was a tie in electoral votes; neither won a majority, and the matter was handed to the House of Representatives for a final decision. Ironically, the Federalists, despite their major defeat in the congressional elections of 1800, still controlled the lame-duck Congress (which did not expire until March 1801) and therefore were in a position to help decide which Republican would serve as president and which as vice president. At the urging of Alexander Hamilton, who disagreed with Jefferson on policy matters but distrusted Burr personally, some of the

Federalist representatives eventually cast blank ballots, which permitted the Republican legislators to choose Jefferson as president on the thirty-sixth ballot.

One result of this bizarre chain of events was the ratification in 1804 of the Twelfth Amendment, stipulating that electors cast separate ballots for president and vice president. The amendment also provides that if no presidential candidate receives a majority of the electoral votes, the House of Representatives, balloting by states, will select the president by majority vote from among the three (instead of five) candidates who receive the highest number of electoral votes. If no vice-presidential candidate receives a majority of electoral votes, similar procedures are to be used by the Senate in choosing between the two persons with the highest number of electoral ballots.

Other changes in the selection of the president followed; however, they did not come by way of constitutional amendments but as political developments that fit within the legal framework of the electoral college. Thus, state legislators, who held the power to determine how electors should be chosen, began to cede this right to the general electorate. By 1832 all states except South Carolina had done so.

Another matter left to the discretion of the states—how their electoral votes would be counted—soon underwent change. States initially were inclined to divide the vote by congressional districts; the candidate who won the plurality of the popular votes (that is, more votes than anyone else) in each district received its electoral vote, and the remaining two electoral votes (representing the two Senate seats) were awarded to the statewide popular winner.

Legislatures soon, however, began to adopt the "unit" or "general-ticket" rule, whereby all the state's electoral votes went to the candidate who received the plurality of the statewide popular vote. Two political considerations prompted this decision. The state's majority party benefited because it did not have to award any electoral votes to a minority party that might be successful in individual congressional districts. Also, this system maximized the influence of the state in the presidential election by permitting it to throw all its electoral votes to one candidate. Once some states adopted this procedure, others, wanting to maintain their influence on the presidential contest, felt they had to follow. As a result, by 1836 the district plan had vanished, and the unit system had taken its place. Since then, a few states have returned to the district plan; Maine has done so for several decades and Nebraska recently adopted the plan for 1992.

Another political development of the era changed the nature of the presidential election contest: the elimination of property qualifications for voting. By the early 1840s white manhood suffrage was virtually complete in the United States. The increasing democratization of U.S. political life was reflected in the procedure for choosing the most important public official. Yet the formal provisions of the electoral college remain the same today as they were in 1804, when the Twelfth Amendment was adopted.

Today these formal provisions provide a strange system for choosing the chief executive. Although most Americans view the presidential election as a popular one, it really is not. When voters mark their ballots for a presidential candidate, the vote actually determines which pledged slate of electors will have the opportunity to cast electoral votes. In mid-December the state electors associated with the winning candidate (party faithfuls who are chosen in primaries, at conventions, or by state committees) meet in their state capitals to cast ballots. (About one-third of the states attempt by law to bind the electors to vote for the popular-vote winner, but there is some question whether such laws are constitutional.) The results of the electoral balloting are transmitted to Washington, D.C.; they are counted early in January of the following year, and the incumbent vice president, as presiding officer of the Senate, announces the outcome before a joint session of the Congress. If, as usually happens, one candidate receives an absolute majority of the electoral votes, the vice president officially declares that candidate to be president. (Because the popular-vote winner usually wins in the electoral college as well, we consider this a "validation" of the popular vote outcome.)

The formal procedure has occasionally created some ironic moments. In January 1961, Richard Nixon declared his opponent, John Kennedy, to be president; eight years later another vice president, Hubert Humphrey, declared his opponent, this time Richard Nixon, to be the chief executive. George Bush had the distinction in 1988 of being the first vice president since Martin Van Buren to declare his own victory.

The electoral college system as it operates today is considered by many students of presidential elections to be not only strange but also grossly unfair; some even consider it dangerous. Chapter 5 assesses the arguments for and against the electoral college; this section examines only the effects the present arrangements have on campaign strategies.

Under the electoral college system, election results are decided state by state. In effect, there are fifty separate presidential contests with a "winner-take-all" principle that puts a premium on a popular vote victory in each state, no matter how small the margin of that victory may be.

A built-in bias in the electoral college works to the advantage of certain states over others. The present system benefits the very small and the very large states. The small states have the advantage of what political scientist Lawrence Longley calls the "constant two" votes, that is, the two electoral votes, representing the two senators, that all states receive, regardless of size.[6] This arrangement—the constant two, plus the additional vote for their House member—means that the smallest states control three electoral votes, even though their population alone might entitle them to just one or two votes. The very large states have an even greater advantage; they benefit from the unit or general-ticket system because all their electoral votes are awarded to their popular-vote winner. Thus in 1988 George Bush, the popular-vote winner in California, received all 47 electoral votes, almost 18 percent of the total 270 electoral votes required for election, although he defeated Michael Dukakis by just 352,684 votes out of the 9.767 million cast, a mere 3.6 percent margin of victory.[7]

Electoral votes were reallocated for the 1992 presidential election reflecting the results of the 1990 census; those figures were finalized in mid-July 1991.[8] Eight states gained seats in the House of Representatives and thirteen lost seats; the states' electoral vote totals were adjusted accordingly. The biggest gains were recorded in California (whose delegation will increase by seven seats), Florida (four seats), and Texas (three seats). On the losing end, New York will lose three seats, while Illinois, Michigan, Ohio, and Pennsylvania each will lose two seats. Eight other states will lose one seat. With the changes, California will become an even greater prize as a candidate can gain fully 20 percent of the electoral votes needed for victory by winning a plurality of popular votes in that state. (See Figure 3-1 for an illustration of the size of the states based on their number of electoral votes for the 1992 election, reflecting changes occasioned by the 1990 census.)

Longley shows that residency in the very small and the very large states of the Far West and, to a lesser extent, the East is an advantage for some ethnic groups. Voters concentrated in urban areas, both central cities and the suburbs, also benefit. In general, however, blacks do not benefit by the rules of the system because the rules put the South, where many blacks live, at a disadvantage. (The South contains a disproportionate number of medium-sized states—those with from four to fourteen electoral votes. Medium-sized states offer candidates neither a great many electoral votes, as the big states do, nor a disproportionately large number of electoral votes, as the small states do.)

Finally, the electoral college benefits certain kinds of candidates. These include not only those of the two major parties, who are in a position to win enough popular votes in a state to be awarded its electoral votes, but also third-party candidates who have a regional appeal sufficient to win some states. At a disadvantage, however, are third-party

Figure 3-1 State Size by Number of Electoral Votes, 1992

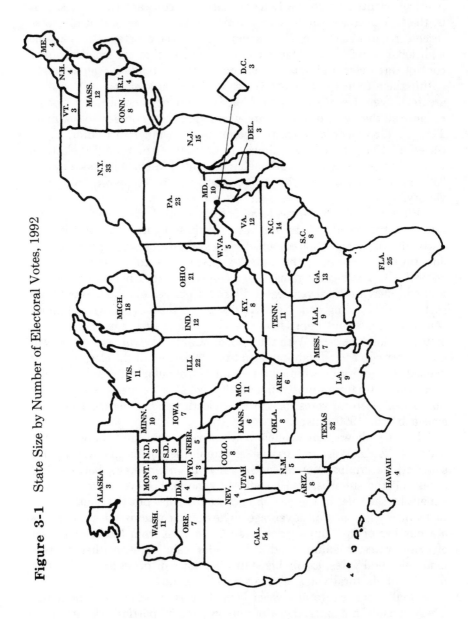

candidates without regional appeal. In 1948, Dixiecrat presidential candidate Strom Thurmond carried four states with a total of thirty-nine electoral votes, even though he won only about 2.4 percent of the national popular vote; that same year the Progressive party candidate, Henry Wallace, with the same percentage of the nationwide vote, did not carry any states and thus received no electoral votes at all.[9] More recently, John Anderson polled 5,720,060 votes in 1980 (five times the total of Thurmond and Wallace in 1948 and 6.6 percent of the total votes cast), but he received no electoral votes because his support was distributed nationally rather than concentrated regionally.

Because candidates wish to maximize the return on limited resources available during the campaign—particularly time and money—they focus heavily on those states likely to contribute the largest number of electoral votes toward a victory. Thus, the electoral map is a critical consideration in formulating their campaign strategy.

Rules Affecting Campaign Finance

The legal provisions for financing the general election differ considerably from those governing presidential nominations. For the general election, complete public financing is provided to nominees of the major parties (those that won 25 percent or more of the popular vote in the last presidential election). In the 1988 presidential election, the federal government allocated $46.1 million to each candidate and $8.3 million to each national committee. To be eligible for that money, nominees must agree not to accept other contributions to their campaign. Candidates of minor parties (those that won between 5 and 25 percent of the vote in the previous election) receive partial public financing. Candidates of parties ineligible for public financing (those that won less than 5 percent of the vote in the previous election) can be partially reimbursed after the current election if they receive at least 5 percent of the vote.

Two provisions of the campaign finance law permit the major party candidates to benefit from campaign expenditures besides those made from public funds. As is true of the nomination process, there is no limitation on independent campaign expenditures, that is, those made by individuals or political committees that advocate the defeat or election of a presidential candidate but that are not made in conjunction with the candidate's own campaign. (Again, however, such individuals and committees must file reports with the Federal Election Commission stating, under penalty of perjury, that the expenditure was not made in collusion with the candidate.) In addition, an amendment to the cam-

Table 3-1   Cost of Presidential General Elections, 1940-1972
(in millions of dollars)

Year	Republican		Democratic	
	Expenditure	Candidate	Expenditure	Candidate
1940	3.45	Willkie	2.78	F. Roosevelt*
1944	2.83	Dewey	2.17	F. Roosevelt*
1948	2.13	Dewey	2.74	Truman*
1952	6.61	Eisenhower*	5.03	Stevenson
1956	7.78	Eisenhower*	5.11	Stevenson
1960	10.13	Nixon	9.80	Kennedy*
1964	16.03	Goldwater	8.76	Johnson*
1968	25.40	Nixon*	11.59	Humphrey
1972	61.40	Nixon*	30.00	McGovern

Source: Excerpted from Herbert E. Alexander, *Financing Politics: Money, Elections and Political Reform* (Washington, D.C.: CQ Press, 1976), Table 2-1, 20.

Note: Asterisk (*) indicates winner.

paign finance law enacted in 1979 permits state and local party organizations to spend money for any purpose except campaign advertising and the hiring of outside personnel; this means that they can engage in grass-roots activities such as distributing campaign buttons, stickers, and yard signs, registering voters, and transporting them to the polls to vote.

Like the provisions for financing presidential nomination campaigns, those governing the general election have brought significant changes in the funding of fall presidential campaigns. The two major party candidates no longer need to depend on wealthy contributors and other private sources to finance their campaigns. (They may still benefit, however, from the independent expenditures of such sources and from the grass-roots activities of state and local parties.) The law also has the effect of limiting and equalizing the expenditures made by the two major party candidates, which is a distinct advantage for the Democrats because, historically, Republican presidential candidates have spent more than their opponents.[10] (Table 3-1 shows that, except for 1948, the Republican presidential candidate outspent his Democratic opponent in every election from 1940 through 1972, the last contest before the enactment of the campaign finance law providing public funding.) Finally, the law benefits the candidates of the two major parties over minor-party candidates, who are entitled to only partial public financing, if any at all.

The General-Election Campaign

Traditionally, U.S. presidential campaigns have begun on Labor Day, but individual candidates are free to choose other times, depending on the political circumstances. Gerald R. Ford, seeking to reorganize his forces after a bruising battle with challenger Ronald Reagan at the 1976 Republican national convention, waited until a week after Labor Day to launch his fall campaign. In contrast, Ronald Reagan, with the Republican nomination locked up in both 1980 and 1984, hit the campaign trail early to counteract the favorable publicity generated by the Democratic national conventions of those two years. George Bush also got started early, but for a different reason: having clinched the 1988 nomination after his decisive victory on Super Tuesday (March 8), public attention focused almost exclusively on the Democrats' battle between Dukakis and Jackson. Dukakis emerged as the probable nominee and led the vice president in trial competitions, producing concern among Bush's advisers that the gap would grow too great to overcome if they delayed launching the campaign until September. Bush previewed his fall strategy when he began to emphasize his eventual opponent's liberalism in June, a full month before the nomination was decided.[11] Thus the conditions under which candidates win their party's nomination, plus the circumstances surrounding their opponent's choice, shape decisions on the beginning of the fall campaign.

Targeting the Campaign

As in the nomination process, presidential candidates must decide in which states they will focus their efforts in the fall campaign.[12] The decision is harder at this stage because the general election takes place simultaneously in all fifty states rather than in stages, and campaign efforts must be concentrated into a much shorter period of time than is available for the nomination campaign. Moreover, in the general election, unlike the nomination process, there are no legal limits on the amount of money presidential candidates can spend in individual states; they therefore have a freer hand in their choices, but those choices are more difficult.

By far the most important consideration in targeting the fall campaign is the electoral college. The candidate's task is clear: to win the presidency, he or she must win a majority (270) of the 538 electoral votes. This fact places a premium on carrying those states with the largest number of electoral votes. In 1992, by winning the eleven largest states—California, New York, Texas, Florida, Pennsylvania, Illinois, Ohio, Michigan, New Jersey, North Carolina, and either Georgia or Virginia—a candidate could win the presidency while losing the other thirty-nine states. Naturally, candidates from both major political parties concentrate their personal visits on the largest states.

Another element that affects candidates' decisions on where to campaign is the political situation in a particular state; that is, whether the state generally goes to one party's candidate or whether it swings back and forth from one election to the next. Distinctly one-party states are likely to be slighted by both of the major party candidates. The party in control does not think it is necessary to waste time there. In 1968, for example, Nixon did not visit or spend money in Kansas; as one campaign aide, Robert Ellsworth, said of his home state, "If you have to worry about Kansas, you don't have a campaign anyway." [13] In contrast, the opposition party is likely to think it futile to exert much effort in what is obviously enemy territory.[14] The "swing" states naturally draw the greatest attention from presidential candidates of both parties.

Since 1968, there has been a major geographic revolution in American politics. Historically, the South has been vital to the electoral fortunes of Democratic candidates, recently playing an essential role in the electoral victories of Kennedy in 1960 and Carter in 1976. In fact, no Democrat has ever won the White House without carrying a majority of Southern states. But since 1968, with the lone exception of 1976, when Jimmy Carter attracted support as a favorite son from Georgia, the Solid South—long a mainstay of Democratic campaigns—has moved into the Republican camp. Humphrey in 1968 and McGovern in 1972 wrote off the region; in 1980, even with Carter on the ticket, only Georgia went for the Democratic candidate.[15] No southern state supported the Democratic ticket in 1984 or 1988; Mondale eventually wrote off the region in 1984 but Dukakis had chosen Lloyd Bentsen, senator from Texas, as his running mate in 1988 partly in the effort to attract southern votes. Several factors contributed to the South's political reorientation: the Democrats' endorsement of aggressive action on civil rights violated a long-standing regional commitment to local control of race relations; the debate among Democrats over Vietnam policy was perceived by many southern voters as unpatriotic; the emergence on the national agenda of law and order and social issues such as abortion and school prayer renewed the salience of the region's deep-seated traditional values; and the influx of new residents attracted by the region's rapid economic growth created a new group of voters who were less closely tied to the traditional Democratic party identification. Thus, the Republicans have added the South to their already substantial support in the West; the

Democrats, if one can say they retain an area of regional strength, have been strongest in the Northeast.

The regions that have been crucial in recent presidential contests are the Middle Atlantic states of New York, Pennsylvania, and New Jersey and the Middle West states of Ohio, Michigan, Illinois, and Missouri. Together, this tier of seven highly industrial states controlled 155 electoral votes in the 1984 and 1988 elections. These states also tend to be highly competitive, which means that campaign efforts there can be very important in deciding which candidate prevails. On the other hand, these states will collectively lose twelve electoral votes for the 1992 election due to reapportionment, and their significance may decline accordingly.

What remains the most systematic plan for targeting a presidential campaign was developed for Jimmy Carter in 1976 by Hamilton Jordan. Jordan assigned points to each state, using three criteria. The first was its number of electoral votes. The second was its Democratic potential based on the number of Democratic officeholders in the state and how well McGovern had done there in 1972. The third was how concerted a campaign was needed in a particular state, taking into account how well Carter had done in the preconvention period, how much time or resources he had previously expended in the state, and how close to Ford he was in the polls. Each campaigner was allocated points as well: for example, a day's campaigning by Carter was worth seven points; by Mondale, five points; and by a Carter child, one point. Jordan then assigned campaigners to states so that scheduling points were matched with those developed under the political-importance formula.[16]

Electoral college considerations remain crucial throughout the entire campaign. Bush's strategy in 1988 sought to solidify expected support in the Southern and Rocky Mountain states and then to confront Dukakis in potential swing states that would be essential for his victory, particularly Ohio and New Jersey. Dukakis, like most candidates, had to adjust his strategy as the competitive situation changed, reallocating effort and resources to that combination of states that offered the best hope of victory. Thus, after the second presidential debate in 1988 when Dukakis still trailed Bush in opinion polls, the Democratic candidate focused his efforts more narrowly on eighteen states that would provide him with 272 electoral votes, barely enough to win, where polls showed that he still had a chance at victory.[17] With such a narrow margin for error, it is not surprising that Dukakis lost the election, but as part of this last-gasp strategy, he managed to win 49 percent of the vote in Illinois, and 48 percent in California, Maryland, and Pennsylvania, all critical to the strategy.

Manipulating Political Appeals

Party Label. Political party labels, unimportant in the nomination process, become a focal point in general election campaigns. Given the Democrats' status as the majority party since the days of Franklin Roosevelt, it is natural that Democratic candidates throughout the years have emphasized their party affiliation and linked their opponents with the minority Republican party. In 1960 John Kennedy stressed that he "stood" with Woodrow Wilson, Franklin Roosevelt, and Harry S. Truman, whereas his opponent, Richard Nixon, "stood" with William McKinley, William Howard Taft, Warren Harding, Alfred Landon, and Thomas Dewey. (Kennedy did not mention popular Republican presidents such as Abraham Lincoln, Theodore Roosevelt, or Dwight D. Eisenhower.) Twenty years later Jimmy Carter pursued a similar strategy, emphasizing that he represented the party of Franklin Roosevelt, Harry Truman, John Kennedy, and Lyndon B. Johnson (leading Ronald Reagan to quip that the only Democratic president Carter was not talking about was himself). In 1984 Walter Mondale sought to link his candidacy with Truman, who, like Mondale, was counted out of the race by pollsters. In one appearance, Mondale held up the famous erroneous headline of the Chicago *Tribune,* "Dewey Defeats Truman." Dukakis also drew on the Truman victory as a way to encourage effort in the closing days of his campaign when it was widely reported that he trailed in the opinion polls.

Over the years, Republican presidential candidates have devised tactics to counteract the partisan advantage enjoyed by their Democratic opponents, with whom a far larger portion of the populace has been willing to identify. (See Chapter 4.) One is to advise the voters to ignore party labels and vote for the "best man." Nixon used this approach in his 1960 campaign, urging Americans to cast their ballots for the person who had experience in foreign affairs, who had stood up to Soviet leader Nikita Khrushchev and bested him in a "kitchen debate" in Moscow. (The informal exchange over the comparative worth of communist and capitalist economic systems took place at a kitchen display at a fair in Moscow.) Another tactic is to suggest that the Democratic presidential candidate does not represent the views of the rank-and-file members of the party. In 1972 Nixon charged that the Democratic convention had rejected the historic principles of that party and implored, "To those millions who have been driven out of their home in the Democratic party, we say come home." Another ploy open to Republican presidential candidates is to associate themselves with past Democratic presidents. In 1976 Gerald Ford tied his candidacy to that of former Democratic chief executive Harry Truman, who, as an underdog incumbent, struggled successfully for the same goal as Ford: election to the office in his own right, not merely by succession. Four years later Reagan linked his desire for major changes in U.S. society with the New Deal, Fair Deal, and New Frontier administrations of Roosevelt, Truman, and Kennedy. In 1984 he participated in anniversary ceremonies for Roosevelt and Truman and held receptions at the White House in honor of Hubert Humphrey and former senator Henry Jackson.[18]

Whether a candidate represents the majority or the minority party, it is important that prominent political figures in the party support his campaign. In 1964 Barry Goldwater's candidacy suffered (although it is unlikely that he could have won the presidency in any event) because leading Republicans dissociated themselves from the party's presidential nominee and conducted independent campaigns of their own. Sen. Eugene McCarthy's lukewarm and belated endorsement of Hubert Humphrey in the last stages of the 1968 campaign did little to help Humphrey avert his narrow defeat that year. And in 1972 large numbers of Democratic candidates for congressional and state offices deliberately dissociated themselves from the McGovern-Shriver ticket.

Incumbency. Incumbent presidents usually find that their office provides more advantages than disadvantages in running for reelection. They are typically better known to the voters than their opponents, who must strive to narrow the recognition gap between the two candidates. The incumbent president frequently assumes the role of statesman, too busy with the affairs of the nation to participate in a demeaning, partisan campaign. Describing the 1972 contest between George McGovern and President Nixon, one journalist remarked, "Around the White House, it bordered on treason to call Nixon a candidate." [19] In 1976 Gerald Ford followed his advisers' recommendation by conducting the early stages of the campaign from the White House Rose Garden—gathering presidential publicity by receiving visitors, signing or vetoing bills, and calling press conferences to make announcements.

While the incumbent is operating above the partisan fray, others are free to make political attacks on the opposition. Frequently, the vice-presidential candidates assume that role, as Humphrey did for the Democrats in 1964 and Robert Dole did for the Republicans in 1976.[20] Or the president's supporters may develop an entire team to carry on the effort. In 1972 the Committee to Reelect the President (note that Nixon's name did not even appear in the title of the committee) organized a special "surrogate's" office to schedule the campaign appearances of thirty-five White House aides, cabinet members, senators, representatives, mayors, and Republican party officials.

The incumbent president is also in a position to use the prerogatives of the office to good advantage during the election campaign. In 1976 President Ford suddenly recommended legislation to expand the national park system and to reduce the amount of the down payments required for mortgages guaranteed by the Federal Housing Administration. The president also can disburse forms of political "patronage" available to the nation's chief executive. In 1980 President Carter announced his support for water projects in Kentucky and Tennessee that he had previously opposed, offered the steel industry protection against foreign imports, approved financial aid to enable residents of Love Canal (the polluted area near Niagara Falls, New York) to move away from that region, and announced federally subsidized loans for drought-stricken farms. Even Chicago—whose mayor, Jane Byrne, supported Edward Kennedy in the primary fight—received its share of national government "goodies," which prompted Byrne to declare that while diamonds are still a girl's best friend, federal grants are next best. In 1984 President Reagan provided assistance to U.S. farmers by allowing the Soviet Union to purchase an extra 10 million metric tons of grain and by changing credit arrangements to grant greater relief to farmers who were heavily in debt. To help his vice president in 1988, President Reagan delayed the announcement of several important changes in domestic programs until after the election.

Incumbent presidents can also use their office to publicize important events in foreign and military policy. During 1972 President Nixon visited both Communist China and the Soviet Union, gathering extensive media coverage in the process. In the spring of 1984, President Reagan went to China; in June of that year he journeyed to the Normandy beaches to lead the fortieth anniversary commemoration of the Allied invasion of France in World War II, an occasion attended by veterans and their families.

Of the last three incumbents who ran for reelection, only Ronald Reagan was successful. The electoral defeats of Presidents Ford and Carter may suggest some disadvantages associated with incumbency particularly if service in the presidency coincides with negative economic developments (such as recession and high inflation) or an unresolved foreign crisis for which the president may be blamed. Thus, if a sitting president's record is considered weak or national conditions seem to have deteriorated under his stewardship, he may be held accountable by voters who cast their ballots retrospectively rather than prospectively, that is, based on a judgment of past performance rather than an estimate of future performance. This has been suggested as the major reason for Carter's defeat in 1980. To illustrate the problem, one can contrast what many perceived to be Carter's failure to resolve the Iranian hostage crisis with the newfound respect many believed the nation enjoyed after Reagan's first term.

Even in these instances, one can argue that incumbency is more beneficial than detrimental. It must be remembered that both the 1976 and 1980 elections were extremely close. In the former, an incumbent who had never run for national office came very close to victory in the final weeks of the campaign; in the latter, polls indicated that Carter and Reagan were virtually neck-and-neck going into the final weekend of the campaign.

Until 1988, incumbency seemed to benefit presidents but not vice presidents. Nixon in 1960 and Humphrey in 1968 failed in their attempts to succeed an outgoing president. George Bush found himself in a far more advantageous position, however. During his final year in office, Ronald Reagan's public approval ratings bounced back from the beating they had taken in 1986-87 following public disclosure of the secret Iran-contra transactions; from a low of 40 percent approval and 53 percent disapproval in February 1987, Reagan's rating rose to 54 percent approval and 37 percent disapproval in September 1988.[21] In contrast, Humphrey was trying to succeed a disheartened and discredited Lyndon Johnson whose approval rating in September 1968 stood at 42 percent (with 51 percent disapproval). Eisenhower's ratings were strong in 1960, although they slipped during the year from 68-21 percent positive in March to 58-31 percent in mid-October.[22] Unlike Eisenhower, who seemed to harbor doubts about Nixon, Reagan unequivocally endorsed Bush as his successor, thereby transferring the mantel of his legacy. Reagan was also an active campaigner, visiting sixteen states to demonstrate his support.[23] Moreover, the Reagan administration, whether rightly or wrongly, was given credit for the peace and prosperity that prevailed in 1988, conditions that reflected well on Bush. Finally, Bush drew upon a number of Reagan's most experienced campaign aides for his own effort in 1988, including campaign chairman James A. Baker and campaign director Lee Atwater. Atwater, later named chairman of the Republican National Committee, had twenty-eight people working for him in 1988 who had experience in two or more successful presidential campaigns.[24] Thus, by drawing closer to his popular predecessor than could Nixon or Humphrey, George Bush turned vice-presidential incumbency into a campaign asset.

Candidate Image. Because the public focuses so much attention in a presidential campaign on the candidates themselves, the personality and character that the aspirants project are particularly important. Each

89

campaign organization strives to create a composite image of the most attractive attributes of its candidate. Although the image necessarily deviates from reality, it must still reflect enough of the essential characteristics of the candidate to be believable. One effective tactic is to take a potential flaw and convert it into an asset. Thus, the somewhat elderly Dwight Eisenhower (he was sixty-six at the time of his second campaign in 1956) was pictured as a benevolent father (or even grandfather) whose mature judgment was needed to lead the nation in times of stress.[25] In contrast, the youthful John Kennedy, who was forty-three when he ran for the presidency in 1960, was characterized as a man of "vigor" who would make the United States "feel young again" after the Eisenhower years.

Presidential candidates frequently take their opponents' images into account when shaping their own. In 1976 Gerald Ford portrayed himself as a man of maturity and experience to counteract Jimmy Carter's emphasis on being a "new face" and an outsider to the Washington scene. Four years later, as the incumbent president, Carter tried to come across as a deliberate and moderate person who could be trusted to maintain his calm in a crisis, in contrast to his supposedly impetuous and irresponsible opponent, Ronald Reagan. Reagan, in turn, presented himself as a decisive leader who could overcome the nation's problems, as opposed to Carter, depicted as an uncertain, vacillating person overwhelmed by the burdens of the presidency and inclined to blame the country's difficulties on the "spirit of malaise" of the American people themselves. George Bush redirected attention in 1988 to the candidates' character and values in response to the cold and colorless emphasis on "competence" that Michael Dukakis had offered. In doing so, Bush was able to paint his own portrait of Dukakis, whose largely favorable public image, Bush's pollsters had discovered, was based on very little information.[26]

Besides molding their own images to balance those of their opponents, candidates also can directly attack the images of the opposition and so put them in a bad light. In 1976, for example, Gerald Ford described Jimmy Carter as follows: "He wavers, he wanders, he wiggles, he waffles." He also charged that his opponent had a strange way of changing his accent: "In California he tried to sound like Cesar Chavez; in Chicago, like Mayor Daley; in New York, like Ralph Nader; in Washington, like George Meany; then he comes to the farm belt and he becomes a little old peanut farmer." During the second debate, after Ford stated that Eastern Europe was not under Soviet domination, Carter countered that the president must have been "brainwashed" when he went to Poland. (Carter was thereby comparing Ford with George Romney, the former Michigan governor whose nomination campaign collapsed in 1968 after he said he had been brainwashed by the military in the course of a trip to Vietnam.) The Georgian also said that during the second debate Ford had shown "very vividly the absence of good judgment, good sense, and knowledge," all qualities expected of a president. In 1980 Carter suggested that a Reagan presidency would divide Americans "black from white, Jew from Christian, North from South, rural from urban" and could "well lead our nation to war." Reagan, in turn, impugned Carter's honesty, saying that the president's promise never to lie to Americans reminded him of a quotation from Ralph Waldo Emerson, "The more he talked of his honor, the more we counted our spoons." In 1984, Walter Mondale was accused of being overly gloomy about the country and its prospects—"Whine on harvest moon," as Vice President George Bush liked to put it. Mondale and Geraldine Ferraro, in turn, attacked President Reagan for being the most "disengaged" president in recent history, one who lacked the knowledge necessary to govern the nation.

At the urging of his campaign advisers, George Bush unleashed one of the most negative strategies in modern presidential campaign history. In an effort to alter favorable public perceptions of his opponent, the Bush campaign portrayed Dukakis as a "card-carrying member of the ACLU" (American Civil Liberties Union), sympathetic to criminals (symbolized by the now infamous Willie Horton, a prison inmate who committed a rape in Maryland after fleeing from a Massachusetts prison furlough program), and of questionable patriotism, as indicated by the governor's veto of a bill that would have required students in Massachusetts schools to pledge allegiance to the flag in a daily exercise. Worse still, Dukakis was a "liberal," portrayed as someone who favored high taxes and big government except in national defense, where he would show his antimilitary colors. This strategy had been carefully planned using "focus group" research techniques where small groups of Democrats who had supported Ronald Reagan in 1980 and 1984 but were leaning toward Dukakis in 1988 were asked to respond to new information about the Democratic front-runner's positions and record on a number of social issues. Those issues that elicited the desired effect— abandoning Dukakis in favor of Bush—became cornerstones of the Bush campaign's advertising and media efforts. Dukakis, not hesitating occasionally to abandon the high road, sought to link Bush to the Iran-contra incident, to the illicit international drug activities of Panamanian leader Manuel Noriega, and to ethics violations committed throughout the Reagan years, but the effort was far less successful.[27]

Social Groups. Fairly early in life many Americans begin to think of themselves as members of ethnic, geographic, or religious groups. As they get older, they also begin to identify with groups associated with their occupations and to consider themselves as businesspeople or farmers or members of labor unions. Sometimes people relate politically to groups to which they do not belong. A well-to-do white liberal, for example, who sympathizes with the underdog in society, may favor programs that benefit poor blacks. Responses to groups can also be negative: a self-made businessperson may have an unfavorable image of labor unions or social welfare organizations. Far from declining in significance, group identifications may be gaining importance as a guide to voter behavior. At the same time, partisanship appears to be losing significance.[28]

Presidential candidates take these group attitudes into account in devising campaign appeals. Since the days of Franklin Roosevelt, the Democratic party has aimed its campaigns at certain groups thought to be particularly susceptible to its political overtures: among these are southerners, members of racial and ethnic groups, organized labor, Catholics, Jews, intellectuals, and big-city "bosses" and their political supporters (hence the quip that the Democratic party has more wings than a boardinghouse chicken). At the same time, the Democrats usually have tried to depict the Republicans as the party of "big business" and the rich.

Until recently, Republican candidates made little use of explicit group appeals in their presidential campaigns. In fact, in 1964 Senator Goldwater conducted an antigroup campaign. The Republican candidate seemed to go out of his way to antagonize particular blocs, speaking in Knoxville against the Tennessee Valley Authority; in retirement communities against Social Security; and in Charleston, West Virginia, near the heart of Appalachia, against the Johnson administration's War on Poverty. (In writing off such groups as "minorities," Goldwater ignored the fact that an aggregation of minorities can make a majority.) In 1968 Richard Nixon tried a different approach, aiming his campaign at the "forgotten Americans who did not break the law, but did pay taxes, go to work, school, church, and love their country." He thereby sought to establish a negative association between the Democrats and groups he considered to be outside the American mainstream, such as welfare recipients, atheists, and war protesters.

Since the Democrats' New Deal coalition began to come apart in the 1970s, Republican presidential candidates have been more inclined to seek the support of specific groups through targeted appeals. In 1972 the Committee to Reelect the President produced campaign buttons for almost thirty nationalities, provided copy for ethnic newspapers and radio stations, and made special appeals to Catholics, Jews, blacks, and

Mexican-Americans. In his 1980 presidential campaign Reagan appealed to union members by pointing out that he had been president of a labor union for six terms; courted the Polish vote by meeting on Labor Day with Stanislaw Walesa, father of the leader of the strike against the Polish government; and wooed blacks by arguing that their high unemployment rate was caused by the sluggish state of the economy. Four years later the Reagan campaign set aside an "ethnic week" to court groups such as Polish-Americans and Italian-Americans (recall that the Democratic vice-presidential candidate, Geraldine Ferraro, was the first person of Italian background to run on a presidential ticket). Reagan also tried to appeal to Jews by criticizing Mondale for not repudiating Jesse Jackson's anti-Semitic remarks. Bush's carefully targeted strategy in 1988 was designed to appeal to former Democratic voters who had supported Reagan in the two preceding elections, particularly southern whites and Catholics. By naming the first Hispanic to a cabinet level post, the Reagan administration also sought to strengthen its appeal to a group whose votes are especially important in California, Texas, and Florida. And during the campaign, President Reagan made campaign appearances in Chicago, before a gathering of community leaders of Polish descent, and in Newark, at an Italian-American Columbus Day celebration. Such attention is typical of the new Republican appeal for group support.[29]

Two other groups took on a special significance in all three presidential elections of the 1980s. Women were thought to be anti-Reagan because of his promilitary stance and his opposition to social programs and the Equal Rights Amendment. Democrats played on such fears by portraying Reagan as "trigger-happy" and as insensitive to the needs of economic and social underdogs; the Republicans tried to assure women that he was a man of peace who looked to the private sector and to state and local governments to provide assistance to the disadvantaged. Work and family issues, such as child care and parental leave, received prominent attention in 1988 as a way to address the concerns of women, who now constitute a majority of registered voters. The Republicans in 1984 and 1988 also appealed to fundamentalist Christians, particularly in the South, by advocating prayer in the public schools and by opposing abortion; Democrats tried to counter such appeals by arguing that prayers should be said in church and the home (not in school), and that the government had no right to interfere with a woman's private decision whether or not to carry a pregnancy to term.

Another group of voters targeted by both political parties in 1984 was young voters. Traditionally Democratic in their sympathies, college-age youth were wooed by Republican promises of job opportunities in an expanding economy and appeals to love of country. The Democrats responded by urging young people to consider those less fortunate than themselves and to express their concern about the dangers of nuclear war. Both parties' candidates made many campaign appearances on college campuses (Mondale gave one of his best speeches at George Washington University), typically with supporters and hecklers alike in attendance.

Issues and Events. Over the years, both major political parties have been associated with certain broad issues in American life. Democratic presidential candidates usually emphasize economic issues: by doing so they can link the Great Depression to the Republican president, Herbert Hoover, who was in office at the time, and can draw on the voters' traditional preference for Democrats over Republicans to handle the economy. In contrast, Republican candidates historically have focused more on foreign policy issues because Democratic presidents were in power at the start of World War I, World War II, and both the Korean and Vietnamese conflicts, leading many voters to conclude that Republicans were better able to keep the peace than Democrats. More recently, the willingness of presidents Reagan and Bush to use military force in Lebanon, Grenada, Libya, Panama, and the Persian Gulf may alter these traditional party images.

Circumstances surrounding particular elections can lead to changes in the traditional politics. In 1980 the poor economic record of the Carter administration led Ronald Reagan to focus on that issue; four years later, as the incumbent president, Reagan continued to emphasize the economy because inflation and interest rates had fallen since he took office. In 1980 President Carter concentrated on foreign policy so that he could raise fears about Reagan's reliability in keeping the nation out of nuclear war. In 1984 Mondale pointed out that President Reagan was the first U.S. chief executive in the atomic era who had not met with a foreign chief of state to advance negotiations on an arms treaty. Bush sought to remind voters in 1988 of the Carter era by linking Dukakis to the brand of Democratic liberalism blamed for high taxes and poor fiscal management. Bush could point to Reagan's summit meetings with Gorbachev as evidence of improved superpower relations. Dukakis sought to shift foreign policy criticism to the Iran-contra incident; on the domestic front he stressed the burgeoning national debt as well as the Republicans' failure to make progress on the environment and education.

Although candidates address major issues in U.S. society, they frequently do so only in very general terms. The party out of power often uses a catchy slogan to link the party in power with unfortunate political events. In 1952, for example, the Republicans branded the Democrats with "Korea, corruption, and communism." The party in power responds in the same way, as when the Democrats defended their record in 1952 by telling the voters, "You never had it so good." In 1976 the situation was reversed; Democrats talked about Watergate, inflation, unemployment, and President Ford's pardon of Richard Nixon. (Carter refused to attack Ford on the issue, but his vice-presidential candidate, Walter Mondale, did.) President Ford asserted that his administration had cut inflation by half, brought peace to the nation ("Not a single American is fighting or dying"), and restored faith, confidence, and trust in the presidency. In 1980, as in 1952, the Republicans attacked the Democratic incumbent: Ronald Reagan blamed President Carter for the nation's mounting economic problems and for allowing the United States to fall far behind the Soviet Union in military preparedness. At the same time the Democratic president pointed with pride to the signing of the Egyptian-Israeli accord, the ratification of the Panama Canal Treaty, and the development of an energy program.

This general sort of attack and defense characterizes most presidential campaigns. The party out of power blames all the ills of American life on the administration; the party in power maintains that all of the nation's blessings have resulted from its leadership. The candidate in the most difficult position is a nonincumbent nominee of the party in power, such as Nixon in 1960 and Humphrey in 1968. Both served as vice president in administrations whose policies they did not fully endorse. Nixon, for instance, did not believe Eisenhower was doing enough in space exploration and national defense. Humphrey opposed the bombing of North Vietnam when it was initiated in 1965. Yet each hesitated to criticize the administration in which he had served. Humphrey's inability to dissociate himself from the Johnson administration's Vietnam policy is considered one of the main reasons for his defeat in 1968.[30]

In sharp contrast, George Bush stressed his commitment to continuing Reagan's policies into the future. This was most memorably expressed in his acceptance speech at the Republican national convention on August 18, 1988. As Bush argued, "In 1940, when I was barely more than a boy, Franklin Roosevelt said we shouldn't change horses in midstream. My friends, these days the world moves even more quickly, and now, after two great terms, a switch will be made. But when you have to change horses in midstream, doesn't it make sense to switch to one who's going the same way?" Bush put a modest amount of distance between himself and Reagan on environmental and education policy, but continuity was more central to his campaign than change.

While addressing political issues in very general terms, presidential candidates typically make few concrete proposals for dealing with such issues.[31] In 1960 Kennedy urged that he be given the chance to "get the nation moving again," but he was very vague about what, specifically, he would do to move the nation forward. Nixon was even more indefinite in 1968; he refused to spell out his plans for dealing with the most important U.S. political issue, Vietnam. His excuse was that doing so might jeopardize the Paris peace talks then being held.

In some presidential campaigns, however, candidates have made specific suggestions for dealing with issues. In 1972 George McGovern proposed that the defense budget be cut by 30 percent; and early in his campaign he advocated that everyone, regardless of need, be given a $1,000 grant by the government. In 1980 Reagan advocated the passage of the Kemp-Roth tax plan, which called for reducing taxes by 10 percent each year over a period of three years. In 1984 Mondale unveiled a plan that called for cuts in defense, health, and agricultural expenditures and tax increases for upper-income earners and corporations so that by 1989 the budget deficit could be reduced by two-thirds. Bush in 1988 reiterated Reagan's position against raising taxes in his now famous statement: "Read my lips—no new taxes!" In 1990 Republican loyalists unleashed a storm of complaints at President Bush when he abandoned this promise and accepted limited tax increases as part of a negotiated budget agreement with the Democratic-controlled Congress, illustrating precisely why most presidential candidates are loathe to make specific commitments.

In manipulating political appeals, candidates usually attempt to develop an all-encompassing theme that will give the voters an overall impression of the campaign. Sometimes the theme focuses on the candidates themselves, as did Humphrey's slogan, "He's a man you can trust"; the Carter-Mondale phrase, "Tested and trustworthy"; and Reagan's 1984 motto, "Leadership that's working." The Dukakis campaign began to pick up support in the closing days of the campaign when it shifted to a new theme, "He's on your side." Alternatively, the appeal can be to a broad group, such as Nixon's "forgotten Americans" who did not break the law but did pay their taxes, go to work, school, and church, and love their country. At other times the theme may be directed at issues and political events ("Korea, corruption, and communism" or "peace and prosperity") or take the form of a general call to action, such as Kennedy's "We've got to get the nation moving again"; McGovern's "Come home, America"; Carter's promise to make the government as "truthful, capable, and filled with love as the American people"; and Reagan's 1980 invitation to a "new beginning." Once the theme is established, candidates try, by constant repetition, to get the electorate to respond emotionally to it. Their success in doing so depends, however, on another important aspect of presidential campaigns: how political appeals are communicated to the American voter.

Communicating with the Public

Because the electorate is more than twice as large as the selectorate and the campaign for the election is much shorter than it is for the nomination, presidential candidates place even more emphasis on the mass media during this latter stage of the process. Advertising expenses are one measure of that emphasis. In the 1984 campaign, for example, Ronald Reagan and Walter Mondale each spent more than half of their $40 million subsidy from the federal government on television, radio, and print advertisements. Of the three types of media, television is by far the most important. Watching takes much less effort than reading, particularly as watching can be combined with other activities but reading cannot.[32] In addition, polls indicate that people are more inclined to believe what they see on television than what they read in the newspapers or hear on the radio. As a result, since 1952, television has been the chief source of campaign information for most Americans.

Over the years presidential candidates have employed several television formats. In 1968 Richard Nixon used sixty-second spot announcements during popular programs such as Rowan and Martin's "Laugh-in." The Republicans also staged appearances of Nixon before panels of citizens who asked questions that he could appear to answer spontaneously. (Nixon's advisers carefully screened both the panels and the questions to avoid possible embarrassment or surprise.)

In the 1972 campaign, the candidates adopted new formats for their televised political communications. Although thirty-second spots remained popular (one of Nixon's, for example, showed a hand sweeping away toy soldiers and miniature ships and planes to symbolize McGovern's proposed cuts in defense), five-minute advertisements became more common. McGovern chose still longer programs to present his addresses on Vietnam and the issue of corruption. Semidocumentary formats, such as a candidate discussing issues with ordinary citizens, were used as well. McGovern was filmed interacting with workers and owners of small businesses, and Nixon's trips to China and the Soviet Union were dramatized for television viewers.

In 1976 President Ford employed the medium more imaginatively than did Carter. The president held an informal television interview, for example, with television personality and former baseball player Joe Garagiola, who tossed him some "gopher-ball" questions: "How many foreign leaders have you met with, Mr. President?" to which Ford mod-

estly replied, "One hundred and twenty-four, Joe." In the last stages of
the campaign, the Ford forces also broadcast short television interviews
with voters in Georgia who described Carter as "wishy-washy." Carter
concentrated on short commercials in which he looked directly into the
camera and talked about various issues, so as to counteract Ford's por-
trayal of him and to present himself as a strong, positive leader with
specific programs.

During the 1980 campaign the television advertisements varied in
length from thirty seconds to thirty minutes, but most were short messages designed to reach peak audiences. The Carter television commercials appeared in three separate stages: the first showed the candidate
being presidential, meeting with foreign dignitaries and working late at
night in the Oval Office; the second consisted of interviews with people
"in the street" saying that Reagan "scared" them; the third showed
Carter being praised by prominent party figures, such as Lady Bird
Johnson and Edward Kennedy, and by rank-and-file Democrats—a
farmer, a steelworker, and a worker in a rubber factory. Most of the
Reagan television advertisements featured the candidate himself, whom
the Republicans considered to be a superb communicator, looking
straight into the camera. They stressed three themes: Reagan's record as
governor of California; his stand on issues, especially the economy; and a
recitation of the record of President Carter, illustrated with graphs of
rising consumer prices.

In 1984 the Republicans aired a nostalgic, half-hour film of President
Reagan riding his horse, walking on a hilltop with Nancy, speaking at the
Normandy beaches, and taking the oath of office. Most of the Republican
commercials, however, were thirty-second ones. The most famous, "It's
morning again in America," showed the sun shining on San Francisco
Bay, people hurrying to and from work, and a bride and groom kissing at
a wedding while a mellifluous voice asked, "Why would we ever want to
go back to where we were less than four short years ago?" The Democrats
relied entirely on thirty-second spots. One showed a roller coaster climb-
ing its tracks (suggesting what will happen tomorrow as a result of record
U.S. deficits), with a voice intoning, "If you're thinking of voting for
Ronald Reagan in 1984, think of what will happen in 1985." Another,
positive commercial pictured a warm, dynamic Walter Mondale talking
to a group of students, urging them to "stretch their minds" and to live
their dreams, telling them he wanted to help them be what they wanted
to be. The most controversial advertisement of 1988 was run by the
National Security Political Action Committee as part of an independent
campaign for the Bush-Quayle ticket. Featuring a police photo of Willie
Horton and widely criticized as racist, the advertisement ran for twenty-

five days on cable television before the Bush campaign disavowed it. Because the advertisement was filmed by a former employee of the Bush campaign's media expert, Democrats charged that there was a link between the committee's effort and the main Republican campaign.

In five elections, televised debates between presidential candidates have been the most important communication source of the campaign.[33] The first occurred in 1960 between Richard Nixon, at that time Eisenhower's vice president, and Sen. John Kennedy. In the first of four debates, Nixon's somewhat uncertain manner and his physical appearance (he had not fully recovered from a recent illness and television accentuated his heavy beard) was contrasted with Kennedy's confident demeanor and bright, alert image (he wore a blue shirt and dark suit that showed up well against the television studio background rather than fading into it as Nixon's light-colored clothes did). Also, unlike Nixon, Kennedy had prepared thoroughly for the debates. As a result, viewers perceived a victory for the young Massachusetts senator.[34] Contributing to that perception was the fact that people had not expected Kennedy to best Nixon, who had gained political prominence in part because of his debating skills in previous campaigns. From that point on, Kennedy's campaign assumed more enthusiasm, and the senator himself credited the debate for his close victory over the vice president.

In 1976, presidential debates again played a major part in the campaign. In this case it was the second of those debates between President Ford and Jimmy Carter that proved crucial. In that debate, Ford stated that he did not consider countries of Eastern Europe (in particular, Yugoslavia, Romania, and Poland) to be under Soviet domination. To make matters worse, the president refused to change his answer even after the startled questioner (a newspaper reporter) gave him the opportunity to do so; in fact, it was not until several days after the debate that the president's staff finally persuaded him to retract his statement. Many political observers considered that gaffe to be the turning point of the contest, the one that ended the dramatic decline in public support for Carter (and the increased support for Ford) that had characterized the previous month of the campaign.

In 1980 the presidential debates became more complicated. The sponsors of the debate, the League of Women Voters, originally extended an invitation not only to President Carter and Ronald Reagan but also to independent candidate John Anderson, whose standing in the public opinion polls exceeded the 15-percent cutoff point established by the League. Carter refused to participate on the grounds that the debate would legitimize the Anderson candidacy, which he asserted was strictly a "creation of the media." In contrast, Reagan, who believed that enhancing Anderson's standing would help his own candidacy, accepted the League's invitation and criticized Carter for refusing to debate.

Just a week before election day, Anderson's public support in the polls having fallen below 15 percent, a single debate was held between the two major candidates. Although both men looked and handled themselves well, and neither made a serious mistake, most observers concluded that Reagan won the debate—on style rather than substance. Carter aides congratulated themselves that the president had kept the focus of the debate on Reagan rather than on his own presidential record, but the tactic apparently backfired. On the one hand, many viewers thought Carter was too aggressive in his accusations; on the other, they felt reassured by Reagan's responses and were convinced that he would not be a trigger-happy president if elected.[35]

In 1984 the Mondale forces requested six separate presidential debates and a format in which the candidates could ask each other questions. The Reagan organization refused that request, and the sides ultimately agreed to two debates between Mondale and Reagan and one between the vice-presidential candidates, Bush and Ferraro. In all three, members of the media would ask the questions. The first presidential debate turned out to be a clear victory for the challenger, Mondale, who projected himself as calm, bright, and confident, while the president appeared confused, inarticulate, and, in his summation, to have lost his train of thought altogether. When the president at one point repeated the line from his 1980 debate with Carter, "There you go again," Mondale turned pointedly to Reagan and asked, "Remember the last time you said that?" and then answered the question himself: "You said it when President Carter said you were going to cut Medicare ... and what did you do right after the election? You went out and tried to cut $20 billion out of Medicare." The debate sent shock waves through the Republican camp not only because the media and most observers (even Reagan supporters) agreed that the president had been defeated decisively, but also because the debate raised the issue of whether his age had slowed him down and made him incapable of handling the demands of the office for the next four years. The second debate, however, ended with a far different result: Reagan prevailed on style, appearing more relaxed and coherent (although he again rambled in his closing remarks). Most important, the president defused the age issue when, in response to a question on the matter, he replied that he did not intend "to exploit my opponent's youth and inexperience," a clever retort that drew a broad smile even from Mondale.

There were two presidential debates and one vice-presidential debate during the 1988 campaign. All were sponsored by a new entity, the

Commission on Presidential Debates, a nonprofit, bipartisan organization created in February 1987 with support from the Democratic and Republican national chairmen. Party sponsorship was presented as a means to ensure that election-year debates would be held, and a plan was developed for four debates to be financed through private contributions. Long before he became the Democrats' nominee, Michael Dukakis committed himself to the plan, but George Bush delayed making a commitment until after the Republican nominating convention, leaving open the possibility that he would refuse to participate. Two of the debates planned for early September were canceled; dates for the remaining sessions had to be worked in around the Olympic Games (NBC eventually agreed to delay broadcast of the games rather than the debate), baseball playoffs, and the World Series.

As in previous instances, questions about debate scheduling and format were decided only after protracted negotiations between the two campaigns that produced a 16-page agreement on rules and procedures. These questions became an issue in early October when the nonpartisan League of Women Voters, sponsors of the presidential candidate debates in 1976, 1980, and 1984, and scheduled to sponsor the last debate of 1988, suddenly withdrew its sponsorship of the second and final presidential debate. The League had fought to preserve a role in 1988 but withdrew when the two major campaigns refused to alter the format agreement already worked out with the commission and employed in the first presidential and the vice-presidential debates. Under the ground rules, candidates faced questions from a panel of three journalists chosen through an elaborate process similar to jury selection that allowed campaigns to challenge nominees. The debaters had two minutes to respond to initial questions and the other candidate then received one minute to rebut; a follow-up question could then be posed to the rebutting candidate and the process would repeat. The League sought to alter these arrangements in several respects, urging more interchange between the candidates and proposing to substitute a single moderator for the panel of questioners used in the earlier debates. The League also objected to several other ground rules: the campaigns maintained a phone link with the producer which, the League charged, could be used to determine what pictures were broadcast (an allegation of influence vigorously denied by the debate producer); the moderator's script was subject to campaign officials' approval; the press would be relegated to the two last rows in the auditorium; and each campaign could recruit supporters to fill the hall and provide sound effects. Recriminations flowed both ways and the new commission stepped in to replace the League, raising the money needed to sponsor the event (nearly $500,000) on short notice.[36]

Many observers considered the 1988 presidential debates less than riveting. Bush and Dukakis loyally echoed the major themes of their campaigns. Dukakis stressed the need for improving access to health care and housing, fighting drug use, and restoring economic health while also touching on symbols of the family, strong leadership, and middle-class opportunity. Bush placed somewhat more emphasis on foreign policy and education than did his opponent but hammered away on symbols related to crime, Democrats, and liberalism, the focus of his controversial campaign ads.[37] Dukakis was widely viewed as having demonstrated mastery of substance in the first debate but as failing to project an attractive personality to his audience. His cold demeanor was painfully apparent at the outset of the second debate when he was asked a blunt question by journalist Bernard Shaw: "Governor, if Kitty Dukakis were raped and murdered, would you favor an irrevocable death penalty for the killer?" Instead of using his response to this horrible prospect as a means to project a more human side, Dukakis patiently and unemotionally repeated his lifelong opposition to the death penalty and proceeded to discuss the need for a stepped-up war on drugs. (Campaign aides later explained that Dukakis had been ill throughout that day and had slept during much of the afternoon.) The debates, in short, provided neither candidate with a "knockout." Dukakis, the trailer in the contest, was not able to reverse the campaign's momentum.

The vice-presidential debate offered the most dramatic moment of all three encounters. In response to the third question he was asked about what he would do if forced to assume the duties of president, Dan Quayle compared the length of his congressional service to that of former president John F. Kennedy. Lloyd Bentsen, the Democrats' vice-presidential nominee, delivered a previously prepared response to the comparison. Bentsen's comments were delivered with withering directness: "Senator, I served with Jack Kennedy. I knew Jack Kennedy. Jack Kennedy was a friend of mine. Senator, you're no Jack Kennedy." Millions of viewers watched as hurt, anger, and astonishment flashed across the youthful features of the Republican candidate whose selection had been so controversial. Quayle's response—"That was really uncalled for, Senator"—sounded lame in comparison.

Televised presidential debates have become the most important campaign events of modern presidential elections. Candidates have recognized the danger of making a mistake or an embarrassing gaffe on live television, a particular danger for incumbents. Challengers have sought to use the opportunity to demonstrate their knowledge of issues and their "presidential" qualities to a large nationwide audience. Kennedy in 1960 and Reagan in 1980 seem to have benefited the most from an opportunity to engage a more experienced opponent, at least in part because they were able to exceed performance expectations and dispel negative impressions. Most candidates prepare extensively prior to the meeting and follow a conservative plan of reemphasizing themes already made prominent during the campaign. As a result, the exchanges frequently seem wooden rather than extemporaneous, an impression heightened by the cautious rules approved by the respective camps. Although there may be good reason to prefer sponsorship by a nonpartisan rather than a bipartisan organization (the former may be better able to resist adopting procedures that help candidates more than voters), the question may be moot. The events surrounding the second presidential debate in 1988 probably put the League of Women Voters out of the general election debate business, particularly if the Commission on Presidential Debates continues to do a reasonable job. Planning is already underway for two debates between presidential candidates and one between vice-presidential candidates to be sponsored by the commission during the 1992 general election. The League of Women Voters will be working with the commission on voter education and is planning a Democratic candidate debate (two in the unlikely event of a Republican contest) to be broadcast by CNN before the New Hampshire primary.

Besides political commercials and debates, a third source of communication in presidential campaigns is the coverage provided by representatives of the mass media themselves, both the broadcast media (television and radio) and print media (newspapers and magazines). These representatives are not nearly as important in general election campaigns, however, as they are in the nomination stage. By the time of the fall election, the campaign is much more structured. The contest essentially has come down to two candidates who by then are fairly well known to the electorate; in addition, the voters at this stage associate the candidates with their respective parties and evaluate them on that basis. Moreover, the candidates have more money to spend on campaign communications than they did in the nomination process; and debates, if held, are more focused (typically involving just two candidates) and reach a wider audience than any that occurred in the nomination campaign.

The media's coverage of the election campaign is similar to their coverage of the nomination stage. Reporters and commentators pay great attention to the election "game," that is, which party candidate is leading in the public opinion polls and by how much, the strategies being pursued by both camps, and the "hoopla" of campaign rallies and the like. The media also tend to focus on "campaign issues"—such as Jimmy Carter's remark in the 1976 campaign that he "lusted after women in his heart" and Ford's comment about Eastern Europe—rather than policy issues. In

1980 the media played up Jimmy Carter's personal attacks on Ronald Reagan and on Reagan's contention that the literal, biblical interpretation of creation should be taught equally with the theory of evolution. In 1984 the media zeroed in on the financial affairs of Geraldine Ferraro and her husband. Dan Quayle's service in the National Guard during the Vietnam era and his admission to law school despite a weak undergraduate record similarly attracted unusual and possibly excessive attention in 1988.

Patterson's study of the 1976 election contest does indicate, however, that the voters became more aware of the candidates' positions on policy issues as the campaign progressed.[38] He attributes some of that increase to their familiarity with the policy tendencies of the Democratic and Republican parties. His analysis also shows that newspaper coverage of policy issues increased voters' awareness of them, particularly for voters who previously had not been highly interested in policy issues. In contrast, the short, superficial coverage of the issues by network news did not raise voters' awareness of the issues. More recent campaign studies, however, do not confirm the superiority of the print media. In their analysis of the 1980 campaign, Robinson and Sheehan conclude that the broadcast networks covered the issues at least as well as the wire services.[39] Moreover, Patterson and Davis found in their study of the 1984 campaign that only 4 of 114 newspaper articles they analyzed mentioned Mondale's charge that Reagan's tax cuts benefited the rich, and none mentioned Mondale's progressive tax plan.[40] Ironically, Patterson finds that the public learns more about candidate policy positions through exposure to campaign advertising than through attention to television news.[41]

Despite the dominance of television in recent presidential contests, the other media continue to play a role in campaigns. Newspapers not only cover the issues in more detail than television but also are free to endorse candidates.[42] The print media are also available for advertisements stressing visual effects. In 1960 the Democrats used pictures of John Kennedy and his attractive wife, Jacqueline, in many of their promotions. In 1976 the Republicans printed full-page advertisements comparing the cover of *Newsweek* magazine that featured President Ford with the cover of *Playboy* magazine that carried the controversial interview with Carter (in which he confessed that he "lusted after women in his heart").

Radio also plays a role in presidential campaigns. It is less expensive than television and can be used in ways that television cannot, such as broadcasting to commuting drivers, as President Ford did in a series of early morning chats during the 1976 campaign. There is also the distinct possibility that a particular candidate will come across better on radio, one possible reason that President Nixon favored the medium over television for his speeches during the 1972 campaign. Moreover, some radio networks, such as National Public Radio, cover presidential campaigns in much greater depth than does television.

The formats available in the various media therefore make it possible for candidates to emphasize different types of appeals and to reach disparate groups. Nimmo distinguishes between two major types of audiences.[43] The first consists of the politically concerned and interested, who use the print media as well as television and radio to obtain information on presidential campaigns. The second comprises less politically involved voters who must be reached through television and sometimes through radio, particularly by means of spot announcements, such as those used by Richard Nixon during his 1968 campaign.

During the 1988 election, there was renewed concern that campaign strategists might be able to control media coverage through adroit staging of events. As Thomas Patterson points out, "Since the candidates decide what they will say, and where they will say it, they frequently can direct the press's attention to what they want it to see." [44] *Sound bites* are brief, punchy lines developed for candidates to deliver with the intent of providing dramatic footage for evening television news broadcasts. Effective campaign managers seek to develop a theme for the day and stage events where their candidate can deliver the pithy lines. Informal and even structured interaction with the press is minimized. One consequence of such a pattern is the trivialization of public issues and candidate positions. Because an effectively managed campaign can make the difference between victory and defeat it is critical to understand how candidates construct a campaign team.

Campaign Organization and Workers

Although the mass media reach more people in the general election campaign than in the nomination contest (more money is spent in a shorter period of time, and some voters become politically interested only after the parties nominate their respective candidates), not everyone follows the election campaign, except perhaps casually on television. These voters depend on those who do follow it to pass along information, such as the candidates' stands on the issues. (Of course, the transmitters often alter the messages in keeping with their own views and biases.) Beyond that, personal contacts are particularly important in persuading many people to make the most basic political decision: whether or not to vote at all. Sometimes citizens' apathy can be overcome only by the dogged determination of persons who see that others register to vote and have transportation to the polls.

Presidential candidates typically start the general election campaign with a core of people who, in effect, constitute their personal organization. If there has been a spirited nomination battle, the principal organizers of the campaign shift their attention to the general election. John Kennedy put his brother Robert in charge of his 1960 campaign against Richard Nixon, and Hamilton Jordan continued as the head of Jimmy Carter's 1976 fall campaign. Many who worked for the candidate in the primary and caucus-convention states also are available for the election campaign. Incumbent presidents frequently assign key members of their administration to work on the fall campaign. In 1972 Richard Nixon initially put his attorney general, John Mitchell, in charge of the Committee to Reelect the President and transferred others in the White House to assignments with the committee. Three important figures in the Carter administration, Robert Strauss, Hamilton Jordan, and Gerald Rafshoon, played significant roles in the 1980 campaign.

Because the electorate for the general campaign is so much broader than the selectorate, which participates in the nomination phase, presidential candidates must increase the ranks of their supporters in the fall to include people who had not been involved previously. One potential source of new recruits is political rivals who had sought the nomination themselves. In 1972 George McGovern asked Hubert Humphrey to campaign for him; Humphrey did so out of personal friendship and party loyalty. In 1984 both Gary Hart and Jesse Jackson worked hard on Mondale's behalf in the fall campaign. In 1976 Ford and Reagan supporters cochaired the general election campaign in many states.[45] In many instances, however, personal loyalties and commitments to issues are so strong that it is not possible to recruit those who supported the other candidates for the nomination. In 1968 the Humphrey organization was not able to persuade many of Eugene McCarthy's supporters to work in the general election campaign after McCarthy lost the presidential nomination. In 1980 many who backed Edward Kennedy's unsuccessful bid for the Democratic nomination did not work for President Carter in the fall campaign; nor in 1984 did many of Gary Hart's supporters campaign for Mondale. Jesse Jackson's role in 1988 was more limited than his supporters would have liked, a factor that may have contributed to the decline in black turnout.

Persons associated with the regular party organization are another potential source of campaign workers. Termed "organizational loyalists" by John Kessel, these are the people who owe their allegiance to the party instead of a particular presidential candidate or set of political issues.[46]

Because of such loyalties, they are often willing to work in the fall campaign for whichever candidate wins their party's nomination, no matter what their personal feelings about the nominee may be. At the same time, because they are pragmatic and not ideological, party loyalists may not work hard for a presidential candidate they believe to be a loser who will hurt the chances of party candidates seeking other political offices. Many Republicans took this attitude toward Goldwater in 1964, as did some Democratic leaders toward Humphrey in 1968, McGovern in 1972, Mondale in 1984, and even Dukakis in 1988.

State and local political parties are another potential source of workers for the presidential general election campaign. For several reasons, however, problems traditionally have arisen in persuading these organizations to work for the presidential candidates. First, state and local races are more important than the presidential contest to local leaders, particularly those in patronage positions. Second, national, state, and local organizations compete for the same resources, such as visits by candidates and financial donations. Finally, the campaign finance legislation passed in the early 1970s to provide public funds for presidential campaigns, prohibited state and local parties from spending money on such campaigns.

The 1979 amendment to the campaign finance legislation, however, permitted state and local party organizations to spend money in presidential campaigns for any purpose except campaign advertising and hiring outside personnel. This legislation enabled both parties in 1980 to develop grass-roots support for their presidential campaigns, although the Republicans clearly outdid the Democrats. Early in the fall campaign Reagan met with Republican members of Congress on the steps of the Capitol to symbolize cooperation among all elements of the party in electing Republicans to public office. As election day approached, the GOP stated that it had half a million Reagan volunteers ringing doorbells and another four hundred thousand staffing telephone banks on his behalf.

Democratic presidential candidates have generally benefited from another major source of campaign workers: those provided by organized labor. In 1968 the AFL-CIO said it had registered 4.6 million voters, printed and distributed more than a hundred million pamphlets, operated telephone banks in 638 localities, sent out seventy thousand house-to-house canvassers, and provided almost a hundred thousand volunteers on election day to transport people to the polls.[47] This effort was extended on Hubert Humphrey's behalf and is credited with winning the votes of a large number of workers who initially planned to vote for George Wallace.

In contrast, the antipathy of George Meany and other AFL-CIO leaders toward George McGovern caused the organization to remain neutral in the 1972 presidential race and to concentrate its efforts instead toward helping Democrats win House seats and state and local offices. In 1976 the AFL-CIO returned to its traditional policy of supporting the Democratic presidential candidate and played an important role in registering its members and their families and in transporting them to the polls to vote for Jimmy Carter. In 1980, although some of its principal leaders backed Senator Kennedy in the Democratic nomination struggle, labor generally did support President Carter; the National Education Association was especially active on his behalf. In 1984, except for the Teamsters, who backed Reagan, labor unions were united on behalf of Walter Mondale, as they were for Michael Dukakis in 1988.

One distinctive feature of the 1984 campaign was the extent to which both political parties sought to register new voters. Initially, observers thought that the Democrats would benefit most from this effort by registering traditionally low-voting groups such as blacks, Hispanics, and the poor. Their registration effort ran into difficulties, however, because of rivalries among organizations attempting to register the same people and the reluctance of some political organizations to add new voters who would later share in deciding which candidates would prevail in Democratic primary contests for various offices. Moreover, the Republican party launched an all-out drive of its own to counteract the rival party's effort. Republicans registered a large number of white southerners, with the assistance of fundamentalist ministers. Key states, such as California, Texas, and Florida, were selected for special registration drives. Most observers considered the parties' 1984 efforts a standoff even though significant registration gains were made among some groups. For example, it is estimated that as many as two million new black voters joined the rolls.[48] Registration efforts were more selectively targeted by the parties in 1988 (for example, Hispanics in Texas) and both parties seemed to devote more time to mobilizing voters, stressing persuasion over registration.

Campaign Finance

Since 1976, campaign reform legislation has significantly influenced general election campaigns. In 1976 both Ford and Carter accepted federal funds ($21.8 million each that year) and were therefore restricted to that figure for the entire campaign (plus another $3.2 million that each national committee could spend on behalf of its presidential candidate). As a result, both sides had to conduct more restricted campaigns than they did in 1972, when the Republicans spent $61 million and the Democrats $30 million. The equal public subsidy provided to both candidates meant that Ford had to forgo the traditional Republican advantage in campaign funds. As the incumbent president, however, he received a great deal of free publicity, and his Rose Garden strategy enabled him to reserve his financial resources for the last ten days of the campaign, in which he spent $4 million on television and radio broadcasting, primarily in airing the television commercials with Joe Garagiola. All told, both candidates spent about half of their total campaign outlay on the mass media, particularly television, and therefore had limited funds available for organizing their grass-roots campaigns. Largely missing from the 1976 contest were fund-raising activities and the buttons, bumper stickers, and yard signs used extensively in previous elections (recall that under the law then in effect state and local parties could not assist the presidential campaign by spending money for such purposes).

The 1980 campaign brought new developments in campaign finance. Again two major party candidates accepted public financing, and each spent about $18 million of the $29.4 million in federal funds on the mass media, which again meant that they had limited funds available for grass-roots activities. In 1980, however, the law permitted state and local parties to make expenditures for such activities. Figures provided by the Federal Election Commission show that Republican state and local committees spent $15 million on grass-roots efforts on Reagan's behalf compared with $5 million spent by Democratic organizations for Carter.

Also of increased importance in the 1980 campaign were the actions of independent groups in support of Reagan. In the summer of 1980 several organizations announced plans to spend up to $70 million on media efforts for the Republican candidate. A citizens' interest group, Common Cause, together with the Federal Election Commission and the Carter-Mondale Presidential Committee, challenged such expenditures on the grounds that the groups were not truly autonomous, as some of their leaders had been closely associated with Reagan in past political campaigns. Although these challenges were unsuccessful, they did impede the fund-raising efforts of the independent groups and forced them to cut back on their original plans. Eventually, independent organizations spent approximately $10.6 million on Reagan's behalf. Although much less than originally anticipated, these expenditures were nonetheless significant: independent groups were estimated to have spent only $28,000 for President Carter, about one-quarter of 1 percent of the amount spent for Reagan.[49] Total independent expenditures increased for 1983-84 to nearly $17.5 million, with $15.83 million spent in efforts favoring the Republican candidates and $800,000 supporting the Democratic ticket.

The overall total declined in 1988 but the party imbalance widened. Total expenditures of $14.13 million were reported to the Federal Election Commission for 1987-88; $10.54 million was spent in support of the Republican cause and $568,000 for the Democrats. Spending to oppose a ticket rose dramatically from $831,000 in the previous election to $3.5 million in 1988, of which all but $150,000 was directed against the Democrats.[50]

In 1984 both presidential candidates again spent a major portion of their federal funds ($40.4 million plus $6.9 million for the national committee) on the mass media. Both parties also expended considerable sums of money on voter registration and get-out-the-vote efforts, making use of a loophole in the campaign finance laws that allows money to be raised and spent for "party building" activities. The Republicans funneled much more money to state parties to assist in the campaign than did the Democrats, a gap that was substantially narrowed in 1988 when it was reported that Republicans spent $69 million and Democrats $60 million on such efforts. Many observers are concerned about the growth in these "soft money" expenditures (referred to as "sewer money" by critics) since there are no limits on the amounts that individuals, corporations and labor unions may contribute and the funds can be channeled into areas critical to the presidential election with only a nominal separation from the presidential campaigns. Reportedly, 270 contributions of $100,000 or more were received by the Republicans in 1988 and the money was clearly targeted, as was the Democrats', to critical state contests.[51] Moreover, the parties' efforts to raise soft money were coordinated by the chief fundraisers for each presidential candidate, Robert A. Farmer, finance chairman of the Dukakis nomination campaign, and Robert A. Mosbacher, Sr., Bush's finance chairman.[52] The growth in soft-money contributions, argue the critics, will reopen the system to abuse.

Both the rules of the game and the campaign strategies and resources developed by the opposing candidates shape the outcome of presidential campaigns. The campaign, however, is only one influence on the way people vote. Chapter 4 examines other influences, as well as patterns of voting in presidential elections.

Notes

1. During the 1988 election, approximately 36.5 million persons participated in primaries or caucuses as part of the nomination process and 91.6 million voted in the general election. Harold G. Stanley and Richard G. Niemi, *Vital*

Statistics on American Politics, 2d ed. (Washington, D.C.: CQ Press, 1990), Tables 3-1, 3-2, 3-3, 3-4, 3-5, 3-6.

2. Max Farrand, *The Framing of the Constitution of the United States* (New Haven: Yale University Press, 1913), 160.

3. Neal Peirce, *The People's President: The Electoral College in American History and the Direct-Vote Alternative* (New York: Simon and Schuster, 1968), 430.

4. Lucius Wilmerding, *The Electoral College* (New Brunswick, N.J.: Rutgers University Press, 1958), chap. 8.

5. John Roche, "The Founding Fathers: A Reform Caucus in Action," *American Political Science Review* 55 (December 1961): 811.

6. Lawrence Longley, "Minorities and the 1980 Electoral College" (Paper delivered at the annual meeting of the American Political Science Association, Washington, D.C., August 28-31, 1980).

7. The 270 electoral votes constitute a majority of the total number of 538, which is the sum of 435 electoral votes representing members of the House of Representatives, 100 representing the senators from the fifty states, and 3 representing the District of Columbia.

8. As part of the settlement in a lawsuit filed against the Census Bureau, a postcensus survey of 165,000 households was conducted to determine the extent of undercounting. Preliminary survey findings suggested that the size of eight state delegations could be adjusted. July 15, 1991, was the deadline for making adjustments in the original census count. On that date, Secretary of Commerce Robert Mosbacher announced that no adjustment would be made. This decision is certain to undergo court challenge but is unlikely to be resolved before the 1992 presidential election.

9. Wallace, however, may have affected the results of the Truman-Dewey contest in some states; Wallace's winning 8 percent of the popular vote in New York State probably drained enough votes away from Truman to allow Dewey to defeat him by about 1 percent of the popular vote in that contest.

10. Although presidential candidates are free to refuse public funds, none has done so in the general election, perhaps because of the difficulty of raising money under the limitations on contributions from individuals and political action committees. Candidates may also think that the American public favors the use of public rather than private funds in the presidential general election.

11. *New York Times,* November 12, 1988, A8. Also see Thomas Weko and John H. Aldrich, "The Presidency and the Election Campaign: Framing the Choices in 1988," in *The Presidency and the Political System,* 3d ed., ed. Michael Nelson (Washington, D.C.: CQ Press, 1990).

12. Although campaign activities are carried in the national media, local media give special publicity to the candidate and thus affect the immediate audience. Moreover, some voters are flattered by the fact that a candidate takes the time and effort to come to their locality to campaign.

13. Lewis Chester, Godfrey Hodgson, and Bruce Page, *The American Melodrama: The Presidential Campaign of 1968* (New York: Viking, 1969), 620.

14. Sometimes, however, presidential candidates venture into states thought to belong politically to their opponents. In 1976 Jimmy Carter made some trips into normally Republican areas to put Ford on the defensive, therefore forcing him to spend time and money in states he expected to carry. Martin

Schram, *Running for President 1976: The Carter Campaign* (New York: Stein and Day, 1977), 247. Carter in 1980 and Mondale in 1984 also visited California, in part to require Ronald Reagan to use some resources to protect his home state. Similarly, by adding Lloyd Bentsen to the ticket in 1988, Democrats hoped to challenge Bush in his home state.

15. John Kessel reports the comment made during the 1972 campaign that "McGovern could not carry the South with Robert E. Lee as his running-mate and Bear Bryant as his campaign manager." John Kessel, "Strategy for November," in *Choosing the President,* ed. James D. Barber (Englewood Cliffs, N.J.: Prentice-Hall, 1974), 109.

16. This carefully thought-out plan is to be contrasted with the pledge Richard Nixon made at the 1960 Republican national convention to visit all fifty states personally. In the closing days of the campaign, Nixon took precious time to fly to Alaska, which he had not previously visited, while his opponent, John Kennedy, was barnstorming through heavily populated Illinois, New Jersey, New York, and the New England states.

17. Marjorie Randon Hershey, "The Campaign and the Media," in *The Election of 1988: Reports and Interpretations,* ed. Gerald Pomper (Chatham, N.J.: Chatham House Publishers, 1989), 94.

18. Thomas Cronin, "The Presidential Election of 1984," in *Election 84: Landslide without a Mandate,* ed. Ellis Sandoz and Cecil Crabb, Jr. (New York: Mentor, 1985), 49.

19. Timothy Crouse, *The Boys on the Bus* (New York: Ballantine Books, 1972), 257.

20. One of the interesting features of the 1980 campaign was that President Carter did *not* use Vice President Mondale much to assault the opposition; instead, the president himself launched frequent personal attacks on Ronald Reagan while for the most part Mondale played the role of the "happy warrior" in the campaign.

21. The approval measure has become standard. It reflects responses to the common question, "Do you approve or disapprove of the way Ronald Reagan is handling his job as President?"

22. James A. Barnes, "Aging Well," *National Journal,* October 8, 1988, 2562.

23. Paul J. Quirk, "The Election," in *The Elections of 1988,* ed. Michael Nelson (Washington, D.C.: CQ Press, 1990), 76.

24. David Broder, "The American Political Scene Could Turn Upsidedown," *Wilmington News Journal,* January 29, 1989, J1.

25. In 1980 the Republicans handled the potential problem of an even older Ronald Reagan, who was almost seventy at the time of the fall campaign, in a very different way: he was depicted as an unusually vigorous man for his age. This image was helped considerably by Reagan's full head of hair, as contrasted to Eisenhower's bald pate.

26. Hershey, "The Campaign and the Media," 78.

27. Hershey, "The Campaign and the Media," 80-83; Quirk, "The Election," 75-76; Weko and Aldrich, "The Presidency and the Election Campaign," 273-275.

28. Martin P. Wattenberg, "From a Partisan to a Candidate-Centered Electorate," in *The New American Political System,* 2d version, ed. Anthony King (Washington, D.C.: AEI Press, 1990).

29. Dick Kirschten, "The Gipper's Last Campaign . . . A Mix of Wit and Harsh

Rhetoric," *National Journal,* October 15, 1988, 2609.
30. A variant of this problem plagued Walter Mondale in 1984. Although he was not the incumbent vice president, he did hold that office from 1977 to 1981 and was associated with the policies of the Carter administration, some of which he did not endorse (for example, placing an embargo on grain shipments to the Soviet Union).
31. One political scientist calls "position issues" those that "involve advocacy of governmental action from a set of alternatives," in contrast to "valence issues," which "merely involve linking of the parties with some condition that is positively or negatively valued by the electorate." Donald Stokes, "Special Models of Party Competition," in *Elections in the Political Order,* ed. Angus Campbell, Philip Converse, Warren Miller, and Donald Stokes (New York: Wiley, 1966), 170-171.
32. Marshall McLuhan, *Understanding Media: The Extensions of Man* (New York: McGraw-Hill, 1964), chap. 1.
33. A problem in holding presidential debates is a provision of the Federal Communications Act of 1934 requiring the networks to provide equal time to *all* candidates, including those of minor parties. In 1960 Congress temporarily suspended the provisions of the act to allow the Nixon-Kennedy debates. In 1976, 1980, and 1984 the debates were sponsored and paid for by the League of Women Voters. The networks supposedly covered them as "news events," a legal fiction that was exposed when the first Carter-Ford debate in 1976 was interrupted for twenty-eight minutes until an audio failure could be repaired.
34. This was especially true of people who watched the first Nixon-Kennedy debate on television. Those who heard that same debate on the radio, however, thought the two candidates came out about equally. Theodore White, *The Making of the President, 1960* (New York: Pocket Books, 1961), 348.
35. Albert Hunt suggests that Reagan convinced many viewers of the debate that he was sufficiently smart to go head-to-head with the president and not crumble. President Carter, however, did not meet the greater expectations the viewers had of his debate performance, namely, that he explain why things had not gone very well in the previous four years and how he would do better in a second term. Albert Hunt, "The Campaign and the Issues," in *The American Elections of 1980,* ed. Austin Ranney (Washington, D.C.: American Enterprise Institute, 1981), 170-171.
36. For press reports of these events see *Los Angeles Times,* October 4, 1988, 23; October 5, 1988, 14; October 6, 1988, 20; October 7, 1988, 19. Also see *Washington Post,* October 4, 1988, 15, 18, and *Christian Science Monitor,* November 7, 1988, 14.
37. See the content analysis of debate transcripts in Hershey, "The Campaign and the Media," 90.
38. Thomas Patterson, *The Mass Media Election: How Americans Choose Their President* (New York: Praeger, 1980), chap. 13.
39. Michael Robinson and Margaret Sheehan, *Over the Wire and on TV: CBS and UPI in Campaign '80* (New York: Russell Sage Foundation, 1983), 166.
40. Thomas Patterson and Richard Davis, "The Media Campaign: Struggle for the Agenda," in *The Elections of 1984,* ed. Michael Nelson (Washington, D.C.: CQ Press, 1985), 116.
41. Thomas E. Patterson, "Television and Presidential Politics: A Proposal to

Restructure Television Communication in Election Campaigns," in *Presidential Selection,* ed. Alexander Heard and Michael Nelson (Durham, N.C.: Duke University Press, 1987).

42. Over the years endorsements have clearly favored Republican candidates, except in 1964, when the press favored Johnson over Goldwater. As a group, newspaper owners and editors, who decide on endorsements, tend to be conservative, possibly because much of their advertising revenue comes from large corporations. Political reporters, by contrast, are widely perceived to be liberal. In 1988, the number of newspaper endorsements fell to the lowest point since *Editor and Publisher* began to track them in 1932. This was taken as an expression of dissatisfaction with the quality of the campaign conducted by the two major party nominees.

43. Dan Nimmo, *The Political Persuaders: The Techniques of Modern Political Campaigns* (Englewood Cliffs, N.J.: Prentice-Hall, 1970), 117-118.

44. Patterson, "Television and Presidential Politics," 312.

45. Jonathan Moore and Janet Fraser, *Campaign for President: The Managers Look at 1976* (Cambridge, Mass.: Ballinger, 1977), 133.

46. John Kessel, "Strategy for November," in *Choosing the President,* ed. James D. Barber (Englewood Cliffs, N.J.: Prentice-Hall, 1974), 179.

47. Theodore White, *The Making of the President, 1968* (New York: Bantam, 1969), 453-454.

48. Rhodes Cook, *Congressional Quarterly Weekly Report,* October 1, 1988, 2704.

49. Herbert E. Alexander, *Financing the 1980 Election* (Lexington, Mass.: D.C. Heath, 1983), 387.

50. The data for 1983-84 and 1987-88 may include minor expenditures made during the nomination stage although the bulk of spending occurred during the general election. *Statistical Abstract of the United States, 1990,* table 447.

51. An example of coordination between party expenditures and presidential campaigns was the Democrats' funneling of more than half the $15.8 million raised from August through October 1988 into California, Illinois, Texas, Pennsylvania, and Michigan—key targets of the Dukakis campaign. *National Journal,* December 17, 1988, 3219. For a discussion of coordination in the Illinois campaign during 1988, see *New York Times,* September 29, 1988, A1.

52. *National Journal,* October 8, 1988, 2516-2517.

Selected Readings

Abramson, Paul R., John H. Aldrich, and David W. Rohde. *Change and Continuity in the 1980 Elections.* Washington, D.C.: CQ Press, 1982.

——. *Change and Continuity in the 1984 Elections.* Rev. ed. Washington, D.C.: CQ Press, 1987.

——. *Change and Continuity in the 1988 Elections.* Rev. ed. Washington, D.C.: CQ Press, 1990.

Chubb, John, and Paul Peterson. *The New Direction in American Politics.* Washington, D.C.: Brookings, 1985.

Election Rules and the Election Campaign

Nelson, Michael, ed. *The Elections of 1984.* Washington, D.C.: CQ Press, 1985.
——. *The Elections of 1988.* Washington, D.C.: CQ Press, 1989.
Ranney, Austin, ed. *The American Elections of 1980.* Washington, D.C.: American Enterprise Institute, 1981.
Robinson, Michael, and Margaret Sheehan. *Over the Wire and on TV: CBS and UPI in Campaign '80.* New York: Russell Sage Foundation, 1983.

Voting in
Presidential Elections ══════4

Rival campaigns spend millions of dollars and untold hours pursuing two objectives: to motivate people to vote on election day and to win their support for a particular candidate. A combination of factors other than campaign appeals will help determine who votes and how they will vote. The ultimate choice voters make among candidates depends on their long-term political predispositions, such as political party loyalties and social group affiliations, and their reactions to short-term forces, such as the particular candidates and issues involved in specific elections.

The first two sections of this chapter explore participation in presidential elections and the various factors that shape the voters' choice of candidates. The final section shifts to other important aspects of presidential elections—their effect on the political party system and on policy making in the United States.

Participation in Presidential Elections

True to the Constitution, members of the electoral college make the official selection of president. Nonetheless, important developments in U.S. politics have substantially altered the selection process. With the formation of rival political parties in the 1790s, electors began to vote the presidential preferences of the electorate instead of exercising independent judgment. Moreover, state legislatures that were granted power by the Constitution to determine how the electors should be chosen soon began to vest that right in the general electorate. In the process, the U.S. presidential election system became less "elitist" and more "democratic."

This development was highly significant, but it left an important question unanswered. Who should be entitled to vote for the presidential electors? The Constitution leaves that decision to the individual states, so that it is possible for some states to allow particular groups to vote for president while other states prevent them from doing so. Consequently, the federal government has sometimes found it necessary to take action in order to force all states to allow certain groups of people to participate in the selection of the chief executive.

An early state barrier to participation in presidential elections was the requirement that voters own *property*. Many legislatures took the position that only property owners would have enough of a "stake" in society to interest themselves in its political affairs. Some legislators also were concerned that the poor would sell their votes to unscrupulous politicians or, worse, use their votes to choose candidates who would proceed to redistribute the wealth of property owners. However, as more and more people acquired property and redistribution of wealth did not happen, state legislatures began to drop the property qualification for voting in presidential and other elections. By the early 1840s such qualifications had generally disappeared at the state level. Thus, the first major expansion of the presidential electorate took place without federal intervention—in contrast to later battles over the composition of the presidential electorate.

The most bitter franchise struggle involved the right of *blacks* to vote in elections, including presidential contests. At the end of the Civil War, as part of a concerted program to bring liberated slaves into the mainstream of American life, the Fifteenth Amendment was passed. It stated that "the right of the citizens of the United States to vote shall not be denied or abridged by the United States or by any state, on account of race, color, or previous condition of servitude." For a short time, blacks did participate in presidential and other elections, but when federal troops withdrew from the South in the 1870s, a systematic disenfranchisement of blacks began. It took many forms, including physical violence; economic coercion; and legal devices, such as excluding blacks from participating in primaries of the dominant Democratic party, assessing poll taxes (which also disenfranchised many poor whites), and selectively administering literacy tests.

The federal government has taken action on many occasions to force states to extend the right to vote to blacks. The earliest pressure came from the federal courts. In a 1915 decision, *Guinn v. United States,*[1] the Supreme Court invalidated the "grandfather" clause of the Oklahoma constitution, which exempted persons from a literacy test if their ancestors were entitled to vote in 1866; the Court viewed this as a deliberate (and not too subtle) attempt to avoid the Fifteenth Amendment's prohibition against denying certain citizens the right to vote. Ultimately, the Court in 1944 also outlawed "white" primaries, ruling in *Smith v.*

Allwright[2] that a primary was a *public* function and not the business of a private organization—the Democratic party—as had been held in 1935 in *Grovey v. Townsend*.[3] Hence, "white" primaries were forbidden under the Fifteenth Amendment.

The two other branches of the national government lagged behind the courts in helping blacks to win the right to vote. Democratic presidents Franklin D. Roosevelt and Harry S. Truman both favored black enfranchisement, but they were unsuccessful in persuading Congress, dominated by southern committee chairmen who could readily block legislation, to move against poll taxes or even to enact an antilynching law. Not until 1957, during the Republican administration of Dwight D. Eisenhower, did Congress finally pass legislation giving the attorney general of the United States the right to seek judicial relief against persons violating the right of individuals to vote. Many southern election officials easily circumvented the law; they continued to harass blacks who tried to vote and destroyed records to cover up their actions. In 1960 Congress passed additional legislation that strengthened the enforcement of voting rights by authorizing courts to appoint voting referees to register persons deprived of the right to vote because of race or color and by making it a crime to destroy election records.

Building on these modest beginnings, Congress in the 1960s launched an attack against the disenfranchisement of blacks. It initiated the Twenty-fourth Amendment outlawing the use of the poll tax in presidential and congressional elections; the states ratified the amendment in early 1964.[4] The following year, Congress responded to President Lyndon B. Johnson's leadership by enacting the Voting Rights Act of 1965, which suspended literacy tests and authorized the appointment of federal examiners to supervise electoral procedures in areas where such tests were in use and where less than one-half the voting-age population was registered to vote or had voted in 1964. The act subsequently was amended in 1970 to cover areas in which a similar situation existed in November 1968. In 1975 the act was extended for seven years, and its provisions were expanded to cover the voting rights of other minorities, including Hispanics, American Indians, Asian-Americans, and Alaskan natives. In 1982, after some initial difficulties,[5] the act was extended for twenty-five years with provisions requiring certain areas of the country to provide bilingual election materials until 1992.

The national government also has taken action to expand the electorate to include two other major groups: *women* and *young people*. Even though some states had acted on their own to enfranchise both groups, Congress ultimately decided to require all states to do so. In 1920 the states ratified the Nineteenth Amendment, which forbade either the

United States or any of the states from denying a U.S. citizen the right to vote "on account of sex." Young people won a major victory in the early 1970s when Congress first passed a law granting eighteen-year-olds the right to vote in national, state, and local elections. After the Supreme Court ruled that a national law could affect voting only in national elections, the Twenty-sixth Amendment was enacted to extend the right to state and local elections.

Congress has initiated other actions to expand the presidential electorate. The Twenty-third Amendment, ratified in 1961, grants residents of the District of Columbia the right to vote in presidential elections, a privilege they had been denied since the capital was located there in 1800. The 1970 act that lowered the voting age to eighteen also provides that people may vote in presidential elections if they have lived at their current residence for at least thirty days.

Thus, the number of people eligible to vote in presidential elections has increased greatly over the years. The right to vote and the actual exercise of that right are, however, two separate matters.

General Trends in Voter Turnout

One of the ironies of U.S. presidential elections in recent years is that as more and more citizens have acquired the right to vote, a smaller and smaller proportion of them have exercised that right. As Table 4-1 indicates, the estimated number of people of voting age has more than doubled since Franklin Roosevelt was first elected to office in 1932. After reaching a peak in 1960, however, the percentage of eligible voters who actually went to the polls declined in the next seven presidential elections except for a modest increase in 1984. In 1988 only 50.2 percent of eligible voters went to the polls, the second lowest turnout recorded for a presidential election in the twentieth century. The most pronounced drop—more than 5 percent—occurred between the 1968 and 1972 elections after eighteen-year-olds were granted the vote.

The recent decline in voter participation runs counter to some of the traditional theories of why people do not vote. Restrictive laws, particularly those pertaining to registration and voting, frequently are said to prevent citizens from going to the polls. Yet many states have eased such restrictions in recent years, and the Congress has facilitated voting in presidential elections for new residents, so that generally it was easier for a person to register and to vote for president in 1988 than it was in 1960. A person's lack of education also is often cited as a reason for not voting; however, the level of education of U.S. citizens has consistently risen as participation has declined. Lack of political information is yet another

Table 4-1 Participation of General Public in Presidential Elections, 1932-1988

Year	Estimated population of voting age (in millions)	Number of votes cast (in millions)	Number of votes as percentage of population of voting age
1932	75.8	39.7	52.4
1936	80.2	45.6	56.0
1940	84.7	49.9	58.9
1944	85.7	48.0	56.0
1948	95.6	48.8	51.1
1952	99.9	61.6	61.6
1956	104.5	62.0	59.3
1960	109.7	68.8	62.8
1964	114.1	70.6	61.9
1968	120.3	73.2	60.9
1972[a]	140.8	77.6	55.1
1976[a]	152.3	81.6	53.6
1980[a]	164.6	86.5	52.6
1984[a]	174.5	92.7	53.1
1988[a]	182.8	91.6	50.1

Source: "Projections of the Voting-Age Population, for States: November 1990," *Current Population Reports,* Series P-25, No. 1059, table no. 5 (Washington, D.C.: U.S. Government Printing Office, 1990).

[a] Elections in which persons eighteen to twenty years old were eligible to vote in all states.

frequently cited explanation; however, because of increased use of the mass media, and particularly because of televised presidential debates, more Americans than ever have been made aware of the candidates and their views on public issues (more than one hundred million tuned in to the 1980 debate). Finally, close political races are supposed to stimulate people to get out and vote because they think their ballot might make a difference in the outcome. Pollsters forecast that the 1964 and 1972 elections would be landslides and that the 1968, 1976, and 1980 elections would be close contests, but a smaller percentage of people voted in 1968 than in 1964, and participation also declined in 1976 and 1980 despite close contests. In 1984 there was a slight increase (one-half of one percentage point) in participation even though the outcome was hardly in doubt, while participation declined in 1988, a closer contest.

It is possible to attribute some of the decline in voter turnout in recent years to the extension of the right to vote to eighteen-year-olds, which first took effect in the 1972 presidential election. Analyses of

Table 4-2 Participation of Various Groups in Presidential Elections, 1972-1988 (Percent)

	Year				
Group characteristic	1972	1976	1980	1984	1988
Male	64.1	59.6	59.1	59.0	56.4
Female	62.0	58.8	59.4	60.8	58.3
White	64.5	60.9	60.9	61.4	59.1
Black	52.1	48.7	50.5	55.8	51.5
Age					
18-20 years old	48.3	38.0	35.7	36.7	33.2
21-24 years old	50.7	45.6	43.1	43.5	38.3
25-43 years old	59.7	55.4	54.6	54.5	48.0
35-44 years old	66.3	63.3	64.4	63.5	61.3
45-64 years old	70.8	68.7	69.3	69.8	67.9
65 and over	63.5	62.2	65.1	67.7	68.8
Residence					
Northeast	NA	59.5	58.5	59.7	57.4
Midwest	NA	65.1	65.8	65.7	62.9
South	55.4	54.9	55.6	56.8	54.5
West	NA	57.5	57.2	58.5	55.6
School year completed					
Grade 8 or lower	47.4	44.1	42.6	42.9	36.7
Grade 9 to 11	52.0	47.2	45.6	44.4	41.3
Grade 12	65.4	59.4	58.9	58.7	54.7
College					
1-3 years	74.9	68.1	67.2	67.5	64.5
4 years or more	83.6	79.8	79.9	79.1	77.6

Note: Data are based on estimated population of voting age. The percentages are based on those *reporting* that they voted and are higher than those who actually voted. NA=Not available.

Source: *Statistical Abstract of the United States,* 1990, table 439 (Washington, D.C.: Government Printing Office, 1990).

participation in that election by age group showed that eighteen- to twenty-year-olds did not vote as much (proportionately to their number) as did people twenty-one and over. (See Table 4-2.) Therefore, some of the overall 5 percent decline in voter turnout between 1968 and 1972 was caused by the addition of people to the potential electorate who were less inclined to vote. This factor, however, does not help to explain the decline in participation between 1964 and 1968 and again in 1976, 1980, and 1988. Moreover, analyses of the 1972 election indicate that people twenty-one and over did not participate as much (proportionately) as they did in 1968.

It is difficult to determine why voting has declined in presidential elections in recent years. Abramson, Aldrich, and Rohde, who analyzed this decline in *reported* turnout in all presidential elections from 1952 through 1980, link it to two major factors.[6] The first is an erosion in the strength of the political party identification of many Americans (the next section contains a discussion of that matter), which may result in less psychological involvement in politics. The second factor is a decline in the sense of political efficacy: over the years, fewer and fewer people have thought that public officials cared about their opinions, and many have felt that as citizens they had little to say about how the government operated. These attitudes, in turn, relate to public disaffection with the government's policies on issues such as race relations, Vietnam, and the Watergate scandals, as well as a general feeling that government has failed to solve the country's economic and social problems.

Group Differences in Voter Turnout

As shown in Table 4-2, participation in presidential elections varies among groups. Blacks and young people—two groups who participate the least—were formerly denied the franchise. One possible reason for this pattern is that some of the "newly" enfranchised may still be affected by the public attitudes that originally denied them the right to vote. Non-whites, especially older people who grew up in the South where formerly they could not vote, may feel that they are not able to make good choices. Some eighteen- to twenty-year-olds may also feel that they are too immature to exercise the right to vote intelligently. In all probability, however, the voting patterns of these two groups are attributable to other factors as well. Many blacks have completed fewer years of education, which, as Table 4-2 shows, is linked to low voting participation. Many eighteen- to twenty-year-olds have not yet settled down and become involved in community affairs, another factor related to voter turnout. It is significant to note that women, another group that traditionally had a comparatively low rate of participation, now vote more than men, a development probably linked to the increased level of education now achieved by women. (In recent years, women have begun to outnumber men among college students.)

Group differences in voter turnout are rooted in psychological feelings that affect all kinds of political participation, including voting. Well-educated people are more likely to be aware of political developments and their significance than poorly educated people. In addition, well-educated people tend to feel politically efficacious. They have a sense of confidence about the value of their opinions and believe that people in public office will listen to them; therefore, they think that what they do has an important effect on the political process. Poorly educated persons, however, are likely to feel that political officials do not care about them or their opinions. General attitudes about other people also affect voting behavior; those who trust people are more likely to cast their ballots than those whose cynicism and hostility toward others make them feel alienated.

The influence of a group is frequently important. Thus, if individuals belong to a business organization or labor union whose members talk much about political affairs, they may develop their own interests in such matters. If so, their political interests probably will lead them to make the effort to vote. Moreover, even if people are not interested in politics, they may feel that it is their duty as citizens to vote. This attitude is much more likely to exist in the upper and middle classes than in the lower classes.

The reasons that prompt some people to vote and lead others to remain at home on election day are, indeed, varied; yet the factors that shape preferences between competing groups of presidential candidates are even more complex.

Voting Preferences in Presidential Elections

Long-term political dispositions that voters begin to acquire early in life, such as party affiliation and social-group loyalties, affect how they vote in presidential elections. So do short-term forces, such as the particular candidates and issues involved in specific elections. Over the years, however, these separate factors have exerted varying degrees of influence in different elections.

Party Affiliation

Analyses of presidential elections in the 1950s by a group of researchers at the University of Michigan indicate that the single most important determinant of voting at that time was the party affiliation of the voter.[7] This general psychological attachment, shaped by family and social groups, tended to intensify with age. For the average person looking for guidance on how to vote amid the complexities of personalities, issues,

Table 4-3 Party Identification, 1952-1988 (Percent)

Party	1952	1956	1960	1964	1968	1972	1976	1980	1984	1988
Strong Democrat	22	21	20	27	20	15	15	18	17	18
Weak Democrat	25	23	25	25	25	26	25	23	20	18
Total	47	44	45	52	45	41	40	41	37	36
Strong Republican	14	14	16	11	10	10	9	9	10	14
Weak Republican	13	15	14	14	15	13	14	14	15	14
Total	27	29	30	25	25	23	23	23	25	28
Independent	22	24	23	23	30	35	37	34	34	36

Source: *Statistical Abstract of the United States,* 1990, table 442 (Washington, D.C.: Government Printing Office, 1990).

and events of the 1950s, the party label of the candidates was the most important reference point. In this era—which voting analyst Philip Converse refers to as the "Steady State" period[8]—partisanship was also fairly constant. When asked, about 45 percent of Americans in 1952 and 1956 said they thought of themselves as Democrats; about 28 percent, as Republicans; for a combined total of nearly three-fourths of the adult electorate. When asked to classify themselves further as "strong" or "weak" partisans, both Republicans and Democrats tended to divide equally between those two categories. Independents in 1952 and 1956 averaged about 23 percent of the electorate.

In the mid- to late 1960s, however, partisan affiliation in the United States began to change. (See Table 4-3.) In 1964, party affiliation among the voters rose about 5 percent for the Democrats but fell about 3 percent for the Republicans; the independents' share of the electorate also declined slightly. Beginning with the 1968 election, the number of independents began to increase, primarily at the expense of the Democrats, until they constituted one-third of the electorate in 1972. Even those voters who stayed with the Democrats were more inclined than formerly to say they were weak rather than strong party members. Moreover, since 1968, more people have identified themselves as independents than as Republicans. This trend progressed one step further in 1988, when some polls found that independents outnumbered Democrats for the first time.

Another indication of the declining importance of political party identification in presidential elections is the increase in recent years in the number of "switchers," that is, people who vote for one party's candidate in one presidential election and for another party's candidate in the following election. Analyses of presidential voting from 1940 to 1960 show that approximately one-eighth to one-fifth of the electorate switched from one election to the next.[9] From 1968 to 1980 the proportion ranged from one-fifth to one-third.[10] A similar phenomenon has occurred in split-ticket voting, that is, voting for candidates of more than one party in the same election. In 1952, some 13 percent of the Americans who voted cast a split ticket in presidential-House races; by 1972, 30 percent did. The number of split-ticket voters declined to 26 percent in 1976, rose to 35 percent in 1980, and declined to 25 percent in 1984. It remained at that point in 1988.[11] Still more significant, even voters who identify with one of the major parties have increasingly displayed partisan disloyalty by switching and ticket splitting.

Thus, independence from political parties, whether measured by voters' expressed attitudes toward the parties themselves or by reports of their actual behavior in the voting booth, has increased in recent years in the United States. This rise in independents is not, however, spread evenly across the voting population.[12] It has occurred primarily among young people, particularly those who entered the electorate in 1964 or later. New voters who came of age since that time are much more likely to be political independents than are voters of earlier political generations.

Independents in the United States not only have grown dramatically in numbers but also have changed in character. In the 1950s, independents tended to be less knowledgeable about political issues and candidates and to participate less in the political process than partisans.[13] Since the early 1960s, however, they have shown themselves to be just as knowledgeable about political matters as Democrats and Republicans.[14] Furthermore, although not as likely to vote as are party identifiers, independents do participate at least as much as partisans in other political activities, such as writing to political officials and voting on referendums. Thus, nonpartisanship, rather than general political disinterest, characterizes many of the younger independents, particularly those with a college education. A new type of independent seems to have joined the ranks of nonpartisans prevalent in the 1950s.

Observers of voting behavior have suggested several possible reasons for the decline in partisanship among U.S. voters. One is a decrease in the transfer of partisanship from one generation to the next; beginning in the late 1960s younger groups became less likely than earlier generations to retain their family partisan affiliation.[15] Two political "shock" periods, as Converse calls them, also weakened partisan loyalties.[16] The first, which began in 1965 and stemmed from the Vietnam War and racial unrest, affected voters of all ages, Democrats somewhat more than Republicans. The second, which began in 1972 and was precipitated by Watergate and the disclosure that led to Vice President Spiro Agnew's resignation, had a distinct impact on older Republicans.

As shown in Table 4-3, however, the decline in partisanship reached its peak between 1972 and 1976. The proportion of independents has not changed significantly in the four presidential elections since then. Since 1980, modest Republican gains of roughly 5-10 percent have been offset by Democratic losses of the same size. Considered in light of their enormous success in winning presidential elections, Republican gains have been limited, although they may still have had an impact on election results. Although the trend away from party affiliation appears to have stopped, the parties have been unable to reestablish firm loyalties within the public. Overall, the picture has remained remarkably stable since 1972, with just under two-thirds of the citizenry expressing a party identification.

Social Groups and Social Class

Analysts of the presidential elections of 1940 and of 1948 found that a fairly close association existed between voters' social group membership and social status and their support for one of the two major parties.[17] Democrats received most of their support from southerners, blacks, Catholics, and people with limited education, lower incomes, and a working-class background. Republican candidates were supported by northerners, whites, Protestants, and people with more education, higher incomes, and a professional or business background.

Table 4-4 shows how various groups voted in presidential elections from 1952 through 1988. The support of many groups for their traditional party's candidates declined over the thirty-six-year period. Especially noticeable for the Republicans was their loss of votes from white-collar workers through 1984 (comparable figures are unavailable for 1988) and Protestants. The most significant drop for the Democrats came in the southern vote in the 1968 and 1972 elections. The party regained this vote in 1976, when Jimmy Carter of Georgia headed the ticket, but lost it again in 1980, 1984, and 1988. Loss of support has been concentrated among southern whites; by 1988, only one in three white votes in the South went to Dukakis and only 26 percent of white males supported the Democrat.[18] The only group that significantly increased its support for its traditional party candidate over the thirty-six-year period was nonwhites, who have been more firmly in the Democratic camp since 1964 than they were in 1952.[19]

Table 4-4 also shows that the circumstances of particular elections can greatly alter group voting tendencies. In 1964, when the very conser-

Table 4-4 Group Voting Patterns in Presidential Elections, 1952-1988 (Percent)

Group	1952 Stevenson	1952 Eisenhower	1956 Stevenson	1956 Eisenhower	1960 Kennedy	1960 Nixon	1964 Johnson	1964 Goldwater
Sex								
male	47	53	45	55	52	48	60	40
female	42	58	39	61	49	51	62	38
Race								
white	43	57	41	59	49	51	59	41
nonwhite	79	21	61	39	68	32	94	6
Education								
college	34	66	31	69	39	61	52	48
high school	45	55	42	58	52	48	62	38
grade school	52	48	50	50	55	45	66	34
Occupation								
professional, business	36	64	32	68	42	58	54	46
white collar	40	60	37	63	48	52	57	43
manual	55	45	50	50	60	40	71	29
Age								
under 30	51	49	43	57	54	45	64	36
30-49	47	53	45	55	54	46	63	37
50 and older	39	61	39	61	46	54	59	41
Religion								
Protestant	37	63	37	63	38	62	55	45
Catholic	56	44	51	49	78	22	76	24
Region								
East	45	55	40	60	53	47	68	32
Midwest	42	58	41	59	48	52	61	39
South	51	49	49	51	51	49	52	48
West	42	58	43	57	49	51	60	40
Members of labor union families	61	39	57	43	65	35	73	27
National	44.6	55.4	42.2	57.8	50.1	49.9	61.3	38.7

Source: Excerpted from *Gallup Report,* November 1988, 6, 7.

Table 4-4 (Continued)

1968			1972		1976		1980			1984		1988	
Humphrey	Nixon	Wallace	McGovern	Nixon	Carter	Ford	Carter	Reagan	Anderson	Mondale	Reagan	Dukakis	Bush
41	43	16	37	63	53	45	38	53	7	36	64	44	56
45	43	12	38	62	48	51	44	49	6	45	55	48	52
38	47	15	32	68	46	52	36	56	7	34	66	41	59
35	12	3	87	13	85	15	86	10	2	87	13	82	18
37	54	9	37	63	42	55	35	53	10	39	61	42	58
42	43	15	34	66	54	46	43	51	5	43	57	46	54
52	33	15	49	51	58	41	54	42	3	51	49	55	45
34	56	10	31	69	42	56	33	55	10	34	66	NA	NA
41	47	12	36	64	50	48	40	51	9	47	53	NA	NA
50	35	15	43	57	58	41	48	46	5	46	54	NA	NA
47	38	15	48	52	53	45	47	41	11	40	60	37	63
44	41	15	33	67	48	49	38	52	8	40	60	45	55
41	47	12	36	64	52	48	41	54	4	41	59	49	51
35	49	16	30	70	46	53	39	54	6	39	61	42	58
59	33	8	48	52	57	42	46	47	6	39	61	51	49
50	43	7	42	58	51	47	43	47	9	46	54	51	49
44	47	9	40	60	48	50	41	51	7	42	58	47	53
31	36	33	29	71	54	45	44	52	3	37	63	40	60
44	49	7	41	59	46	51	35	54	9	40	60	46	54
56	29	15	46	54	63	36	50	43	5	52	48	63	37
43.0	43.4	13.6	38	62	50	48	41	51	7	41	59	46	54

vative Barry Goldwater was the Republican standard-bearer, all groups, including those that typically support the GOP, voted predominantly for the Democratic candidate, Lyndon Johnson. In 1972, when the very liberal George McGovern ran on the Democratic ticket, all of the groups that usually sympathize with that party, except for nonwhites, voted for the Republican candidate, Richard Nixon. In 1984, when Walter Mondale, a traditional, New Deal Democrat, ran against the highly popular Republican president, Ronald Reagan, the Democrats won overwhelming support only from nonwhites and eked out a narrow victory among voters with a grade school education and members of labor unions, traditional elements of the New Deal coalition.

Michael Dukakis did better than Mondale among several traditionally Democratic groups. Dukakis won increased support from labor, Catholics, and the less educated, but lost ground among nonwhites, although the Democratic margin in this last group remained enormous. Dukakis even won a majority of votes in one region—the East—something that neither Carter nor Mondale had been able to do in the two previous elections. Despite these improvements among major elements of the Democratic coalition, Dukakis lost because the Democrats' base has shrunk appreciably, because there are higher rates of desertion among its identifiers, and because nonvoting is especially prevalent among blacks and the poor, two of the party's major constituencies. One cannot conclude, however, that a higher turnout would have produced a Democratic victory. One study analyzed the partisan and policy preferences of nonvoters for 1988 and concluded "there is no reasonable scenario under which increased turnout would have altered the outcome of the presidential election." Democrats, the authors conclude, suffer from low support more than low turnout.[20]

Table 4-4 also makes clear the extent of Ronald Reagan's attraction to voters. In 1984, after serving four years as president, Reagan won a greater percentage of voters in every category than when he first ran for the office in 1980. The increases were particularly pronounced among voters under age thirty (19 percent); Catholics (14 percent); and males, professional and business people, and southerners (11 percent each).[21] To further illustrate the point, Bush surpassed Reagan's totals only among nonwhites and those under 30, although some polls found Bush's support slipping with the latter group.

Party identification and group affiliation, therefore, have not meant as much in recent presidential voting as they once did. With a large part of the electorate having lost their partisan *anchor,* other forces, such as candidates, issues, events, and presidential performance are now more important in the political world of the American voter.

Recent Trends in Race and Sex

Since 1964 African-American voters have become a mainstay of the Democrats' presidential electorate. Black voters have consistently supported the Democratic presidential candidate in overwhelming numbers. In 1988, black voters bucked the trend among other traditionally Democratic groups and gave Dukakis less support than Mondale received in 1984. Black support for Dukakis was estimated at 86 percent in the CBS News/*New York Times* exit poll and 90 percent in the National Election Study (NES) survey. Abramson, Aldrich, and Rohde found that blacks gave Dukakis a large majority across the board—that is, regardless of differences in social class, income, or other politically significant social categories.[22] Approximately 12 percent of black voters supported Bush in 1988, an increase over Reagan's support in 1984 but only slightly more than the level of black support received by every Republican presidential candidate since Barry Goldwater in 1964. Turnout among both blacks and whites dropped in 1988, but it decreased more among blacks—down 11 percentage points from 1984. Some blacks reportedly stayed away from the polls because Jesse Jackson and his supporters felt slighted at the Democratic convention and because Jackson was not included on the Democratic ticket.

During the period following World War II, the Democratic party actively pursued civil rights reform despite considerable opposition from the party's southern wing. The consequences of this support were substantial: regional challenges were mounted to the national ticket in 1948 and 1968, and southern whites have converted to Republican allegiance in massive numbers, at least in presidential elections. More recently, the Republican party has made numerous attempts to win black support, especially as the party has continued to make inroads with other groups that traditionally have supported the Democratic party. In 1977 the Republican National Committee (RNC), under the direction of Bill Brock, attempted to expand the party's base by initiating a black outreach program. The firm of Wright-McNeill and Associates was awarded an initial $257,300 contract and, subsequently, more than $1 million over the following three years to run the committee's Black Community Involvement Division.[23] But, even in the 1980 and 1984 Reagan victories, black support for the Democratic party candidate remained the strongest of all of the traditional Democratic voting groups. President Bush and the RNC have sought to gain support among blacks through the appointment of African-Americans to jobs in the administration and in the party apparatus. As Pearl T. Robinson suggests, the success of the Republican party in securing the support of black voters will depend upon whether conservative Republican ideology can accommodate the economic interests of the black middle class and support for civil rights.[24] Otherwise, the weak performance of the GOP among blacks since 1964 is likely to continue.

In the last three presidential elections gender has become an important group difference. During the 1980s men were more likely to vote Republican than were women, a phenomenon labeled *the gender gap.* One explanation offered for the differences in voting behavior between women and men in 1980 was Reagan's "macho" stand on many issues. Throughout Reagan's term in office men consistently reported a higher presidential approval rating than women. Early in the 1988 campaign Dukakis led Bush among women by a margin of 43 percent to 35 percent. In the end, however, the Democratic nominee failed to convince voters, including women, that he could manage economic problems. [25] Once the campaign moved to issues other than the economy, thereby diminishing the salience of the economic vulnerability felt by women, Dukakis's advantage among women dwindled. As indicated in Table 4-4, women gave more support to Dukakis than did men, but both provided a majority for Bush. In contrast to 1984, however, when the difference between male and female support for Reagan was 9 percent, the gap in 1988 was only 4 percent.

Another potentially important difference may emerge in the next decade. Abramson, Aldrich, and Rohde's analysis of the NES survey and the CBS News/*New York Times* exit poll found clear behavioral differences among women in 1984 and 1988.[26] Married women were more likely to vote for Bush in 1988 than were single women. Similarly, married men were more likely to vote for Bush. These findings suggest that marital status may well become a factor in presidential elections in the 1990s—a *marriage gap.*

Candidates

The precise influence of candidates on the outcome of elections is difficult to determine. It is easier for observers to focus on the specific qualities of a particular candidate, such as Eisenhower's personal warmth, Kennedy's youth and Catholicism, and Johnson's expansive style, than it is to compare candidates systematically over a series of elections. [27]

Recognizing these limitations, scholars nonetheless have made overall comparisons of voters' reactions to candidates from 1952 through 1988. Each presidential election year, the University of Michigan Center for Political Studies asked people whether there was anything about the major candidates that would make them want to vote for or against that person. The total number of favorable and unfavorable comments were

Figure 4-1   Appeal of Presidential Candidates, 1952-1988

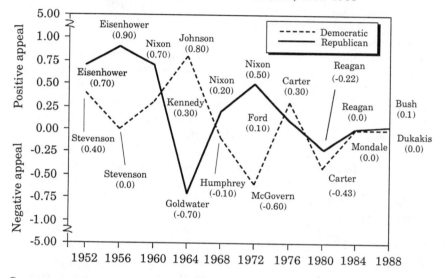

Sources: *American National Election Studies Data Sourcebook, 1952-1986* (Cambridge: Harvard University Press, 1987), table 2.42; 1988 data provided by the Center for Political Studies, University of Michigan.

Note: 5.00 and −5.00 are the greatest possible positive and negative scores because 5 is the maximum number of comments tabulated over the election series. The numbers in the figure are the candidates' composite scores.

tabulated for each candidate; the more numerous the favorable comments about a candidate, the more positive the score. The overall scores, positive and negative, of the Republican and Democratic party candidates can be compared with one another to determine the relative appeal of the nominees in each election year. (See Figure 4-1.)

Three significant findings are revealed in Figure 4-1. First, voters' attitudes toward the candidates are highly variable. The differences in candidate appeal were much less pronounced in 1952, 1960, 1968, and in the last four elections than they were in 1956, 1964, and 1972. Second, except for 1964, 1976, and, surprisingly, 1984, voters evaluated the Republican candidate more favorably than the Democratic candidate. It is somewhat surprising to find that voters evaluated Nixon more highly than Kennedy in 1960, and far more surprising to find that Ronald Reagan did not hold a substantial advantage over Mondale in 1984. This leads to the third finding: candidate appeal is generally declining with even the winning candidates in the last three elections having less appeal for voters than was true in previous contests. Both Reagan and Carter received negative scores in 1980, the only time this has occurred since the surveys began; the appeal of Reagan and Mondale was neutral in 1984; Bush eked out a bare preference over Dukakis in 1988.

Herbert Asher has suggested that the advantage often enjoyed by Republican candidates may stem from several factors. As the minority party, Republican hopes for success have hinged on nominating attractive candidates who have also been advantaged by the nature of the times. Democratic candidates in 1952 and 1968 were forced to defend their party's record on the Korean and Vietnam wars while hostilities had been concluded or had virtually disappeared when the Republicans were the incumbent party in 1956 and 1972.[28] In 1980, the Democratic administration was beset with the Iranian crisis and high inflation caused by rising oil prices. More difficult to explain is the general decline in candidate appeal. One possible explanation is the decline in the importance of parties as a structure that mediates voters' relations with politics: with fewer citizens having a strong relationship to the parties, voters may now scrutinize candidates more directly and evaluate them more harshly.[29]

The survey by the Michigan Center for Political Studies suggests that voters' attitudes toward candidates stem from diverse sources: the party affiliations of the candidates, their stands on issues, voters perceptions of how the candidates managed or would manage the government, and their personality and character traits. In order to focus more particularly on personal qualities alone, in its 1984 study the Michigan group asked respondents to evaluate Reagan and Mondale on twelve specific traits, which they combined into four summary measures: (1) leadership (commands respect, is inspiring, provides strong leadership); (2) competence (is hard-working, intelligent, and knowledgeable); (3) integrity (is decent, is moral, sets a good example); and (4) empathy (is compassionate, is kind, "really cares about people like you"). In contrast to some expectations, Reagan was favored over Mondale on just leadership and integrity. Mondale prevailed on competence and empathy. Only on leadership was the president's margin substantial.[30]

A 1988 election day poll asked voters about positive and negative characteristics of the candidates that influenced their vote. Bush's experience and competence were widely cited—fully 97 percent of the people who said that experience was important to them voted for the vice president. Voters who wanted a more caring president and one more likely to introduce change disproportionately supported Dukakis. On the negative side, voters citing Dukakis as too liberal went overwhelmingly for Bush, as did those who saw the Democrat as "too risky." Dukakis was supported disproportionately by voters who commented on candidates running a dirty campaign. Among voters who cited the vice-presidential candidates as a reason for their ticket choice, 86 percent supported

Dukakis. Their support contributed an estimated 7 percent of Dukakis's vote total.[31] Overall, Bush seems to have derived greater benefit from candidate characteristics but members of the Democratic ticket derived some advantages as well.

Issues, Events, and Presidential Performance

Michigan researchers in the 1950s suggested that issues influence a voter's choice only if three conditions are present.[32] First, the voter must be aware that an issue or a number of issues exist. Second, issues must be of some personal concern to the voter. Third, the voter must perceive that one party better represents his or her own thinking on the issues than the other party does.

When these three conditions were applied to U.S. voters in the 1952 and 1956 presidential elections, researchers found that these criteria existed for relatively few voters. About one-third of the respondents were not aware of *any* of the sixteen principal issues about which they were questioned. Even the two-thirds who were aware of one or more issues frequently were not personally concerned about them. Finally, a number of those who were aware and concerned about issues were not able to perceive differences between the two parties' positions on them. The conclusion of the analysis was that issues determined the choice of no more than one-third of the electorate. (The proportion who actually voted as they did because of the candidates' stances on issues could have been, and probably was, even less.)

Studies of political attitudes in the 1960s[33] and 1970s[34] show that issues had become more important to voters. In this period the number and types of issues of which voters were aware increased. Voters during the Eisenhower years had exhibited some interest in traditional domestic matters (welfare, labor-management relationships) and in a few foreign policy issues (the threat of communism, the atomic bomb); beginning with the 1964 election, however, voters' interests broadened to include concerns such as civil rights and Vietnam. Vietnam in particular remained a prominent consideration in the 1968 and 1972 contests and was joined by new matters such as crime, disorder, and juvenile delinquency (sometimes referred to collectively along with race problems as the "social issue").

The connection between voters' own attitudes on issues and their perceptions of where the parties stand on them has grown closer since the early 1960s. Gerald Pomper's analysis of voters' attitudes on issues from 1956 through 1972 shows that beginning with the 1964 presidential election attitudes became more aligned with partisan identification.[35]

Democrats were more likely to express the "liberal" position on economic, civil rights, and foreign policy issues than were Republicans. Also, voters in the 1960s perceived more clearly than voters in the 1950s the differences between the general approaches the two parties take on issues. During this decade a consensus developed that the Democratic party takes a liberal stand, and the Republican party, a conservative one. With these developments, the potential for voting on the basis of issues has increased in recent years. Correlations of voters' attitudes on issues with the way they voted in presidential elections in the 1960s and 1970s show that this potential for issue voting was converted into actuality.

Recent analyses also reveal a change in the way the American people think about politics. When voters in the 1950s were asked to indicate what they liked or disliked about the candidates and the parties, only about one in ten responded in ideological terms by linking personal attitudes on such matters to political issues or by mentioning such general concepts as "liberal" or "conservative" to describe differences between candidates and parties. Far more people made references to group benefits—such as Democrats helping the worker, Republicans helping business—or to the nature of the times, linking Democrats to foreign wars and Republicans to economic downturns and depressions. More than one-fifth of the voters in the 1950s gave replies that had no issue content at all, such as "I just like Democrats better than Republicans" or "Ike's my man." In the 1960s and early 1970s, however, the number of "ideologues" increased considerably, to as much as one-third of the electorate in 1972, for example.[36] Particularly noticeable was a movement away from the perception of politics primarily from the vantage point of group benefits and toward a broader view of issues and general political ideas.

In addition to this broadening of the conceptualization of politics, voters increasingly related political issues to one another as liberal or conservative. Studies of the electorate in the 1950s showed that voters were inconsistent in this respect; that is, people who took the "liberal" position that government should take an active role in providing welfare for the needy did not necessarily think it should assume a similar role in encouraging racial integration in the schools.[37] Nor were voters' attitudes on either of these domestic matters related to their opinions on the foreign policy issue of what stand the U.S. government should take toward the threat of communism in the world. Beginning with the 1964 election, however, voters' attitudes were more often correlated, showing consistency among domestic issues as well as between domestic and foreign issues.[38]

Many observers assumed that the decline in the social unrest produced by the U.S. involvement in Vietnam and the racial tensions of the late 1960s and early 1970s would mean a return to a less ideological and issue-related presidential election in 1976. A study of that election by political scientists Arthur Miller and Warren Miller indicates, however, that this did not occur.[39] Using the same criteria that were used to discern the development of ideological thinking in the earlier period—voters' liberal and conservative attitudes on issues, their perceptions of party differences on such matters, and a correlation among their attitudes on issues—Miller and Miller concluded that ideological thinking declined only slightly between 1972 and 1976. Economic matters were much more important to the electorate in 1976 than social or cultural issues; Democrats in particular were concerned over the rise in unemployment before the election. Because many people believed that the Democratic party would do a better job than the Republican party in dealing with unemployment, and because Carter emphasized economic issues over noneconomic ones in his campaign, many voters distinguished between the two parties and their respective candidates on economic grounds. As Miller and Miller stated, the results of the 1976 election ultimately turned on "incumbent performance [Ford's] versus partisan ideology [Democratic]."

Analysis of the 1980 election shows that economic issues were again more important to the electorate than were social and cultural issues, with inflation being the most important concern for many voters. Arthur Miller attributes President Carter's defeat primarily to voter dissatisfaction with his performance in office, particularly his inability to deal with the economy and, to a lesser extent, with a perceived decline in U.S. prestige in the world.[40] Warren Miller, too, sees dissatisfaction with the incumbent's performance in office as an important element in his defeat but also believes that many people voted for Reagan because they agreed with his conservative policies.[41] Other analysts also conclude that dissatisfaction with Carter's performance in office and evaluations of the policy stands of the two major candidates were reasons for Reagan's victory, but dissatisfaction with Carter was somewhat more important than ideological considerations.[42]

The economy was again on the minds of the U.S. electorate in 1984, although government spending had replaced inflation as the major source of concern, and Reagan's perceived success in coming to grips with this issue was a major reason for his overwhelming victory over Mondale. The voters were generally more satisfied with their family's financial situation and with national economic conditions than they were in 1980, and they credited President Reagan with bringing about those positive changes. In fact, there was an optimistic feeling about the general state of the nation, which again was attributed to the president's leadership. As in 1980, the performance of the incumbent significantly influenced the voting decisions of the electorate, but in 1984 the incumbent's performance was the primary reason for *retaining* rather than *removing* the president from office. Moreover, Mondale's vice presidency in the Carter administration allowed the electorate to compare the performance of the present administration with the previous one, rather than choosing between the incumbent and an unfamiliar and untested challenger.[43]

The electorate also evaluated the candidates' policy positions differently in the 1984 and the 1980 elections. In 1980, voters generally approved of Reagan's conservative policies, but in 1984, voters were actually closer to the liberal views of Mondale on desired policy *changes* than they were to the conservative views of the president (especially on cutting defense spending, increasing government aid to women, and avoiding involvement in Central America).[44] At the same time, the electorate was in general agreement with the *current* policies of the Reagan administration.[45] Between 1980 and 1984 it seems that the Reagan administration shifted government policies in the direction of increasing spending for defense and reducing domestic programs, and by 1984 the electorate had decided that the shift had gone far enough and should not be continued.

In 1988, economic concerns again preoccupied the electorate and were cited by 45 percent as the most important problem, but this represented a significant decline from 1976 when fully 76 percent had identified them as most important. For the first time since 1972, social issues regained prominence, being named by more than one-third; foreign and defense problems were identified as most important by only 10 percent of the electorate.[46] Budget deficits and government spending, drugs, and homelessness were the leading issues of public concern. Unlike the situation in 1984, however, a majority (56 percent) of respondents in the University of Michigan's National Election Study thought the government was doing a poor job in handling the most important problem, a level of negative evaluation approaching that suffered by the Carter administration in 1980, when 61 percent felt the government's performance was poor.[47] Unlike 1980, however, when the Republicans established themselves as a viable alternative, Democrats were unable to convince voters that they were likely to perform better. In fact, a majority of respondents (54 percent) felt there was no difference in how the parties would perform in handling the most important problem with the remainder dividing almost evenly between the two alternatives. Similarly, neither party gained an advantage from voter perceptions of their stands on the issues. Abramson, Aldrich, and Rohde found that "the average citizen was almost exactly halfway between the two candidate placements" on six issues, with the average respondent closer to Bush on three and closer to Dukakis on three.[48] Even though voters perceived a clear choice between the candidates and roughly half could place both themselves and the candidates on an issue scale, neither party benefited.

Two factors seem to account most fully for Bush's victory in 1988: evaluations of Reagan's performance and shifts in the partisan preferences of the electorate. At the time of the election, sixty percent of the electorate approved of the way Reagan was handling his job and Bush was regarded as the candidate most likely to continue the Reagan policies.[49] Voters, in other words, were moved by a subtle combination of retrospective and prospective evaluations—judgments about past performance and likely action on policy promises, respectively. In addition, gains made by Republicans in party identification among whites, approximately 10 points between 1982 and 1988, were probably critical: had Bush confronted the same electorate that Reagan did in 1980, his share of the popular vote would probably have been 5 percentage points less, placing him behind Dukakis with 47 percent of the popular vote.[50] This view of the outcome is not inconsistent with Gerald Pomper's "ideological interpretation" of the 1988 election, according to which George Bush served as "the champion of traditionalist values" now broadly associated with the Republican party.[51]

Many forces, therefore, influence voting behavior in presidential elections. Over the years the two major parties have developed different characteristics, and voters associate candidates with those characteristics. Democratic candidates have been favorably regarded for their party affiliation, their attitudes toward social groups, and their stands on domestic issues. In contrast, Republicans have benefited from their positions on foreign policy issues, their party philosophy, their perceived ability to manage the government, and a generally favorable assessment of them as candidates. Although the mix of these factors varies significantly from election to election, Republican victories in five of the last six presidential elections (two by landslides) and in seven of the last eleven has raised questions about the Democrats' capacity to compete successfully.

Consequences of Presidential Elections

The most immediate and most obvious consequence of a presidential election is the selection of a leader of the country for the next four years. As the following discussion indicates, presidential elections have other political effects as well.

139

Effect on the Political Party System

Campbell and his associates categorized presidential elections according to three clusters of electoral factors.[52] A *maintaining election* is one in which the long-term partisan orientation of the electorate keeps the traditional majority party in power. The majority party candidate wins primarily because the people vote according to their traditional party loyalties. Short-term forces, such as candidates and issues, are present, but instead of determining which party wins, they contribute to the size of the majority party's victory. When they favor the majority party, as they did in 1964 when Goldwater was the Republican nominee, the vote margin separating the two major candidates is larger than usual. If short-term forces are in balance, as they were in 1948, the vote division approximates the proportion of voters who identify with the two parties.

A *deviating election* occurs when short-term forces benefit the minority party and override the long-term partisan preferences of the electorate. An especially appealing candidate or an outstanding issue, event, or type of presidential performance allows the minority party candidate to win with the support of some majority party members, independents, and a good share of new voters. The electorate does not, however, change its basic party preferences. Examples of deviating elections are those of 1952, 1956, 1968, and 1972: they were won by the Republican candidates, Eisenhower and Nixon, but the commitment of many voters to the majority party—the Democrats—was unaltered.[53]

An election that brings about major political change is a *realigning election*. These elections entail a major realignment of electoral support among blocs of voters who switch their traditional party affiliation. An unusually large number of new voters may also enter the electoral arena and cast their ballots disproportionately for one party's candidate. Unlike the deviating election, the effects of the realigning election persist in the form of durable loyalties to the advantaged party. Political historians usually include five elections in the realigning category: 1800, 1828, 1860, 1896, and 1932.

Immediately after the 1980 election, many observers concluded that the decisive Reagan victory (51 percent of the popular vote to 41 percent for Carter), plus the unexpected Republican capture of the Senate and their gain of thirty-three seats in the House of Representatives, four governorships, and more than two hundred state legislative seats, meant that 1980 was a realigning election. Moreover, social groups that traditionally voted Democratic—including Catholics, blue-collar workers, and voters with no college education—cast their ballots for the Republican nominee, giving further credence to the contention that the liberal New

Deal era in U.S. politics was over and a new Republican majority had finally been formed.[54] When President Reagan embarked successfully on a series of major policy changes, and when by mid-1981 the percentage of voters declaring themselves to be Republicans equaled that of Democrats, some observers became even more convinced that a party realignment had taken place.

Subsequent events, however, indicated that the 1980 election was not a realigning one. As President Reagan began to have problems with the Congress and the economy took a downturn, the number of voters identifying with the Republican party declined, and those declaring themselves to be Democrats rose again until the gap between the two major parties approached its traditional 5-3 ratio. In the 1982 elections the Democrats picked up 26 seats in the House of Representatives, a net gain of 7 governorships, and some 160 additional seats in state legislatures, showing that many Democrats had not permanently deserted their traditional party.

Although we now have two additional presidential elections to provide perspective on a possible realignment, the situation remains unclear. The results of the 1984 presidential election, in which President Reagan captured 59 percent of the popular vote (compared with Mondale's 41 percent) and the electoral votes of forty-nine states (Mondale carried only his home state of Minnesota and the District of Columbia), suggested that 1984 was the long-awaited realigning election. Several developments were evident in the middle of the 1980s that one would expect to find if a realignment of significant magnitude were occurring: younger voters and newly registered ones tended to be Republicans; many traditional Democrats were deserting the party because they agreed more with the Republicans on issues such as economic growth and opportunity, the necessity of building up the national defense, and social concerns (prayer in the public school, abortion, busing); and the number of political independents appeared to have leveled off or even declined.[55]

Other developments of the mid-1980s, however, did *not* point in the direction of a realigning election. Although President Reagan won by a large margin in the 1984 election, the Republican party actually lost two seats in the Senate, and the fourteen seats it picked up in the House of Representatives did not compensate for the twenty-six it lost in the 1982 elections. Moreover, despite the presidential landslide, Democrats still controlled thirty-four of the nation's fifty governorships and both houses of the legislature in twenty-eight states, compared with eleven for the Republicans. In late 1985, a Gallup poll found that the Democrats were on the rise again; 40 percent of the American public identified with that party compared with 33 percent who said they were

Republicans.[56] Finally, in the 1986 congressional elections, the Democrats unexpectedly picked up eight seats in the Senate to regain control of that body by a 55-45 margin and added five seats in the House of Representatives.

Indications were similarly mixed after 1988. Bush's 7.7 percentage point margin of victory over Dukakis was smaller than Reagan's 9.7 percent margin over Carter in 1980 and far smaller than the 18.2 point victory over Mondale in 1984. "The victory was broad, but shallow," concludes Gerald Pomper; Bush won seven states by less than 5 percent and five more by margins of 5-10 percent. Moreover, the magnitude of Bush's win compares poorly with other Republican victories in the twentieth century.[57]

It was also the first time since 1960 that the party winning the presidency simultaneously lost seats in the House of Representatives (a loss of three placed the party balance at 260-175 in favor of the Democrats); the Republicans also lost one seat in the Senate (enabling the Democrats to regain a 55-45 margin) as well as one governorship. On the other hand, this was the third Republican victory in a row, the first time either party has achieved such success since 1952. Republican gains among white voters have been steady so that they now claim a majority of those declaring a partisan identification. Support is even stronger among young party identifiers.[58]

If the 1980, 1984, or 1988 election is compared with the previous realigning elections (1800, 1828, 1860, 1896, and 1932), some major differences appear. The new majority party that emerged in each of these five earlier elections captured not only the presidency but also both houses of Congress (not just the Senate). With the exception of the first instance (1800), the emerging party controlled the House of Representatives in the session preceding the key presidential election (the Republicans did not do that in 1978, 1982, or 1986). Moreover, two years after the presidential race, the new majority party maintained control of both houses of the Congress in what one writer calls "cementing" elections.[59] In contrast, the Republicans in 1982 failed to capture the House of Representatives, lost control of the Senate as well as seats in the House to the Democrats in 1986, and lost additional seats in 1990 in both the House (8) and Senate (1). Finally, voting participation generally increased in past realigning elections, but participation in the 1980 election declined from the 1976 contest. Despite major registration efforts of both parties in 1984, voter turnout rose by less than 1 percent. Participation resumed its decline in 1988, sinking to its lowest level in more than half a century.

What actually has occurred since the the late 1960s is what Kevin Phillips terms a "split-level" realignment.[60] The Republican party has become the dominant party in presidential elections, winning five of the last six contests, three of them (1972, 1980, and 1984) by substantial margins. Meanwhile, the Democrats are clearly the majority party in the House of Representatives (the Republicans last controlled that body in the 1953-1955 session). Since 1980 only the Senate can properly be termed a "two-party" institution.

Other analysts, such as Walter Dean Burnham, prefer to characterize the recent era as one of party "decomposition" or "dealignment." [61] Traditional loyalties of the American public to political parties have declined greatly, and therefore the party affiliation of candidates is no longer the principal factor in voting decisions, as it once was. Instead, short-term forces, such as the candidates themselves, issues, events, and incumbent performance, shape how people cast their ballots. As a result, voters switch their votes in presidential elections from one party's candidate to another and split their ballots for different party candidates running for separate offices in the same election. As Burnham explains, "Electoral disaggregation carried beyond a certain point would, after all, make critical realignment in the classical sense impossible." [62]

Everett Carl Ladd has suggested that contemporary developments do not represent an either/or situation; rather, the best description of the "post-New Deal system" is a combination of realignment and dealignment, with the latter a feature of the new partisan alignment.[63] In this view, we should not expect the next (or current) realignment to be just like the last one. Instead, the adjustments are likely to take different forms and manifest themselves in different ways.

At this writing (mid-1991), evidence is mounting that a fundamental change has taken place, even though a classic realignment has yet to appear. Although the Republicans have failed to capture control of both houses of Congress to complement their mastery of the presidency, they did manage to break the Democrats' stranglehold on the Senate during much of the 1980s. Moreover, the 1992 election may present Republicans with the best chance to achieve congressional majorities in recent memory. Retirement of incumbents and the creation of new districts following reapportionment may produce as many as one-hundred vacant seats in the House, seats for which incumbents will not enjoy their usual competitive advantage. Combined with George Bush's high approval ratings and recent Republican gains in party identification, this circumstance presents a golden opportunity for the minority party. It remains to be seen, however, whether voters will abandon the practice of splitting their tickets, which recently has produced divided-party government and heightened concern over the president's ability to lead his political party and the nation. Because presidential elections also affect the making of public policy in the U.S. political system, classic realignment could have enormous consequences for the nation.

Effect on Policy Making

The strongest influence voters in presidential elections can exercise on policy making in the United States is to send the winning candidate a clear message that identifies the issues they believe to be most important and that specifies the policies the candidate should follow in dealing with those issues. Such a message is called a *mandate*—a set of instructions to the new president on how to govern the nation. As Pomper suggests, the theory of the mandate "has been particularly associated with the Labour party of Great Britain, although it is supported in other nations as well." [64]

For many reasons presidential elections may not meet the requirements of a mandate. As discussed in preceding sections, issues often have little to do with a voter's choice of candidate. Some people vote according to traditional loyalties—they simply choose the candidate who represents the political party with which they identify. Others base their decision on the personal qualities of the competing presidential candidates; they vote for the candidate whose qualities they like or for the opponent of a candidate they dislike (the "lesser of two evils").

Even when voters choose a candidate because of issues, the election may not produce a mandate. Voters differ on the particular issues they are interested in: some may be concerned over the state of the domestic economy; others, the U.S. position in the world community. Thus, a candidate may garner a plurality of the votes cast by issue-conscious voters, without any single issue having majority support. Moreover, it is one thing for voters to be interested in an issue and quite another for them to be able to suggest specific policies to deal with it. Finally, individual policies favored by voters may conflict with one another. Voters may favor, for example, increased government expenditures for national defense but also support a tax cut and a balanced budget. Similarly, voters may wish to minimize taxes but hope to maintain the benefits derived from government programs, even when costs continue to increase. If it proves to be impossible to carry out all these policies simultaneously (as was true during Reagan's presidency), the electorate may provide no clear message on which policy has the highest priority.

The failure of a presidential election to produce a mandate does not mean that the election has no effect on the making of public policy in the United States. As one observer explains, elections are in effect a "retrospective" judgment on the performance of the incumbent. [65] When voters reelect the officeholder, they are showing their general satisfaction with the way the administration has been handling the principal issues facing the country. Voters may also use this evaluation of past performance to shape their expectations of a president's future performance.[66] In 1984, for example, people who voted for President Reagan approved of the way he had handled major problems (especially the economy) and assumed he would continue to handle those problems successfully in the next four years. Yet they gave little guidance on the specific policies the administration should follow, something that should not be surprising given the nature of that campaign. As discussed in a preceding section, on several major issues the electorate more often agreed with Mondale than with Reagan. Moreover, in the 1984 campaign the president made few specific promises about how he would address the major economic issue (the budget deficit), except to say that he would raise taxes only as a "last resort." Thus, a vote to keep a president in office is primarily a favorable judgment both on his past performance and on the prospects of achieving particular *outcomes* (such as a prosperous economy); it is not an assessment of the *means*, that is, the specific policies, necessary to reach those outcomes.

Retrospective voting may result in the ouster of an administration primarily because voters are so dissatisfied with its past performance and so pessimistic about its future performance that they are willing to give the opponent the opportunity to do a better job. Most observers agree that this happened in 1980. Beyond this message, however, the election usually offers the new president little guidance. The electorate indicates the overall *goal* that it wants the president to achieve but typically cannot specify the policies he should follow to reach that goal. In the 1968 election the voters did not instruct Richard Nixon to follow any particular course of action in extricating the nation from Vietnam, but they did give him the message that he should somehow reach that goal. The electoral message also may suggest that the new president should not continue to follow the policies of his predecessor on the issue. It may also indicate the *general direction* of the public policies the newly elected president should pursue. For example, Warren Miller believes that the 1980 presidential election not only constituted a negative assessment of the performance of President Carter in office but also expressed a general preference for more conservative policies on government spending, government services, and federal income taxes, among other matters. Miller makes it clear, however, that the election did not provide a mandate for President Reagan's specific positions on each issue.[67]

Aside from the question of what policy directions (if any) presidential elections offer successful candidates, presidents themselves frequently interpret the election results as a mandate to pursue the policies they favor. As presidential adviser George Reedy put it, "President Johnson and most of his close advisors interpreted the election result [the 1964 landslide victory of Johnson over Goldwater] as a mandate from the people not only to carry on the policies of the Johnson administration but any other policies that might come to mind." [68] The same tendency applies when the candidate of the party out of power wins an election. When Ronald Reagan assumed the presidency after his victory over Jimmy Carter in 1980, he claimed a mandate from the people to embark on a broad range of conservative policies, some of which—such as reduced rates of government expenditures on health, education, and environmental protection and opposition to the Equal Rights Amendment and abortion—ran counter to voters' preferences.

The indefinite guidance the electorate offers the winner of presidential elections gives the president great freedom in initiating public policies. In recent years new presidents often have sought to enact the pledges made in their party platforms.[69] Lyndon Johnson and Richard Nixon acted on more than half of the promises they made in campaign speeches in 1964 and 1968,[70] as did Dwight Eisenhower and John Kennedy on the promises they made in their 1952 and 1960 campaigns.[71] A positive relationship does exist, therefore, between what presidential candidates say they will do if elected and the policies they actually follow after they assume office, whether or not the electorate has supported them for that reason.

At the same time, U.S. presidents must strive to keep their policies in line with the preferences of the voters. If their new policies go further than their supporters intended, or if the favored policies do not succeed, presidents face the possibility of being removed from office at the next election. As political scientist V. O. Key points out, "Governments must worry, not about the meaning of past elections, but about their fate at future elections." This means that "the electorate can exert a prospective influence if not control" over government policy.[72]

The type of presidential election has some bearing on the policies enacted after the election. Maintaining elections not only keep the majority party in power but also typically result in the continuation of its policies, which have met the general approval of the electorate. Deviating elections provide the opportunity for some change in policies but not a radical departure from the past. The Eisenhower administration, for example, slowed down and modified some of the policies of previous Democratic administrations, but it did not try to repeal the New Deal. Realigning elections typically result in major changes in public policy. An analysis of statutes enacted from 1789 to 1968 shows that those passed in the period immediately following a realigning election departed most from policies of the past.[73]

The elections of 1984 and 1988 illustrate how the conduct of a campaign can contribute to or detract from an election's policy significance. As Thomas Weko and John Aldrich point out, the candidates' campaign strategies, in framing the choices that confront voters during an election, also shape the choices that confront members of Congress after the election.[74] Presidents who run a campaign devoid of issues will have difficulty framing a legislative agenda once in office, a fate that befell Ronald Reagan in his second term and George Bush in January 1989. In the latter case, the voters sent a blurred message on their preferences for the future; by locating themselves between the two candidates and identifying about evenly with their respective issue positions, the voters precluded simple interpretations. Moreover, the campaign further contributed to a mixed retrospective judgment: a majority of the electorate regarded the incumbent administration as doing a poor job on major problems, but the challenger was not viewed as likely to provide a significant improvement. Bush's victorious campaign emphasized areas in which the president's powers are limited—crime and punishment are principally state and local concerns. The clearest commitment Bush made in 1988 was to hold the line on taxes, a position he abandoned in 1990. Thus, waging a "framing" campaign can have advantages after the votes have been counted. Unless an agenda is spelled out during the campaign, the victor can make only minimal claims to having received a mandate. The problem is exacerbated when the electorate speaks with two voices, choosing a president from one party and a Congress dominated by the other, a condition faced by all Republican presidents since Eisenhower.

Notes

1. 238 U.S. 347 (1915).
2. 321 U.S. 649 (1944).
3. 295 U.S. 45 (1935).
4. In *Harper v. Virginia State Board of Elections*, 383 U.S. 663 (1966), the Supreme Court eliminated the payment of a poll tax as a requirement for voting in state elections by ruling that it violated the equal protection clause of the Fourteenth Amendment.
5. A major issue was whether voting rights violations should require actual proof of the "intent" to discriminate (as favored by the Reagan administration), or whether it was sufficient that an election law or procedure merely "result" in

discrimination (as favored by civil rights groups). Sen. Robert Dole (R-Kan.) led in developing an acceptable compromise on the issue.

6. Paul R. Abramson, John H. Aldrich, and David W. Rohde, *Change and Continuity in the 1980 Elections* (Washington, D.C.: CQ Press, 1982), chap. 4.

7. Angus Campbell, Philip Converse, Warren Miller, and Donald Stokes, *The American Voter*, abr. ed. (New York: Wiley, 1964).

8. Philip Converse, *The Dynamics of Party Support: Cohort-Analyzing Party Identification* (Beverly Hills: Sage, 1976), 34.

9. V. O. Key, *The Responsible Electorate: Rationality in Presidential Voting* (Cambridge, Mass.: Belknap Press, 1966).

10. Based on data provided by the University of Michigan Center for Political Studies.

11. Harold G. Stanley and Richard G. Niemi, *Vital Statistics in American Politics*, 2d ed. (Washington, D.C.: CQ Press, 1990), 132. One possible reason for the high percentage of ticket splitting between presidential and House races in 1980 was the presence of independent John Anderson in the presidential contest that year. In most states Anderson's supporters did not have the option of voting for an independent House candidate.

12. Norman Nie, Sidney Verba, and John Petrocik, *The Changing American Voter* (Cambridge, Mass.: Harvard University Press, 1979), chap. 4.

13. Campbell et al., *The American Voter*, 83-85.

14. Gerald Pomper, *Voter's Choice: Varieties of American Electoral Behavior* (New York: Dodd, Mead, 1975), chap. 2.

15. Nie, Verba, and Petrocik, *Changing American Voter*, 70-72.

16. Converse, *Dynamics of Party Support*, chap. 4.

17. For the 1940 election, Paul Lazarsfeld, Bernard Berelson, and Hazel Gaudt, *The People's Choice* (New York: Columbia University Press, 1944); for the 1948 election, Paul Lazarsfeld, Bernard Berelson, and William McPhee, *Voting* (Chicago: University of Chicago Press, 1954).

18. Gerald M. Pomper, "The Presidential Election," in *The Election of 1988: Reports and Interpretations*, ed. Gerald M. Pomper (Chatham, N.J.: Chatham House Publishers, 1989), 136.

19. Another group whose significance in national politics has increased greatly is white fundamentalist or evangelical Christians. This group has become solidly Republican and in 1988 comprised nearly as large a proportion of the voting population as blacks (9 percent vs. 10 percent). See poll results reported in Pomper, "The Presidential Election," 134.

20. Paul R. Abramson, John H. Aldrich, and David W. Rohde, *Change and Continuity in the 1988 Elections* (Washington, D.C.: CQ Press, 1990), 111. Also see polling data reported by Pomper, "Presidential Election," 136, indicating that Bush was favored over Dukakis among nonvoters by 50 percent to 34 percent.

21. It should be pointed out that one reason for the Reagan increases was the absence in 1984 of a third-party candidate, such as John Anderson, to drain off votes. This factor also contributed to Mondale's winning a greater percentage of votes than Carter did among several groups, although only that of white-collar workers exceeded 5 percent.

22. Abramson, Aldrich, and Rohde, *Change and Continuity in the 1988 Elections*, 122-123.

23. Pearl T. Robinson, "Whither the Future of Blacks in the Republican Party?" *Political Science Quarterly* 97:2 (Summer 1982), 217.
24. Ibid., 231.
25. Barbara G. Farah and Ethel Klein, "Public Opinion Trends," in *The Election of 1988: Reports and Interpretations,* ed. Gerald M. Pomper, 121-125.
26. Abramson, Aldrich, and Rohde, *Change and Continuity in the 1988 Elections,* 126.
27. Warren Miller and Teresa Levitin, *Leadership and Change: The New Politics and the American Electorate* (Cambridge, Mass.: Winthrop, 1976), 42.
28. Herbert Asher, *Presidential Elections and American Politics: Voters, Candidates and Campaigns since 1952* (Homewood, Ill.: Dorsey, 1976), chap. 5.
29. Martin P. Wattenberg, "From a Partisan to a Candidate-Centered Electorate," in *The New American Political System,* 2d version, ed. Anthony King (Washington, D.C.: AEI Press, 1990).
30. J. Merrill Shanks and Warren Miller, "Policy Direction and Performance Evaluation: Complementary Explanations of the Reagan Elections" (Paper delivered at the annual meeting of the American Political Science Association, New Orleans, August 29-September 1, 1985), 60, 69.
31. Pomper, "The Presidential Election," 143. The results of this CNN/*Los Angeles Times* poll can also be found in *National Journal,* November 12, 1988, 2854.
32. Campbell et al., *The American Voter,* chap. 7.
33. Pomper, *Voter's Choice.*
34. Nie, Verba, and Petrocik, *Changing American Voter.*
35. Pomper, *Voter's Choice,* chap. 8.
36. Nie, Verba, and Petrocik, *Changing American Voter,* chap. 7.
37. Philip Converse, "The Nature of Belief Systems in Mass Publics," in *Ideology and Discontent,* ed. David Apter (New York: Free Press, 1964).
38. Norman Nie and Kristi Anderson, "Mass Belief Systems Revisited: Political Change and Attitude Structure," *Journal of Politics* 36 (August 1974): 540-591.
39. Arthur Miller and Warren Miller, "Partisanship and Performance: Rational Choice in the 1976 Presidential Election" (Paper delivered at the annual meeting of the American Political Science Association, Washington, D.C., September 1-4, 1977).
40. Arthur Miller, "Policy and Performance Voting in the 1980 Election" (Paper delivered at the annual meeting of the American Political Science Association, New York, September 3-6, 1981).
41. Warren Miller, "Policy Directions and Presidential Leadership: Alternative Interpretations of the 1980 Presidential Election" (Paper delivered at the annual meeting of the American Political Science Association, New York, September 3-6, 1981).
42. Abramson, Aldrich, and Rohde, *Change and Continuity in the 1980 Elections.*
43. Martin Wattenberg, "The Hollow Realignment: Partisan Change in a Candidate-Centered Era" (Paper delivered at the annual meeting of the American Political Science Association, New Orleans, August 29-September 1, 1985).
44. Paul R. Abramson, John H. Aldrich, and David W. Rohde, *Change and Continuity in the 1984 Elections,* rev. ed. (Washington, D.C.: CQ Press, 1987), chap. 6.

45. Shanks and Miller, "Policy Direction and Performance Evaluation."
46. Abramson, Aldrich, and Rohde, *Change and Continuity in the 1988 Elections,* 157.
47. Ibid., 183-184.
48. Ibid., 161-162. Bush was closer to the median position identified by respondents on the issue scales of government spending and services, jobs and standard of living guarantees, and aid to minorities. Dukakis was closer on defense spending, health insurance, and the role of women. Respondents were almost precisely located at the midpoint between the candidates' perceived positions on relations with the Soviet Union.
49. Ibid., 193, 195. Gerald Pomper reads the results somewhat differently. As he reports, Bush received overwhelming support from those who wanted "to continue Reagan's policies," minimal support from those who wanted to "change these policies," and a comfortable majority (57 percent) among those who claimed that Reagan's policies had not influenced their vote. Pomper, "The Presidential Election," 140, 151 n. 19. The data he cites are from a CBS News/*New York Times* exit poll.
50. Abramson, Aldrich, and Rohde, *Change and Continuity in the 1988 Elections,* 222.
51. Pomper, "The Presidential Election," 144-150.
52. Campbell et al., *The American Voter,* chap. 16.
53. Analysts refer to an election following a deviating period as a *reinstating* one, because it reinstates the usual majority party. Examples are the 1960 and 1976 elections, when the Democrats returned to power after the two Eisenhower and the two Nixon victories. A reinstating election, therefore, is like a maintaining one in that long-term partisan factors determine the result.
54. See, for example, Kevin Phillips, *The Emerging Republican Majority* (New Rochelle, N.Y.: Arlington House, 1969).
55. Thomas Cavanaugh and James Sundquist, "The New Two-Party System," in *The New Direction in American Politics,* ed. John Chubb and Paul Peterson (Washington, D.C.: Brookings, 1985), chap. 2.
56. *The Gallup Report,* October-November 1985, 42-44.
57. Pomper, "The Presidential Election," 132.
58. Abramson, Aldrich, and Rohde, *Change and Continuity in the 1988 Elections,* 206-207. Among white identifiers 18-24 years of age, 65 percent were Republicans in 1988.
59. Wattenberg, "The Hollow Realignment," 4.
60. This term is used in Phillips's biweekly newsletter, *The American Political Report* (January 11, 1985), as cited in Abramson, Aldrich, and Rohde, *Change and Continuity in the 1984 Elections,* 287.
61. Walter Dean Burnham, *Critical Elections and the Mainsprings of American Politics* (New York: Norton, 1970), chap. 5.
62. Ibid., 91-92.
63. Everett Carl Ladd, "On Mandates, Realignments, and the 1984 Presidential Election," *Political Science Quarterly* 100:1 (Spring 1985); Ladd, "The 1988 Elections: Continuation of the Post-New Deal System," *Political Science Quarterly* 104:1 (Spring 1989). On the concept of realignment more generally see David G. Lawrence and Richard Fleisher, "Puzzles and Confusions: Political Realignment in the 1980s," *Political Science Quarterly* 102:1 (Spring 1987).

64. Gerald Pomper, with Susan Lederman, *Elections in America: Control and Influence in Democratic Politics,* 2d ed. (New York: Longman, 1980), 212.
65. V. O. Key, Jr., *The Responsible Electorate: Rationality in Presidential Voting* (Cambridge, Mass.: Belknap Press, 1966).
66. Anthony Downs, *An Economic Theory of Democracy* (New York: Harper and Row, 1957); and Morris Fiorina, *Retrospective Voting in American National Elections* (New Haven: Yale University Press, 1981).
67. Miller, "Policy Directions and Presidential Leadership."
68. George Reedy, *The Twilight of the Presidency* (New York: New American Library, 1970), 66.
69. Pomper, *Elections in America,* chap. 8.
70. Fred Grogan, "Candidate Promise and Presidential Performance" (Paper delivered at the annual meeting of the Midwest Political Science Association, Chicago, April 21-23, 1977).
71. Arnold John Muller, "Public Policy and the Presidential Election Process: A Study of Promise and Performance" (Ph.D. diss., University of Missouri-Columbia, 1986).
72. Key, *The Responsible Electorate,* 77.
73. Benjamin Ginsberg, "Elections and Public Policy," *American Political Science Review* 70 (March 1976): 41-49.
74. Thomas Weko and John H. Aldrich, "The Presidency and the Election Campaign: Framing the Choice in 1988," in *The Presidency and the Political System,* 3d ed., ed. Michael Nelson, (Washington, D.C.: CQ Press, 1990), 279.

Selected Readings

Campbell, Angus, Philip Converse, Warren Miller, and Donald Stokes. *The American Voter.* Abr. ed. New York: Wiley, 1964.
Key, V. O., Jr. *The Responsible Electorate: Rationality in Presidential Voting.* Cambridge, Mass.: Belknap Press, 1966.
Miller, Warren, and Teresa Levitin. *Leadership and Change: The New Politics and the American Electorate.* Cambridge, Mass.: Winthrop, 1976.
Nie, Norman, Sidney Verba, and John Petrocik. *The Changing American Voter.* Cambridge Mass.: Harvard University Press, 1979.
Pomper, Gerald, with Susan Lederman. *Elections in America: Control and Influence in Democratic Politics.* 2d ed. New York: Longman, 1980.

Summary and Assessment of Presidential Contests 5

Over time, numerous changes have been made in the way Americans choose their president. In some cases changes have been made through formal mechanisms (constitutional amendments and federal statutes); in others they have emerged through informal changes in party practices and public expectations. This final chapter reviews recent concerns about the presidential selection process and assesses several proposals for reform.

Although critics have focused on many different features of the present process, nearly all of them have sought ways of making the process more democratic or more effective. Although disagreement naturally exists over the definition of these criteria and how they relate to one another, a widely accepted concept of democracy underlies several of the important proposals for reform. According to this concept, any process that involves broader participation by the public is more democratic. There is less agreement about what would constitute greater effectiveness. For some, eliminating the possibility of having the system malfunction would make it more effective. For others, selecting candidates with the best chances of winning or those best qualified to serve as president would represent greater effectiveness. Unfortunately, reforms designed to enhance democracy do not necessarily improve effectiveness, however defined.

The chapter's first section focuses on the nomination stage of the presidential contest; the second section targets the general election stage.

The Nomination Process

As discussed in Chapter 1, parties have used a variety of means to select their candidate for the general election contest. Influence over the nomination shifted first from party leaders in Congress to local and state party figures, and finally to party and candidate supporters among the general public. These changes have made the selection process progressively more democratic in the sense that decisions have come to be made through ever broader participation. National conventions, developed as a means to aggregate local concerns and produce a nominee, continue to prevail today, although they have been significantly altered by the spread of presidential primaries. Although the public's role has been enhanced over time, its influence remains indirect; participants in primaries and caucuses determine the composition of the national convention, which officially names the presidential candidate.

The changes that occurred from the early days of the nation's history until the mid-1960s, a span of nearly two centuries, were gradual; those that have occurred since then have been abrupt. From 1968 to 1980, what political scientist Byron Shafer calls a "quiet revolution" took place in the process by which the parties (especially the Democrats) chose their presidential candidates.[1] Alterations in the rules of the game during those years transferred the choice of candidates from caucus-conventions dominated by elected and party officials to popular primaries in which an increasing number of rank-and-file voters choose delegates to the national convention, delegates pledged to support specific presidential candidates. In addition, the private financing of nomination campaigns by large contributors gave way to a system of government subsidies that match the donations of small donors. New political elites also emerged during this period of flux: political amateurs, mobilized to campaign for candidates, and members of the media replaced governors, senators, House members, and state party leaders as the most influential forces in the nomination of presidential candidates. Moreover, as Shafer points out, the new political elites within the Democratic party spoke for a white-collar electorate, in contrast to the older rank-and-file of blue-collar voters represented by the party professionals.[2]

No one is fully satisfied with the nomination process that has emerged. Several areas of continuing concern and several possible solutions are reviewed below.

Restoring Peer Review

The 1980s witnessed a partial, short-lived "counterrevolution" in nomination politics. Between 1980 and 1984, six states abandoned presidential primaries in favor of caucus-conventions. As a direct consequence, the proportion of Democratic convention delegates chosen in primaries fell from almost three-fourths to slightly more than half. These actions reflected a consensus that the democracy-enhancing reforms of the previous decade had gone too far. One of the major casualties was *peer review,* the opportunity for knowledgable politicians to assess the relative merits of contestants and select as the party's nominee the person most likely to win or best qualified to serve as president. Complementing the retreat from primaries, professionals were brought back into the nomination process in the form of superdelegates, who constituted one of seven delegates at the 1984 Democratic national convention. In the battle over the 1988 rules, a balance was struck: the professionals once again prevailed over the amateurs by winning an increase in the number of superdelegates attending the convention, but at the same time the Democrats returned to their previous reliance on primaries as the principal method for selecting 1988 convention delegates. Although an agreement reached in 1988 to reduce the number of superdelegates at the 1992 convention fell through, the spirit of participatory reform that arose following 1968 remains dominant in the Democratic party.

The result of this revolution, counterrevolution, and response—created over two decades of continual reform in the Democratic party—is a mixed nomination system. It selects delegates by both the primary and caucus-convention methods. Its participants include professionals representing blue-collar constituencies, such as organized labor, as well as amateurs who speak largely for white-collar constituents. The 1984 nomination process vividly reflected these differences: Mondale generally was favored by party professionals, Democratic loyalists, blue-collar workers, and older people; Hart was supported by amateurs, political independents, white-collar workers, and younger voters. With Hart's early departure from the 1988 race, Jesse Jackson remained the principal candidate of nonprofessionals but the battle lines within the party were less clearly drawn than in the past.

One of the unfortunate features of this ongoing internal dynamic has been the tendency for Democratic rules to be *candidate-driven*—adopted as a means to facilitate the chances of one candidate over another.[3] As a consequence, the Democrats have suffered even greater intraparty conflict than the selection process would ordinarily generate. With the emergence of relative stability after 1988, the party faithful hope that struggles over rules will become subordinate to finding ways to win general elections.

The mixed nomination system has a number of desirable features, notably its blend of political amateurs, who are primarily concerned with the candidates' stands on issues, and party professionals, who bring distinctive "peer" perspectives to bear on the candidates' ability to work effectively with the other officials with whom they will govern the nation.

Professionals are in a position to assess how successful candidates are likely to be in shaping compromises among the many increasingly assertive groups in U.S. society. Yet presidential primaries place a premium on candidates who possess the personality and communications skills needed to attract the support of rank-and-file voters, skills especially important for modern presidents, who find it increasingly necessary to pursue their goals by "going public" rather than through the traditional vehicle of bargaining.[4] The variegated nomination process may be especially important for the Democrats, the more heterogeneous party, for whom it is critical "to dampen conflict and resolve tensions among the elements of their coalition."[5]

Not all features of the mixed system are likely to prove permanently beneficial. Democrats, in creating and maintaining the system of superdelegates, may be playing with political fire. Making up just 16 percent of the convention delegates, these restored professionals can determine the party's nominee only if the convention reaches an impasse. At a deadlocked convention—one in which the nomination has *not* been decided by the time the party convenes and where a first-ballot nomination is unlikely—uncommitted superdelegates probably would play a critical role. Although such a deadlock has not occurred in either party since 1952, despite the presence of a larger pool of candidates to divide party preferences, a nominee chosen by an old-style "open convention" rather than "by the people" (as the process has operated recently) runs the risk of having the legitimacy of his or her candidacy called into question. Of the two major parties, the Democrats, with their system of superdelegates, are closer to that possibility. At its foundation, the nomination system remains one of *indirect* public participation even though the public's role has increased and has proved decisive since 1968. In running the risk of violating new public expectations, today's system is susceptible to a *nomination misfire* in much the same way as the electoral college is susceptible to a *general election misfire.*

The Schedule of Competition

The election calendar has been another source of continual dissatisfaction and adjustment. A recurrent complaint has been the privileged position of Iowa and New Hampshire, which are able to influence party decisions far more than their size would merit simply because they hold their caucus-convention and primary contests earlier than any of the other states. This special standing has been sanctioned by the Democratic party and is justified as giving lesser known, poorly financed competitors a chance to compete in the labor-intensive, small state contests. Although the electorates of both states are grossly unrepresentative of the nation and even of the parties, winners of the Iowa and New Hampshire contests receive a boost of media attention, the label of being a "winner," and the associated benefits in raising funds.

Several challenges have been mounted against the present calendar. In 1988, southern Democrats sought to enhance their own impact and hoped to boost the chances of moderate candidates by creating the first true *regional primary*. However, "Super Tuesday," the day in early March 1988 when twenty states concentrated in the South and Midwest held their state primaries or caucuses, proved far more important for the Republican contest, enabling George Bush virtually to sew up his party's nomination by burying his principal opponent, Robert Dole. The Democratic vote, in contrast, was divided three ways. A number of southern states have responded to this disappointment by reconsidering their commitment to a common date. Full-scale regional contests, long advocated by many critics of the presidential nomination process, may not appear quite so attractive after this first experiment, although states in the Pacific Northwest may arrange their own regional primary in 1992.

Throughout much of 1990, it looked as if California would move its primary to the first Tuesday in March to enhance the state's impact on the nomination. Democrats hoped the move would improve the chances of their national ticket in November as candidates in the nation's "megastate" undertook media campaigns to reach the heterogeneous California electorate. A side-effect of the shift would have been to offset the advantage enjoyed by unknown and less well-funded candidates in Iowa and New Hampshire. The first attempt at rescheduling failed when state legislators were unable to reach agreement on other issues allowed to appear on the 1992 primary ballot. More recently, California Democrats approved splitting their delegate-selection procedure into an early caucus-convention, at which one-third of the delegation would be chosen, and a later primary to select the remainder, but further changes may be considered up to the eve of the 1992 contest.

The final schedule of contests for 1992 will not be known until late in 1991; at that time candidates will adjust their strategies accordingly. (The 1992 schedule as it stood in September 1991 can be found in Appendix A.) Prospective candidates in both parties may reassess the accepted wisdom about how to win the nomination. Neither Richard Gephardt nor Robert Dole secured his party's nomination despite finishing first in Iowa, and there may be a reevaluation of the significance of early contests. The 1992 contest has been remarkably short of "early birds"—aspirants who "announced their candidacy by the end of February in the year preceding the national convention." [6] Each contest since 1972 has seen at least one such candidate, and three have gone on to garner the nomination (all Democrats). Yet by the end of February 1991 no such candidates had emerged. The first candidate to declare for the race, former senator Paul Tsongas (D-Mass.), did not do so until the last day of April. No others had declared by the end of August. Aspirants in both parties may have been scared off by the strong public approval ratings enjoyed by President Bush following the successful Persian Gulf conflict. But the inability of Gephardt and Dole to translate early victory into success may also have been important. In 1992 presidential hopefuls may find it essential to establish their political appeal in a broad range of states rather than concentrate on the two small ones that have dominated the early media coverage in the past. As the states continue to jockey for greater prominence, candidates will be obliged continually to reassess their competitive situation.

Campaign Financing

People seem content with the system of partial federal funding available to presidential contestants, but a new problem has emerged—insolvency. At the end of 1990, only $115 million remained in the fund used to support the presidential nomination campaign, to provide a convention subsidy, and to finance the general election. In 1988, sixteen candidates received a combined $67.5 million in matching funds, and total spending rose to $178 million, an increase of almost 35 percent over 1984. However, the percentage of taxpayers participating in the checkoff system has steadily declined from a high of 28.7 percent in 1980 to 19.9 percent in 1989. Moreover, because the payments to candidates are indexed for inflation but contributions are not, the matching-funds ceiling has steadily increased but the checkoff has remained at one dollar since it was introduced in 1976.

Several proposals have been developed to deal with the impending shortfall, projected to be most severe in 1996 but already dangerously close in 1992. One proposal for 1992 would set aside the funds needed to finance conventions (projected at $11 million each); and major-party nominees (projected at $55 million each); barely $15 million would remain for the primary election stage, a total that would disadvantage the Democrats far more than the Republicans since President Bush can expect little competition within his own party for the nomination.[7]

Of the many reforms introduced over the past quarter-century, we believe that the public-financing provisions possibly have been the most beneficial. The reforms, in essence, democratized campaign financing by providing public funds and encouraging broad-based contributions. The demise of this system would once again open the presidential race to the highest bidder and damage public trust. Thus, efforts to preserve the system are critical.

Media Coverage

Dissatisfaction persists over mass-media coverage of the nomination process. The media continue to concentrate on the "horse race" aspect of the campaign and devote little effort to providing in-depth information on the issues of the campaign or on the records of candidates in previous office. This is particularly bothersome to the many observers who believe that "the news media have assumed the parties' traditional function of assessing candidates and selecting issues" [8] as the contest has come to accentuate appeals for broad public support. Thus, in the view of some, "judgment by peers is yielding to an 'audition' by the media." [9] The contest has shifted "from smoke-filled rooms to rooms filled with the bright lights of ever-present television cameras." [10]

Evidence of the media's substantial influence may never have been greater than in the 1988 contest, from which two prominent Democratic contenders, Gary Hart and Joseph Biden, withdrew before the race began. Hart entered 1987 as the front-runner; Biden was carefully honing a message that he hoped would inspire a new generation of Democrats. Each soon confronted a storm of controversy over purported character flaws. Hart exacerbated his problems by challenging reporters to look into his personal life, but many questioned whether the press overstepped its role by staking out the candidate's private residence; Biden's problems were triggered when John Sasso, campaign manager for Michael Dukakis, provided the press with a videotape of public statements by Biden containing unattributed passages from the speeches of British Labour party leader Neal Kinnock. In each instance, the media-created controversy derailed the candidate's campaign.

Media coverage of the campaign can, however, be helpful, as illustrated by the recent proliferation of debates among the competing candidates, a development that was especially important for the Republicans in 1980 and the Democrats in 1984 and 1988. Such encounters enable the voters to judge the candidates' ability to think on their feet and to see how the participants handle common questions (in regular campaign speeches, the candidates frequently talk past one another). Michael Dukakis, for example, engaged in thirty-nine televised debates during the 1988 nomination contest.[11] While such encounters force candidates to take stands on many controversial issues, they may also help to sow the seeds of party discord in November and thereby prove to be counterproductive.

Summary of Recent Changes in the Nomination Process

Although the current nomination process is far from ideal (for example, most observers consider it too long), it has undergone substantial change, probably for the better. Moreover, there is little one can do about some of the remaining problems, such as the way the media in a free society choose to cover the campaign. Finally, as the recent record of the Democratic party demonstrates, there is real danger in constantly revising the rules of the game: unintended and unfortunate consequences can result from such changes.[12] Everyone has benefited from the hiatus over the last two elections in the quest for perfection in the presidential nomination process.

How effectively has the system functioned in selecting nominees? Are we finding candidates qualified to serve as president, and have recent changes in the selection process produced different kinds of nominees? John Aldrich argues that the nomination system established since 1968 has not changed the *kinds* of candidates who run but has changed *how* they run. Candidates are still drawn from the ranks of governors, senators, and vice presidents, as they have been historically.[13] As a group, these candidates are probably no more or less qualified than those who have pursued the office under the old rules. Looking at the pool of successful candidates, Richard Rose has compared American presidents to heads of government in three major European parliamentary systems. According to Rose, the system used to select the former "gives too much weight to learning to campaign, and too little to learning to govern." [14] In short, the selection process rewards persons possessing the skills needed to win election but not necessarily those needed to govern effectively. As a consequence, presidents customarily enter office knowing how to mobilize public support but have far less experience than their parliamentary counterparts in managing the party and the legislature and in overseeing national security and economic policy. Despite the many recent changes in the nomination process, this bias against extensive governmental experience persists, but one also needs to recognize that by rewarding campaign skills the process may produce presidents with greater ability to mount public appeals, a quality needed in the media age.[15]

One measure of campaign effectiveness is victory, and Democrats have been upset that their nominees have not gone on to become winners. A party suffering electoral defeats is naturally more inclined to seek additional changes in the selection process in hopes of finding the way to produce a winner, a pattern true of the Democrats over the past two decades. But it is worth noting that the Republicans, to a large degree, have had to conduct their nominations by the same rules as the Democrats and have been rewarded by an impressive string of victories. Thus, the Democrats' fascination with changing the process may be misdirected effort.

As the nomination process has become longer and more complex, support has grown for a simpler method of selecting party nominees. Sixty-five percent of the public favored holding a single, nationwide primary in 1988 that would completely bypass the traditional party conventions.[16] Such a plan offers the advantages of simplicity and direct-ness but would remove peer review altogether and weaken the mixed character of the present nomination process. Moving the selection of nominees fully into the hands of the public through a national primary might seem to be the next logical step in making the nomination process more democratic, but it would result in serious damage to the national party structures. Presidential nominating conventions have long func-tioned as the central mechanism for creating nationwide coalitions. Re-moving this *raison d'être,* we believe, would do irreparable harm to these already fragile structures. Moreover, part of the difficulty that modern presidents have faced in working with Congress probably stems from the fact that neither institution plays a role in the other's selection. Superdelegates—though they may pose certain risks and may appear to represent a step backwards in the democratization of the selection pro-cess—ultimately may contribute to greater cooperation between the exec-utive and legislative branches. Because we believe that strong parties and legislative-executive harmony are essential to democracy, we oppose the proposal for a national primary.

The General Election Process

Recent changes in the election of the president have not been as sweeping as the changes in the nomination process; however, two in particular have had a significant effect on the general election process. The first has to do with the financing of presidential contests; the second pertains to the increased use of candidate debates in the fall campaign.

Public Financing of Presidential Elections

The public financing of presidential elections has the advantages of equalizing the resources available to the two major party candidates and of sparing them the potential abuses associated with raising funds from large contributors. However, new, minor candidates (such as John Ander-son in 1980) must wait until after the election to determine whether they will receive any public subsidy (a person must win at least 5 percent of the popular vote to qualify), a requirement that makes it difficult for them to raise money when it is most needed—during the campaign itself. Some observers contend that the law should be changed to provide public funds for candidates who reach a certain level of support in the public opinion polls (such as 15 percent) at some designated time during the campaign.

Of greater concern has been the exploitation of two loopholes allowed under the present financing rules: *independent expenditures* and *soft-money contributions*. Under current campaign finance laws, groups and individuals are permitted to spend as much as they wish in behalf of or in opposition to a candidate. However, such efforts must be independent of the favored candidate's campaign. Over the past three presidential campaigns, independent expenditures have averaged more than $15 million, with efforts on behalf of Republican candidates far outdistancing those for Democrats. During the 1988 election, the tone of such efforts changed as the proportion of expenditures used to deliver negative messages surged: nearly 25 percent of 1988 expenditures were devoted to efforts targeted *against* candidates (including the notorious Willie Horton commercial), a five-fold increase over the previous two presidential elections.[17] Moreover, questions persist about whether such efforts are truly independent of the presidential campaigns.

Beyond the $46.1 million in public funds received by the Dukakis and Bush campaigns for the fall election and the $8.3 million that the parties were permitted to contribute to these efforts, each party raised and spent somewhere between $50 and $100 million in additional funds, commonly described as soft money.[18] These totals compare to estimates of $9 million in comparable funds raised by the Republicans and $4 million by the Democrats in 1980. Contributions to so-called "party building activities" are not subject to the annual limit of $25,000 on donations to federal candidates and committees. Thus, many of the contributions come in denominations of $100,000 or more, and, because many are made to state party organizations, they are nowhere reported. Such funds—used for buildings, equipment, staff salaries, and the development of computerized voting lists—were strategically coordinated with presidential campaign efforts during 1988.

We share the view of many observers that the trends in both independent expenditures and soft-money contributions are undesirable. Establishing a system of public financing for presidential elections was one of the few developments of the 1970s that succeeded in countering the growing cynicism and distrust of public officials. By failing to place limits on soft-money contributions and failing to enforce rigorous guidelines for independent expenditures, the Federal Election Commission may have placed these advances in jeopardy. It is essential that these developments be carefully tracked over the next election cycle and in the future.

Presidential Debates

On the whole, presidential debates have been a beneficial development in recent elections. Televised debates provide the public with direct exposure to the candidates and thereby stimulate interest among members of the electorate, particularly those less attentive to other campaign efforts. The encounters help to acquaint viewers with the candidates' views on a variety of political issues and enable the vast audience to reach conclusions on the participants' personal qualities. On the other hand, some observers feel that these events encourage the media as well as voters to focus on style more than substance, to wait breathlessly for a single slip of the tongue that might doom a campaign to failure, and to become fixated on the question of who won the contest as though it were a sporting event. The most severe critics suggest that "debate" is an inappropriate term for what usually amounts to little more than a joint press conference in which the two major party nominees mouth campaign slogans, a criticism widely applied to the meetings between Bush and Dukakis in 1988. Although we believe that even the most recent sessions were valuable, there are several ways to improve campaign debates.

First, the rules should allow for face-to-face exchanges between the candidates rather than restricting communication to members of the panel asking questions. Candidates and their advisers worry that direct exchanges might increase the chances of a blunder or allow the opponent to gain some advantage, but voters are most interested in observing the candidates and evaluating their relative merits, a task made easier by direct exchanges. Unfortunately, sponsorship by the present Commission on Presidential Debates—a creation of the Democratic and Republican parties—is likely to preclude more open interaction.

Second, we see no reason for limiting the panel of questioners to journalists; other knowledgeable persons, such as economists, political scientists, or public officials, if included, might help direct candidates' attention to substantive concerns. Again, candidates are likely to oppose such a change, as they are more accustomed to dealing with journalists and may fear the technical expertise of others. Alternatively, to facilitate interaction between the candidates, the panel might be replaced by a single moderator, as the League of Women Voters had urged in 1988.

Third, we believe that participation in the debates should be mandatory rather than optional. Presidents Johnson and Nixon refused to debate on the grounds that it might hurt their candidacies, but Gerald Ford established a precedent of incumbent participation that was followed by his successors (although Carter opted not to participate in the first 1980 debate, which took place between Ronald Reagan and John Anderson). Creation of the Commission on Presidential Debates was supposed to have resolved this issue, as both national parties endorsed the new structure, but Bush's delayed commitment in 1988 put the guarantee into question. Because the major purpose of presidential debates is to educate the electorate, and not to strengthen or weaken a particular candidacy, participation in the debates should be made a condition for the receipt of federal campaign funds.

Finally, we believe that a nonpartisan organization (such as the League of Women Voters, which sponsored the 1976, 1980, and 1984 presidential debates) or a truly public commission, rather than the present bipartisan commission, should sponsor the debates. On the positive side, under present conditions party sponsorship increases the likelihood that the debates will take place. The cost, however, is that each candidate's list of conditions is likely to be accepted, thereby preventing the encounters from reaching their full potential. Moreover, the bipartisan mechanism virtually ensures that major third-party candidates will be excluded from participating in the centerpiece of modern campaigns.

Electoral College Misfires

The most serious problem in electing the president continues to be a latent one. The electoral college was devised as a means of allowing knowledgeable elites in the states to choose a "continental" character for president, but this purpose was altered with the rise of political parties (see Chapter 1). The present system enables voters to register a nationwide verdict but suffers from several weaknesses and potential dangers. Many proposals have been made to reform the system. Most reformers have claimed that their changes would remove an undemocratic feature of the presidential selection process and make the process more effective.

The electoral college as it operates today violates important tenets of political equality central to our contemporary understanding of democracy. Presently, each citizen's vote does not count equally: the influence one has in the election of the president depends on the political situation in one's state. For the many Americans who support a losing candidate in their state, it is as though they had not voted at all, because under the general-ticket system all the electoral votes of a state go to the candidate who wins a plurality of its popular votes. Other citizens who live in populous, politically competitive states have a premium placed on their vote because they are in a position to affect how large blocs of electoral votes are cast.

Three possibilities for an electoral college misfire remain, although the Twelfth Amendment (ratified in 1804) removed an important loophole (see Chapter 3). The electoral college still does not ensure that the candidate who receives the most popular votes will win the presidency: John Quincy Adams in 1824, Rutherford B. Hayes in 1876, and Benjamin Harrison in 1888 went to the White House even though they trailed their respective political opponents, Andrew Jackson, Samuel Tilden, and Grover Cleveland in the total popular vote. In 1976 Jimmy Carter nearly became the first twentieth century victim of such an electoral college misfire: if some nine thousand voters in Hawaii and Ohio had shifted their ballots to President Ford, Ford would have edged out Carter 270-268.

If no candidate wins an electoral college majority, selection of the president will be thrown into the House of Representatives. This occurred in the elections of 1800, 1824, and 1876, and it has come dangerously close to being repeated several times over the past fifty years. In 1948 Harry S. Truman defeated Thomas Dewey by more than two million popular votes, but if just twelve thousand people in California and Ohio had voted for Dewey rather than Truman the election would have been decided by the House of Representatives. The same would have occurred in 1960 if some nine thousand people in Illinois and Missouri had voted for Richard Nixon instead of John F. Kennedy, and again in 1968 if approximately forty-two thousand people in Missouri, New Jersey, and Alaska had cast their ballots for Hubert Humphrey rather than President Nixon.[19] Permitting the House of Representatives, voting by states, to select the president of the United States is not consistent with the "one person, one vote" principle that has become a central tenet of modern American democracy.

The 1968 election also illustrates another danger of the electoral college system: an elector need not cast his or her ballot for the candidate who wins the plurality of votes in the elector's state. This problem of the *faithless elector* occurs occasionally (most recently in 1988 when one elector from West Virginia cast her presidential vote for Lloyd Bentsen rather than Michael Dukakis) and is not particularly dangerous when individual electors refuse to follow the result of their state's popular vote. But the possibility of widespread desertion from the popular choice is another matter. If the popular vote outcome had made it clear in 1968 that Nixon was unlikely to win a majority of the electoral votes in 1968, third-party candidate George Wallace would have been in a position to bargain with Nixon before the electoral college balloting took place.

Wallace could have asked his forty-five electors to cast their ballots for Nixon, which would have given Nixon enough electoral votes to gain victory.[20] (Wallace's forty-five electoral votes would have made little difference for Humphrey, who would not have had a majority even if he had carried the close contests in Missouri, New Jersey, and Alaska, but the Alabama governor could have tried to bargain with Humphrey by offering to influence southern members of the House of Representatives to choose Humphrey over Nixon.)

Proposals to Reform the Electoral College

Over the years, actual and potential problems have created a great deal of dissatisfaction with the electoral college. The sentiment for changing it has increased recently, particularly after the near misfires of 1948, 1960, 1968, and 1976. Although agreement on the need to change the electoral college is widespread, there is marked disagreement over what form that change should take. Five plans have been suggested as substitutes for the present system.

The *automatic plan,* designed to eliminate the possibility of "faithless electors," would make the least change in the present system. A state's electoral votes would automatically be cast for the popular-vote winner in that state. If no candidate received a majority of the electoral votes, a joint session of Congress would choose the winner. Each representative and senator would have one vote. Under the *district plan,* states would return to the method used early in the nation's history. This method, used for some time by Maine and recently adopted by Nebraska, awards one electoral vote to the presidential candidate who wins the plurality vote in each House district, with the remaining two electoral votes going to the statewide popular winner. If no candidate received a majority of the electoral votes, senators and representatives, sitting jointly and voting as individuals, would choose the president from the three candidates having the highest number of electoral votes. Members of Congress and private groups from rural areas have been the principal supporters of this plan which would, if adopted, shift attention to the most politically competitive congressional districts where the two major parties traditionally divide the vote 55 to 45 percent.

A third proposal, known as the *proportional plan,* would divide each state's electoral votes in proportion to the division of the popular vote in the state: a candidate receiving 60 percent of the popular vote would receive 60 percent of its electoral votes. A plan of this type was passed by the Senate in 1950 but not by the House. It would eliminate the present advantage enjoyed by the large states, which are able to throw all their electoral votes to one candidate. Proportional division of the electoral votes, if fairly evenly split between the two major candidates, increases the possibility that neither candidate would receive a majority; hence, there would be a greater likelihood that an election would enter the House for decision.[21] This possibility would be removed if the president were chosen through *direct popular election,* the fourth plan. In 1969 the House passed a constitutional amendment providing that the president (and vice president) be elected by a minimum of 40 percent of the popular vote and, if no candidate received so large a vote, that a runoff be held between the two leading contenders. The Senate failed to pass the amendment, however, despite the efforts of its major sponsor, Birch Bayh (D-Ind.). After Carter's narrow electoral college victory, Bayh introduced the same measure in 1977, but it failed to clear the Congress that year. No such proposal subsequently has been enacted.

Finally, a proposal advanced by the Twentieth Century Fund, a research group, is known as the *national bonus plan.*[22] It would award the nationwide popular winner 102 "bonus" votes (two for each state plus two for the District of Columbia), which would be added to the electoral votes received under the present state-by-state system. To win the election a candidate would have to receive a majority of 640, the new total number of electoral votes (the former total of 538 plus the 102 bonus votes). If no one received 321 electoral votes, a runoff would be held between the two front-runners. Thus, the proposal retains the electoral college system but ensures that the total electoral vote will better reflect the nationwide popular vote. It also allows the voters, rather than the House of Representatives, to make the final choice of the president if no candidate receives a majority of the electoral votes.

Conclusions

As we have argued, proposed reforms of the nominating and election processes share a general concern with extending democracy and enhancing effectiveness, despite disagreements over how to define and balance these goals. Americans now select the president through a *doubly indirect process:* the popular will is mediated by the convention delegates who select the party nominees and by the electors who determine the winner of the general election. Democracy, some argue, would be better served by removing these mediating elites through a system of national primaries or a direct popular election plan. Moreover, because each stage of the present process is susceptible to a misfire that might thwart the people's will, reform might also improve system effectiveness.

We remain unconvinced by these arguments.

Although misfires are possible in both stages of the process, the system has evolved over the past four decades so that first-ballot nominations have become routine. Over the past century electors have validated the outcome of the popular vote. It is possible, of course, that the selection process could break down during any election, a possibility that is of greater concern in the general election, where the danger of violating popular preferences has been more narrowly averted. Nonetheless, we remain unconvinced that any of the plans designed to replace the electoral college or the mixed nominating system will provide an optimal solution. None of the plans currently under consideration is foolproof. Moreover, their adoption would sacrifice an important quality provided by the present "flawed" system: continuity with the past. Despite their problems, the present nomination and election processes confer a degree of legitimacy upon their outcomes, something that may be lost in the process of change. The Democrats' experience in redesigning their delegate selection procedures is instructive in this regard. Advocates of reform might point out that the new "mixed system" represents a distinct improvement over its predecessor. On the other hand, opponents of reform can point to the disruption (often unintended) and loss of legitimacy occasioned by reform proposals advanced to favor or obstruct particular candidates. Although it leaves open the possibility of repeating a past failure, remaining true to the traditional system brings with it the strength of continuity.

We have consciously chosen a very conservative position on this issue. It is not that change must be avoided. Rather, we believe that change should be introduced only after cautious and thorough assessment of the probable consequences, unintended as well as intended. Our system of presidential selection is remarkably complex and has proved, over time, to be surprisingly responsive to new forces in American society. Adjustments have been made periodically and most have introduced welcome changes. We are confident that responsiveness will remain an important characteristic of the system. But continuity is a virtue as valuable as change.

Notes

1. Byron E. Shafer, *Quiet Revolution: The Struggle for the Democratic Party and the Shaping of the Post-Reform Politics* (New York: Russell Sage Foundation, 1983).

2. Ibid., 524.
3. James W. Ceaser, "Political Parties—Declining, Stabilizing, or Resurging?" in *The New American Political System,* 2d ed., ed. Anthony King (Washington, D.C.: AEI Press, 1990), 112.
4. Samuel Kernell, *Going Public: New Strategies of Presidential Leadership* (Washington, D.C.: CQ Press, 1986).
5. Ceaser, "Political Parties," 113-114.
6. *Congressional Quarterly Weekly Report,* February 28, 1987, 380.
7. *Congressional Quarterly Weekly Report,* March 2, 1991, 558-559.
8. Dom Bonafede, "Scoop or Snoop?," *National Journal,* November 5, 1988, 2793.
9. Wilson Carey McWilliams, "The Meaning of the Election," in *The Election of 1988,* ed. Gerald M. Pomper (Chatham, N.J.: Chatham House, 1989), 180.
10. Martin P. Wattenberg, "From a Partisan to a Candidate-Centered Electorate," in *The New American Political System,* ed. King, 140.
11. Ibid., 143.
12. A book dealing with such consequences is Nelson Polsby, *Consequences of Party Reform* (New York: Oxford University Press, 1983).
13. John Aldrich, "Presidential Selection: A Critical Review" (Paper presented at Presidency Research Conference, University of Pittsburgh, November 11-14, 1990). Also see John Aldrich, "Methods and Actors: The Relationship of Processes to Candidates," in *Presidential Selection,* ed. Alexander Heard and Michael Nelson (Durham, N.C.: Duke University Press, 1987).
14. Richard Rose, "Learning to Govern or Learning to Campaign?" in *Presidential Selection,* ed. Heard and Nelson, 73.
15. One might argue that George Bush could claim equal if not more extensive government experience than John Major, selected to succeed Margaret Thatcher as British Prime Minister in November 1990.
16. *Gallup Report,* March 1988, 9-11.
17. For 1988, a total of $14.13 million in independent expenditures was reported to the Federal Election Commission, with $10,054,000 favoring the Republican ticket and $568,000, the Democrats. Negative spending was $146,000 against the Republicans and $3,499,000 against the Democrats. *Statistical Abstract of the United States, 1990,* table no. 447 (Washington, D.C.: Government Printing Office, 1990).
18. *Congressional Quarterly Weekly Report,* December 17, 1988, 3526-3527; Carol Matlack, "Backdoor Spending," *National Journal,* October 8, 1988, 2516-2519.
19. In each of these elections, persons other than the two major party candidates received electoral votes. The losing candidates, Dewey, Nixon, and Humphrey, therefore could have carried the key states named in the text and still not have had a majority of the electoral votes.
20. Although Wallace actually earned forty-five electoral votes, he received forty-six because one elector in North Carolina (which went for Nixon) cast his vote for the Alabama governor. In 1960, 1972, and 1976, single electors in Oklahoma, Virginia, and Washington also cast their ballot for a candidate other than the one who received the popular-vote plurality in their state.
21. Most of the proportional plans have suggested lowering the winning electoral-vote requirement from a majority to 40 or even 35 percent to avoid the possibility of having the election go to the House. They have also proposed

that, if no candidate receives the requisite proportion of electoral votes, the two houses of Congress, meeting jointly and voting as individuals, should choose the president.

22. *Winner-Take-All: Report of the Twentieth Century Task Force on Reform of the Presidential Election Process* (New York: Holmes and Meier, 1978), 4-6.

Selected Readings

Best, Judith. *The Case Against the Direct Election of the President: A Defense of the Electoral College.* Ithaca, N.Y.: Cornell University Press, 1975.

Diamond, Martin. *The Electoral College and the American Idea of Democracy.* Washington, D.C.: American Enterprise Institute, 1977.

Lawrence Longley and Alan Braun. *The Politics of Electoral College Reform.* New Haven, Conn.: Yale University Press, 1975.

Peirce, Neal. *The People's President: The Electoral College in American History and the Direct-Vote Alternative.* New York: Simon and Schuster, 1968.

Appendixes:
Guide to the 1992
Presidential Race

Schedule of 1992 Presidential Primaries and Caucuses ⎯⎯A

To a far greater degree than usual, state and national committees delayed decisions about the schedule of competition for 1992. Without the likelihood of a challenge to President Bush, some Republican state committees felt little compulsion to make delegate selection decisions. Democrats lacked candidates for much of the preceding year and waited until late September 1991 to settle disputes among several states over their position in the calendar.

Date	State	Procedure	Parties participating
Feb. 10	Iowa	Caucus	Dem./Rep.
Feb. 18	New Hampshire	Primary	Dem./Rep.
Feb. 23	Maine	Caucus	Dem.
Feb. 25	S. Dakota	Primary	Dem./Rep.
March 3	Colorado	Primary	Dem./Rep.
	Idaho	Caucus	Dem.
	Maryland	Primary	Dem./Rep.
	Minnesota	Caucus	Dem./Rep.
	Rhode Island	Caucus	Dem./Rep.
	Washington	Caucus	Dem.
March 5	N. Dakota	Caucus	Dem.
March 7	Arizona	Caucus	Dem.
	S. Carolina	Primary	Dem.
	Wyoming	Caucus	Dem.
March 8	Nevada	Caucus	Dem.
March 10	Delaware	Caucus	Dem.
	Florida	Primary	Dem./Rep.

	Georgia	Primary	Dem./Rep.
	Hawaii	Caucus	Dem.
	Louisiana	Primary	Dem./Rep.
	Massachusetts	Primary	Dem./Rep.
	Mississippi	Primary	Dem./Rep.
	Missouri	Caucus	Dem.
	Oklahoma	Primary	Dem./Rep.
	Tennessee	Primary	Dem./Rep.
	Texas	Primary	Dem./Rep.
March 15	Puerto Rico*	Primary	Dem./Rep.
March 17	Illinois	Primary	Dem./Rep.
	Michigan	Primary	Dem./Rep.
March 24	Connecticut	Primary	Dem./Rep.
March 28	Virgin Islands	Caucus	Dem./Rep.
March 31	Vermont	Caucus	Dem.
April 2	Alaska	Caucus	Dem.
April 7	Kansas**	Primary	Dem./Rep.
	New York	Primary	Dem./Rep.
	Wisconsin	Primary	Dem./Rep.
April 11	Virginia	Caucus	Dem.
April 20	Utah	Caucus	Dem./Rep.
April 28	Pennsylvania	Primary	Dem./Rep.
May 5	Dist. of Columbia	Primary	Dem./Rep.
	Indiana	Primary	Dem./Rep.
	N. Carolina	Primary	Dem./Rep.
	Ohio	Primary	Dem./Rep.
May 12	Nebraska	Primary	Dem./Rep.
	West Virginia	Primary	Dem./Rep.
May 19	Oregon	Primary	Dem./Rep.
May 26	Arkansas	Primary	Dem./Rep.
	Idaho	Primary	Rep.
	Kentucky	Primary	Dem./Rep.
June 2	Alabama	Primary	Dem./Rep.
	California	Primary	Dem./Rep.
	Montana	Primary	Dem./Rep.
	New Jersey	Primary	Dem./Rep.
	New Mexico	Primary	Dem./Rep.

*Changes to the schedule and format still possible.
**If the Kansas legislature fails to appropriate funds for the April 7 primary, then a Democratic caucus will be held on March 21.

Profiles of Prospective Democratic Candidates in the 1992 Presidential Contest ____ B

Edmund G. (Jerry) Brown, lawyer, former governor of California

Unsuccessful in two previous bids for the presidency (1976 and 1980), Brown dropped from national attention after losing a race for the U.S. Senate in 1982. During his two terms as governor of California (1975-1983) Brown's popularity initially surged but later declined precipitously. He is best remembered for a distinctive—some say flaky—lifestyle and an "antipolitics" approach to office that is illustrated by his shunning the use of the governor's mansion and official limousine. Despite being the son of a liberal governor who had been defeated by Ronald Reagan in the 1960s, Brown expressed doubt about big government and emphasized the need for policies to adjust to environmental and economic limits. His late effort to stop Jimmy Carter's drive for the nomination in 1976 produced three primary victories, including California, but his effort in 1980 was far less successful. After losing the Senate contest by a wide margin, Brown traveled extensively and returned to politics as chairman of the California Democratic party. His decision to enter the presidential contest came as a surprise since it followed months of preparation for California's 1992 Senate election.

Bill Clinton, lawyer, governor of Arkansas

Clinton has occupied the governor's mansion for all but two years since his initial victory in 1978 (his bid for reelection failed in 1980). After flirting with a possible presidential candidacy in 1988, he settled for a role as sole nominator of Michael Dukakis at the convention, delivering an oration distinguished only by its length. With degrees from the Georgetown University School of Foreign Service and the Yale law school, as well as a Rhodes scholarship to his credit, Clinton brought impressive credentials to a hard-charging political career. Now serving as chairman of the centrist and conservative Democratic Leadership Council, Clinton has focused on domestic issues. His candidacy would appeal to southern and borderstate voters, who have abandoned the Democrats in all but one of the last six presidential elections. But the South's collective clout in the 1992 nomination campaign—and Clinton's prospects—were reduced when several states chose to abandon a common primary date. His reelection to the governorship in 1990 means that an unsuccessful bid in 1992 would not mean leaving politics.

Mario Cuomo, lawyer, governor of New York

Perhaps the field's most eloquent speaker, Cuomo has also been its most enigmatic noncandidate. Although the press constantly speculates on his intentions, Cuomo has persistently avoided running. He became a hero of his party's liberal wing with a stirring defense of traditional Democratic programs and values in the 1984 convention keynote address. However, as governor of a state that has recently confronted severe fiscal problems, Cuomo has initiated major cuts in a wide array of social programs including education and health care. After several unsuccessful attempts in the 1970s, Cuomo became governor of the nation's second largest state in 1982. He won reelection by a record margin in 1986 and again, but less decisively, in 1990. Cuomo would be favored to win in New Hampshire and would probably outdistance all other contenders in raising campaign funds, giving him an advantage in the numerous primaries scheduled for the first half of March.

Tom Harkin, lawyer, U.S. senator from Iowa

Although some observers thought his 1990 Senate reelection bid was in trouble, Harkin won by 54 to 46 percent and became the first Iowa Democrat to secure consecutive Senate terms. Because of this recent success, he would be an odds-on favorite to win in Iowa's February 1992 caucuses. This might discourage other candidates from campaigning there. Harkin openly endorses a traditional progressive agenda for the party and the nation. During his ten years in the House and seven years in the Senate he has generally been rated a liberal, especially on foreign policy. Strongly supported by organized labor in his reelection bid, Harkin (whose father was a coal miner) would appeal most strongly to traditional elements of the Democratic coalition, although his populist style could carry broader appeal. The key questions surrounding Harkin's candidacy are his prospects for success beyond Iowa and whether another liberal candidate (such as Cuomo or Jackson) might prove more appealing.

Jesse Jackson, minister, civil rights activist, U.S. senator (nonvoting) from the District of Columbia

The only 1988 Democratic candidate not to have held elected public office, Jackson nonetheless led briefly in the polls and finished second to Michael Dukakis. Jackson considers himself the leader of the "coalition of the rejected," which includes blacks, the unemployed, and failing farmers. The most liberal of the candidates, he is highly critical of the moderate wing of the Democratic party. He did well in 1988 among black voters and was given an opportunity to bask in the political spotlight during the Democrats' convention. He has sought to develop a political base in Washington, D.C. Criticized in the past for not holding public office, Jackson now serves as the District of Columbia's nonvoting member of the U.S. Senate (he was elected in 1990). He has made the fight against drugs, care for the homeless, and D.C. statehood his major priorities. He gained national exposure as host of a syndicated television talk show and reportedly is exploring a return to television.

Robert Kerrey, restaurateur, U.S. senator from Nebraska

Competing for office as a relative newcomer would not be new for Robert Kerrey. Kerrey entered politics as an unknown challenger for the Nebraska governorship when he narrowly won election in 1982. He left office after a single term with high public approval ratings which were parlayed into a Senate victory in 1988. As a first-term senator from a sparsely populated midwest state, Kerrey achieved his greatest national recognition during the winter of 1990 when he vocally opposed the use of military force to oust Iraq from Kuwait. A veteran of the Vietnam War who lost a leg and won the Congressional Medal of Honor, Kerrey has since suggested that his wartime experience may have excessively influenced his judgment. Democratic party activists could be attracted by his liberal voting record and antiwar position, especially in neighboring Iowa, but Kerrey has already felt the heat of Republican criticism during several sharp exchanges following the brief war. Kerrey has demonstrated the ability to win votes from a Republican-leaning electorate and offers a fresh face to Democrats, but he is untested on the national scene and may be a more promising candidate for the future.

Paul Tsongas, lawyer, former U.S. senator from Massachusetts

After his stunning departure from the Senate in 1984 to wage a reportedly successful battle against cancer, Tsongas has returned to the national scene as an unlikely candidate. As a liberal Greek from Massachusetts campaigning on the need for a new national industrial policy to revitalize America's economic base, Tsongas will remind many of Michael Dukakis in 1988. On April 30, 1991, he became the first candidate for the 1992 contest and had raised more than $500,000 by the end of June. His campaign is built upon the need to restore America's competitiveness in the international marketplace. Tsongas proposes a targeted cut in the capital-gains tax, tax credits to stimulate research and development, and relaxed antitrust laws. One can also expect to hear more of the doubts about liberalism that Tsongas first voiced in 1980, a theme that may be especially appropriate for a party reexamining its purpose. Now 50, Tsongas combines experience in local government and service in the Peace Corps with ten years in the U.S. Congress, six as a senator. His sabbatical from national politics gave him the opportunity to reflect on national as well as personal priorities, but he must be considered a long shot to capture the nomination.

L. Douglas Wilder, lawyer, governor of Virginia

The grandson of a slave, Wilder became the first elected black governor in the nation's history when he was inaugurated in 1990. Limited by statute to serving a single term as governor, there had been considerable speculation that Wilder would seek a place on the national ticket. As demonstrated by his success in winning statewide elections, Wilder would be expected to attract broader support than Jesse Jackson. His highly visible 1989 stand in favor of abortion rights is said to have gained him broad appeal among white voters. As governor, he has urged fiscal responsibility, endorsing an austerity budget of program cuts and public employee layoffs to deal with a $2 billion state deficit and refusing to raise taxes. Wilder authorized an exploratory committee to raise funds for his 1992 campaign, but his candidacy was hurt by his political feud with Virginia's other presidential hopeful, Sen. Charles S. Robb. The careers of both men were damaged by the series of charges, countercharges, and revelations given extensive coverage by the national media.

Results of 1988
Presidential Primaries _____ C

Table C-1 Democratic Presidential Primary Returns, 1988

State (date)	Turnout	Dukakis	Jackson	Gore	Gephardt	Simon	Others	Uncommitted
New Hampshire (2/16)	123,360	35.8%	7.8%	6.8%	19.8%	17.1%	12.8%	—
South Dakota (2/23)	71,606	31.2	5.4	8.4	43.5	5.6	5.9	—
Vermont (3/1)	50,791	55.8	25.7	—	7.7	5.2	5.6	0.4%
Alabama (3/8)	405,642	7.7	43.6	37.4	7.4	0.8	2.7	7.1
Arkansas (3/8)	497,544	18.9	17.1	37.3	12.0	1.8	5.7	6.2
Florida (3/8)	1,273,298	40.9	20.0	12.7	14.4	2.2	3.7	1.2
Georgia (3/8)	622,752	15.6	39.8	32.4	6.7	1.3	3.0	3.3
Kentucky (3/8)	318,721	18.6	15.6	45.8	9.1	2.9	4.6	—
Louisiana (3/8)	624,450	15.3	35.5	28.0	10.6	0.8	9.7	2.8
Maryland (3/8)	531,335	45.6	28.7	8.7	7.9	3.1	3.1	1.7
Massachusetts (3/8)	713,447	58.6	18.7	4.4	10.2	3.7	2.7	3.5
Mississippi (3/8)	361,811	8.3	44.4	33.3	5.4	0.6	4.6	1.3
Missouri (3/8)	527,805	11.6	20.2	2.8	57.8	4.1	2.3	2.4
North Carolina (3/8)	679,958	20.3	33.0	34.7	5.5	1.2	3.0	—
Oklahoma (3/8)	392,727	16.9	13.3	41.4	21.0	1.8	5.6	1.7
Rhode Island (3/8)	49,029	69.8	15.2	4.0	4.1	2.8	2.5	0.5
Tennessee (3/8)	576,314	3.4	20.7	72.3	1.5	0.5	1.1	—
Texas (3/8)	1,766,904	32.8	24.5	20.2	13.6	2.0	7.0	1.7
Virginia (3/8)	364,899	22.0	45.1	22.3	4.4	1.9	2.6	—
Illinois (3/15)	1,500,928	16.3	32.3	5.1	2.3	42.3	1.6	—
Puerto Rico (3/20)	356,178	22.9	29.0	14.4	3.0	18.2	12.5	0.8
Connecticut (3/29)	241,395	58.1	28.3	7.7	0.4	1.3	3.4	0.3
Wisconsin (4/5)	1,014,782	47.6	28.2	17.4	0.8	4.8	1.0	0.7
New York (4/19)	1,575,186	50.9	37.1	10.0	0.2	1.1	0.1	—
Pennsylvania (4/26)	1,507,690	66.5	27.3	3.0	0.5	0.6	2.2	—
District of Columbia (5/3)	86,052	17.9	80.0	0.8	0.3	0.9	0.1	—
Indiana (5/3)	645,708	69.6	22.5	3.4	2.6	1.9	—	—

Ohio (5/3)	1,376,135	62.7	27.5	2.2	—	1.1	6.6	—
Nebraska (5/10)	169,008	62.9	25.7	1.5	2.9	1.2	2.9	2.8%
West Virginia (5/10)	322,148	78.9	14.0	3.6	—	0.7	2.8	—
Oregon (5/17)	388,932	56.8	38.1	1.4	1.7	1.2	0.7	—
Idaho (5/24)	51,370	73.4	15.7	3.7	—	2.7	—	4.5
California (6/7)	3,089,164	60.8	35.2	1.8	—	1.4	0.8	—
Montana (6/7)	120,962	68.7	22.1	1.8	2.8	1.3	—	3.2
New Jersey (6/7)	640,479	63.2	32.9	2.8	—	—	1.1	—
New Mexico (6/7)	188,610	61.0	28.1	2.5	—	1.5	5.2	1.7
North Dakota (6/14)	3,405	84.9	15.1	—	—	—	—	—
Total	23,230,525	42.4	29.1	13.7	6.0	4.7	3.1	1.0

Note: "—" indicates that the candidate or the uncommitted line was not listed on the ballot. No Democratic candidates filed to appear on the ballot for the June 14 North Dakota primary; write-in votes only. Four states have both caucus and primary results (see also Table 3-5, this volume): Idaho, North Dakota, and Vermont held nonbinding primaries and selected convention delegates through caucuses; Texas selected delegates through caucuses, but those delegates were bound to reflect voter preferences as revealed in the primary vote.

Source: *Congressional Quarterly Weekly Report* (1988), 1894, 1950.

Table C-2 Republican Presidential Primary Returns, 1988

State (date)	Turnout	Bush	Dole	Robertson	Kemp	Others	Uncommitted
New Hampshire (2/16)	157,625	37.6%	28.4%	9.4%	12.8%	11.8%	—
South Dakota (2/23)	93,405	18.6	55.2	19.6	4.6	0.6	1.3%
Vermont (3/1)	47,832	49.3	39.0	5.1	3.9	2.7	—
South Carolina (3/5)	195,292	48.5	20.6	19.1	11.5	0.3	—
Alabama (3/8)	213,515	64.5	16.3	13.9	4.9	0.3	—
Arkansas (3/8)	68,305	47.0	25.9	18.9	5.1	1.0	2.1
Florida (3/8)	901,222	62.1	21.2	10.6	4.6	1.4	—
Georgia (3/8)	400,928	53.8	23.6	16.3	5.8	0.5	—
Kentucky (3/8)	121,402	59.3	23.0	11.1	3.3	1.4	1.8
Louisiana (3/8)	144,781	57.8	17.7	18.2	5.3	1.0	—
Maryland (3/8)	200,754	53.3	32.4	6.4	5.9	2.0	—
Massachusetts (3/8)	241,181	58.5	26.3	4.5	7.0	2.3	1.4
Mississippi (3/8)	158,872	66.0	16.9	13.5	3.4	0.2	—
Missouri (3/8)	400,300	42.2	41.1	11.2	3.5	0.7	1.4
North Carolina (3/8)	273,801	45.4	39.1	9.8	4.1	0.5	1.0
Oklahoma (3/8)	208,938	37.4	34.9	21.1	5.5	1.0	—
Rhode Island (3/8)	16,035	64.9	22.6	5.7	4.9	0.8	1.1
Tennessee (3/8)	254,252	60.0	21.6	12.6	4.3	0.6	0.9
Texas (3/8)	1,014,956	63.9	13.9	15.3	5.0	0.7	1.2
Virginia (3/8)	234,142	53.3	26.0	13.7	4.6	0.8	1.6
Illinois (3/15)	858,256	54.7	36.0	6.8	1.5	1.0	—
Puerto Rico (3/20)	3,973	97.1	2.7	0.1	—	0.1	—
Connecticut (3/29)	104,171	70.6	20.2	3.1	3.1	—	3.1
Wisconsin (4/5)	359,294	82.2	7.9	6.9	1.4	1.0	0.7
Pennsylvania (4/26)	870,549	79.0	11.9	9.1	—	—	—
District of Columbia (5/3)	6,720	87.6	7.0	4.0	—	1.4	—
Indiana (5/3)	437,655	80.4	9.8	6.6	3.3	—	—

State	Votes						
Ohio (5/3)	794,904	81.0	11.9	7.1	—	—	—
Nebraska (5/10)	204,049	68.0	22.3	5.1	4.1	0.5	—
West Virginia (5/10)	143,140	77.3	10.9	7.3	2.7	1.8	—
Oregon (5/17)	274,451	72.9	17.9	7.7	—	1.5	—
Idaho (5/24)	68,275	81.2	—	8.6	—	—	10.2
California (6/7)	2,240,387	82.9	12.9	4.2	—	—	—
Montana (6/7)	86,380	73.0	19.4	—	—	—	7.5
New Jersey (6/7)	241,033	100.0	—	—	—	—	—
New Mexico (6/7)	88,744	78.2	10.5	6.0	—	2.4	2.9
North Dakota (6/14)	39,434	94.0	—	—	—	6.0	—
Total	12,169,003	67.9	19.2	9.0	2.7	0.7	0.5

Note: "—" indicates that the candidate or uncommitted line was not listed on the ballot. Montana, Vermont, and Virginia held nonbinding primaries but selected convention delegates through caucuses. Republicans did not hold a preference vote in New York; the April 19 primary was for election of delegates only.

Source: *Congressional Quarterly Weekly Report* (1988), 2254.

Results of Presidential Contests, 1932-1988 — D

Year	Republican nominee (in *italics*) and other major candidates	Democratic nominee (in *italics*) and other major candidates	Election winner	Division of popular vote[a] (percent)	Division of electoral vote[b]
1932	*Herbert Hoover* (incumbent president) Joseph France (former senator from Missouri)	*Franklin D. Roosevelt* (governor of New York) Alfred Smith (former governor of New York) John Garner (representative from Texas and Speaker of the House)	Roosevelt (D)	57-40	472-59
1936	*Alfred Landon* (governor of Kansas) William Borah (senator from Idaho)	*Franklin D. Roosevelt* (incumbent president) None	Roosevelt (D)	61-37	523-8
1940	*Wendell Willkie* (Indiana lawyer and public utility executive) Thomas E. Dewey (U.S. district attorney for New York) Robert Taft (senator from Ohio)	*Franklin D. Roosevelt* (incumbent president) None	Roosevelt (D)	55-45	449-82
1944	*Thomas E. Dewey* (governor of New York) Wendell Willkie (previous Republican presidential nominee)	*Franklin D. Roosevelt* (incumbent president) Harry Byrd (senator from Virginia)	Roosevelt (D)	53-46	432-99

Year	Losing candidate (and running mates)	Winner	Popular vote (%)	Electoral vote
1948	*Thomas E. Dewey* (governor of New York) / Harold Stassen (former governor of Minnesota) / Robert Taft (senator from Ohio)	Truman (D)	50-45	303-189
1952	*Dwight D. Eisenhower* (general) / Robert Taft (senator from Ohio)	Eisenhower (R)	55-44	442-89
1956	*Adlai Stevenson* (governor of Illinois) / Estes Kefauver (senator from Tennessee) / Richard Russell (senator from Georgia)	Eisenhower (R)	57-42	457-73
1960	*Adlai Stevenson* (previous Democratic presidential nominee) / Averell Harriman (governor of New York)	Kennedy (D)	49.7-49.5	303-219
	John F. Kennedy (senator from Massachusetts) / Hubert Humphrey (senator from Minnesota) / Lyndon B. Johnson (senator from Texas)			
1964	*Richard Nixon* (vice president) / None			
	Lyndon B. Johnson (incumbent president) / None	Johnson (D)	61-39	486-52
	Barry Goldwater (senator from Arizona) / Nelson Rockefeller (governor of New York)			

Harry S. Truman (incumbent president) / Richard Russell (senator from Georgia)

Year	Republican nominee (in italics) and other major candidates	Democratic nominee (in italics) and other major candidates	Election winner	Division of popular vote[a] (percent)	Division of electoral vote[b]
1968	*Richard Nixon* (former Republican presidential nominee) Ronald Reagan (governor of California)	*Hubert Humphrey* (incumbent vice president) Robert F. Kennedy (senator from New York) Eugene McCarthy (senator from Minnesota)	Nixon (R)	43.4-42.7	301-191
1972	*Richard Nixon* (incumbent president) None	*George McGovern* (senator from South Dakota) Hubert Humphrey (senator from Minnesota) George Wallace (governor of Alabama)	Nixon (R)	61-38	520-17
1976	*Gerald R. Ford* (incumbent president) Ronald Reagan (former governor of California)	*Jimmy Carter* (former governor of Georgia) Edmund Brown, Jr. (governor of California) George Wallace (governor of Alabama)	Carter (D)	50-48	297-240
1980	*Ronald Reagan* (former governor of California) George Bush (former director of Central Intelligence Agency) John Anderson (representative from Illinois)	*Jimmy Carter* (incumbent president) Edward M. Kennedy (senator from Massachusetts)	Reagan (R)	51-41	489-49

1984	Ronald Reagan (incumbent president) None	Walter F. Mondale (former vice president) Gary Hart (senator from Colorado)	Reagan (R)	59-41	525-13
1988	George Bush (vice president) Robert Dole (senator from Kansas)	Michael S. Dukakis (governor of Massachusetts) Jesse Jackson (civil rights activist)	Bush (R)	53-46	426-111

[a] Division of popular vote is between the Republican and Democratic nominees. Percentage may not add to 100 due to rounding.
[b] Division of electoral votes is between the Republican and Democratic nominees.

Index